The Lord is My Shepherd

A 12 Step Journey through PSALM 23

DISCOVERY
DECISION
DESIRES

Marcy Hawkins
LAADC, CADC IL, CCGC

Foreword

Today when you hear that someone is in an addiction recovery program, you naturally think that they are in a 12 Step program. That's because The Twelve Steps have been so successful in treating many types of addictions. What is not so widely known is that this program was initially based on biblical principles.

The Lord is My Shepherd: A 12 Step Journey through PSALM 23 brings alive the connection between what actually works in real life struggles with addiction and what God has revealed to us. The book masterfully connects a part of the Psalm with one of the steps. Expanding upon the metaphor of the shepherd and his sheep, the workbook in a very practical way takes one through the emotions, issues, and barriers that usually surface as one walks through the twelve-steps.

The curriculum in this workbook groups the recovery process into three major parts: DISCOVERY, DECISION, and DESIRE. This progression appropriately follows a biblical path for entering into the freedom of life with God at the center (e.g. Jesus' treasure parables in Matthew 13:44-46). It also walks each participant through a variety of questions, exercises and journaling to help internalize each step and its implications.

Marcy Hawkins has lived the struggle of healing from addiction, and she has experienced the new life that comes from putting Christ at the center of her life. For ten years now she has devoted herself to helping others overcome their addictions. In the past year she has taken these experiences, along with her love of God's Word, to create this unique resource for addiction recovery.

Many people are already benefiting from ***The Lord is My Shepherd: A 12 Step Journey through PSALM 23*** and if you are considering starting a 12 Step group, I urge you to consider using this guide. I believe that it will be especially helpful for Christ-followers to better understand the spiritual basis for the 12 Steps. My prayer is that it also might lead people to discover the One who cannot only deliver them from addiction but give them the abundant life that can be found only in dependence upon the true Good Shepherd.

Sid Niemeyer
Executive Pastor
Valley Community Church, Pleasanton

My Mother, Eileen
who committed PSALM 23 to memory as a young girl

My Sister, Mindy
who led me to The Good Shepherd by loving me when I could not love myself.

This workbook is also dedicated to the reader.
May your assurance be built upon
God's words of assurance to you and
May you boldly say, as David did,

*"The Lord is my Shepherd,
I shall not want."*
Psalm 23:1(NASB)

TABLE OF CONTENTS

HOW IT WORKS

DISCOVERY: Chapters 1, 2, and 3

My DISCOVERY of God and His kingdom and the baby steps I took holding His hand got me sober.
I was like the man who found the treasure hidden in a field from the parable Jesus told in Matthew 13:44.
It was an incredible treasure and I wanted to claim it as my own!

> *"The kingdom of heaven is like treasure hidden in a field. When a man found it, he hid*
> *it again, and then in his joy went and sold all he had and bought that field."*
>
> Matthew 13:44

Step 1, Step 2, and Step 3 of Alcoholics Anonymous cover the DISCOVERY process in a similar way.
We come to understand in our hearts that we need God's treasure and that He will restore our sanity. In our joy, we seek God's will for our lives. The DISCOVERY in the first three Steps is life changing. We become aware that our personal resources are incredibly limited and only God is capable of meeting our every need. Only the cross of Jesus has the power over our sin which restores our relationship with God.

DECISION: Chapters 4, 5, 6 and 7

This incredible news about the kingdom of God is a treasure. It's "music to our ears!" We make a DECISION to live "in tune" with God's beautiful rhythm, *one note at a time*, letting it flow over us, *one day at a time*. The DECISION requires us to DO THE WORK planned in Steps 4 through Step 7. The Good Shepherd takes care of us and moves us forward. "He leads me beside the quiet waters" where we proceed to write our stories and take our personal inventories (Step 4). In Step 5 we speak our truth to God, ourselves, and to others and are taught in Psalm 23 that God promises to shepherd us all along the way. He will restore our souls.

> *"The kingdom of heaven is like treasure hidden in a field. When a man found it, he hid*
> *it again, and then in his joy went **and sold all he had** and bought that field."*
>
> Matthew 13:44

We "sell out for Jesus" because we want to make room for the abundance of His Treasure! The Shepherd is with us even though we walk through the valley of the shadow of death. It is difficult work walking the steps of recovery up to the peaks and down in the valleys of life. As we "keep in tune" with God's song and His will for us, we are reminded that David knew he had God's song written on his heart and he did not fear. ♫

DESIRES: Chapters 8, 9, 10, 11, and 12

Our Shepherd has prepared a table for us and has prepared us for the life-long journey with Him. Relationships are restored and we discover the kind of life that God wants to live through us. We continue to learn how to listen to the Holy Spirit which frees us to make healthy choices. *We experience the* DESIRES *of our heart* with the development of character, integrity and concern for our fellows.

> *"Surely goodness and loving kindness will follow you all the days of your life!"*
>
> Psalm 23:6 NASB

DISCOVERY, DECISION, DESIRES

Matthew 13:44: *"The kingdom of heaven is like treasure hidden in a field. When a man found it, he hid it again, and then in his joy went and sold all he had and bought that field."*

DISCOVERY: *"The kingdom of heaven is like treasure hidden in a field. When a man found it, he hid it again*

The Lord is my Shepherd,
Step 1- We admitted that we are powerless over our dependencies - that our lives had become unmanageable.

I shall not want.
Step 2- We came to believe that a Power greater than ourselves could restore us to sanity.

He makes me lie down in green pastures;
Step 3- We made a decision to turn our will and our life over to the care of God.

DECISION: *.....and then in his joy went and sold all he had*

He leads me beside the quiet waters.
Step 4- We made a searching and fearless moral inventory of ourselves.

He restores my soul;
Step 5- We admitted to God, to ourselves, and one other human being the exact nature of our wrongs.

He guides me in the paths of righteousness for His name's sake.
Step 6- We were entirely ready to have God remove all of these defects of character.

Even though I walk through the valley of the shadow of death, I fear no evil; for Thou art with me;
Step 7- We humbly asked God to remove our shortcomings

DESIRES: *....and bought that field."*

Thy rod and Thy staff, they comfort me.
Step 8- We made a list of all the persons we had harmed and became willing to make amends to them all.

Thou preparest a table before me in the presence of my enemies;
Step 9- We made direct amends to such people wherever possible, except when to do so would injure them or others.

Thou hast anointed my head with oil; My cup overflows.
Step 10- We continued to take personal inventory and when we were wrong promptly admitted it.

Surely goodness and loving-kindness will follow me all the days of my life,
Step 11- We sought through prayer and meditation to improve our conscious contact with God, praying only for knowledge of His will for us and the power to carry it out.

And I will dwell in the house of the Lord forever.
Step 12- Having had a spiritual awakening as a result of these steps, we tried to carry this message to others and to practice these principles in all our affairs.

Psalm 23 (ASV and NASB)

PSALM 23

David penned this beautiful poem under the guidance of God's Spirit. Every word is precious and overflows with meaning. He composed it from **his** personal experience, and we capture the truth of his words in **our** daily experiences. The twenty-third psalm was read aloud at the beginning of my mother's memorial service by my younger sister, Mindy. Moments later, Mark, my older brother referred to it again as he shared that Mom had memorized Psalm 23 at the of age five. The rest of the day flowed over me as I let the love of family and friends sustain me. In the days that passed, God gave me a deep longing to hear the words of David's twenty-third psalm, and I, in the image of my mother, memorized it.

The truth of Psalm 23 walks us through the steps to healthy living with Jesus as our Shepherd. David paints a picture and puts you and me within it. We are able to use David's words as our own. On that day in February 2005, I could not see the printed words of Psalm 23 through my tears as Mindy read them aloud, but God, The Shepherd allowed me to see myself as part of a flock, a "one of a kind" lamb that needed a Shepherd to restore my soul.

The 12 Steps

The Lord is My Shepherd: A 12 Step Journey through PSALM 23 is a 12 Step, 12-month recovery workbook that comes alive with scripture found in the 12 lines of Psalm 23. The words of David enshrine the memories and metaphors of his early years as a shepherd, along with his obsession and preoccupation with his love of God. ***The Lord is My Shepherd: A 12 Step Journey through PSALM 23*** places us close to David as we walk with him through a shepherd's year. We allow our Shepherd to guide us through the seasons of our recovery, always protecting and loving us. We can trust the love of God who is the same yesterday, today, and always. God is Yahweh. He is our Shepherd.

The Oxford Group, from which AA was adapted, had the desire to take a healing message to people caught in unwholesome lifestyles. ***The Lord is My Shepherd: A 12 Step Journey through PSALM 23*** brings God's healing message to speak to our brokenness through written and spoken words. When we continue to soak in the Godly principles found in Scripture, we will heal, grow, and bear good fruit as God intended. PSALM 23 recovery groups are forming across the country to study the 12 Steps from a Christian perspective and PSALM-partners are partnering to work the steps together. Let us be obsessed with God's love, love one another and invest time in the healing ***relationships of recovery***!

ISAIAH 40:11 "The Lord tends his flock like a shepherd; He gathers the lambs in His arms and carries them close to His heart; He gently leads those that have young."
PSALM 95:7 " for He is our God and we are the people of His pasture, the flock under His care."

"And I will dwell in the house of the Lord forever."

Amen.

INTRODUCTION to THE 12 STEPS
of Alcoholics Anonymous (AA)

History

The story of AA's roots begins with the visits of alcoholic Roland Hazard with Dr. Carl Jung in Switzerland. The famous psychiatrist told him he could not be cured from alcoholism but needed a conversion through religious association. The search for such a conversion led Roland to the Oxford Group and his drinking was over. The Oxford Group was a life-changing Christian Fellowship of the First Century that believed in God and in Jesus Christ. It was lead by Episcopal Rector Samuel M. Shoemaker Jr. and was founded by Lutheran Minister Frank N.D. Buchman. By applying The Oxford Group principles its members witnessed to others, eventually reaching a fellow New Yorker, William Griffith Wilson (known by AA's as "Bill W."). While in the hospital undergoing treatment for alcoholism, Bill was visited by Ebby Thatcher, who explained the principles of the Group. Twenty years later, Bill W. described his conversion experience of that night in this way:

"My depression deepened unbearably and finally it seemed to me as though I were at the very bottom of the pit. I still gagged badly at the notion of a Power greater than myself, but finally, just for the moment, the last vestige of my proud obstinacy was crushed. All at once I found myself crying out, "If there is a God, let Him show Himself! I am ready to do anything, anything!"
Suddenly, the room lit up with a great white light. I was caught up into an ecstasy which there are no words to describe. It seemed to me, in my mind's eye, that I was on a mountain and that a wind not of air but spirit was blowing. And then it burst upon me that I was a free man. Slowly the ecstasy subsided. I lay on the bed, but now for a time I was in another world, a new world of consciousness. All about me and through me there was a wonderful feeling of Presence, and I thought to myself, "So this is the God of the preachers!" A great peace stole over me and I thought, "No matter how wrong things seem to be, they are still all right. Things are all right with God and His World."(*Alcoholics Anonymous Comes of Age: A Brief History of AA.* p. 63)

On a business venture to Akron, Ohio Bill W. seriously considered drinking again. He located the Oxford Group and met Dr. Robert Holbrook Smith (affectionately known as "Dr. Bob" by AA's). They discussed Bible principles, prayer, Oxford Group's ideas, love, and service. On June 10, 1935, Dr. Bob took his last drink and they set out to find drunks to help. And so AA was founded. Dr. Bob stated that AA's basic ideas were taken from their study of the Bible. He stressed the Book of James, Jesus' Sermon on the Mount, and 1 Corinthians 13 as "absolutely essential" to the program of recovery.

By 1938, some forty alcoholics, mostly from the Akron area, were sober. Bill W. received authorization to write a book about the cure. The original manuscript contained mention of God, Jesus Christ, the Bible, sin, and deliverance, but these terms were ultimately eliminated or replaced with "higher power", "spirituality", and "shortcomings". Mr. Clarence H. Snyder got sober in 1938 and was sponsored by Dr. Bob. He started a splinter group of AA's in Cleveland and limited it to alcoholics and their families. It was the first group to use the name of Alcoholics Anonymous. Clarence wrote materials on sponsorship and took thousands through the Steps over the years. He and his wife, Grace Moore, began spiritual retreats taking participants through all Twelve Steps in an afternoon, to the end that they may come to believe and receive the truth, healing, and recovery available through AA and the Good Book (The Bible). Christians sponsored by Clarence Snyder are still conducting spiritual retreats today. See Our A.A. Legacy to the Faith Community by Dick B. for more information.

Spiritual Principles of Recovery

- *Self-acceptance*
- *Trust*
- *Courage*
- *Self-discipline/self-control*
- *Commitment*
- *Faith*
- *Honesty*
- *Surrender*
- *Willingness*
- *Open-mindedness*
- *Humility*
- *Perseverance*
- *Integrity*
- *Unconditional love*
- *Selflessness*
- *Steadfastness*
- *Patience*
- *Forgiveness*
- *Acceptance*

The Promises

1. *We are going to know a new freedom and a new happiness.*
2. *We will not regret the past nor wish to shut the door on it.*
3. *We will comprehend the word serenity.*
4. *And we will know peace.*
5. *No matter how far down the scale we have gone, we will see how our experience can benefit others.*
6. *That feeling of uselessness and self pity will disappear.*
7. *We will lose interest in selfish things and gain interest in our fellows.*
8. *Self seeking will slip away.*
9. *Our whole attitude and outlook on life will change.*
10. *Fear of people and of economic insecurity will leave us.*
11. *We will intuitively know how to handle situations that used to baffle us.*
12. *We will suddenly realize that God is doing for us what we could not do for ourselves.*

PSALM 23

THE SHEPHERD'S MANY NAMES

The LORD is my Shepherd,
(Jehovah-Roi, my protector)

I shall not want.
(Jehovah-Jireh, my provider)

He makes me lie down in green pastures;
(Jehovah-Adonai, my Master)

He leads me beside quiet waters.
(Jehovah-Shalom, my Peace)

He restores my soul;
(Jehovah-Rapha, my Healer)

**He guides me in the paths of righteousness
for His name's sake.**
(Jehovah-Tsidkenu, my righteousness)

**Even though I walk through the valley
of the shadow of death,**
(Jehovah-Shammah, my divine Presence)

I will fear no evil; for Thou art with me;
(Jehovah-Tsebaoth, my Warrior)

Thy rod and Thy staff, they comfort me.
(Jehovah-El Elyon, my Defender)

**Thou preparest a table before me in the
presence of my enemies;**
(Jehovah-Nissi, my Encourager)

**Thou hast anointed my head with oil;
my cup overflows.**
(Jehovah-el Shaddai, my Nourisher)

**Surely goodness and lovingkindness
will follow me all the days of my life,**
(Jehovah-El Elohim, my Protector)

And I will dwell in the house of the Lord forever.
(Jehovah-El Olam, my Eternity)

(ASV and NASB)

THE LORD'S PRAYER

Our Father who art in heaven,
Hallowed be thy name.
Thy kingdom come,
Thy will be done,
On earth as it is in Heaven.
Give us this day our daily bread.
And forgive us our debts, as we
also have forgiven our debtors.
And do not lead us into temptation,
But deliver us from evil.
For thine is the kingdom,
and the power,
and the glory, forever.

Amen.

New American Standard Version

THE SERENITY PRAYER
Reinhold Niebuhr

God grant me the serenity

to accept the things I cannot change:

Courage to change the things I can;

and wisdom to know the difference.

Living one day at a time;

enjoying one moment at a time;

accepting hardship as the pathway to peace;

Taking, as he did, this sinful world as it is,

not as I would have it;

Trusting that he will make all things right,

if I surrender to his will;

That I may be reasonably happy in this life,

and supremely happy with Him forever in the next.

Amen.

Past 30 Days Reflection

As I begin this workbook, I will reflect on the past 30 days of my life and write about the reasons I'm choosing to begin this *12 Step Journey through PSALM 23*:

Today's date is _______________________________.

HOW DO YOU FEEL?

Each time you use this workbook, check-in with yourself or with the group
if you are in a Psalm 23 bible study group. Pick at least 2 feelings that you are feeling today.

Love	Joy	Potency	Criticized	Inadequate	Anger	Depression	Distress	Anxiety
admired	amused	able	abused	broken	agitated	abandoned	afflicted	afraid
adorable	at ease	adequate	belittled	cowardly	aggravated	alienated	anguished	agitated
affectionate	blissful	assured	branded	crippled	aggressive	alone	awkward	alarmed
agreeable	brilliant	authoritative	criticized	debilitated	annoyed	awful	baffled	anxious
big-hearted	calm	bold	deflated	defective	antagonistic	blue	bewildered	apprehensive
brotherly	cheerful	brave	depreciated	deficient	arrogant	cast off	blameworthy	bashful
caring	comical	capable	diminished	demoralized	tempered	crushed	clumsy	desperate
comforting	contented	competent	discredited	disabled	callous	defeated	confused	dread
congenial	delighted	confident	disgraced	exhausted	cantankerous	discouraged	constrained	embarrassed
cooperative	ecstatic	caring	humiliated	exposed	cool	dismal	disgusted	fearful
cordial	enthusiastic	determined	ignored	feeble	cranky	downcast	disliked	fidgety
courteous	excellent	durable	jeered	flimsy	critical	downhearted	displeased	frightened
dedicated	excited	dynamic	lampooned	fragile	cross	downtrodden	dissatisfied	hesitant
devoted	fantastic	effective	laughed at	frail	disagreeable	dreadful	distrustful	horrified
easy-going	fine	energetic	minimized	harmless	discontented	estranged	disturbed	ill at ease
empathetic	fit	fearless	mocked	helpless	envious	excluded	doubtful	insecure
fair	glad	firm	neglected	impotent	fierce	gloomy	foolish	intimidated
faithful	glorious	forceful	overlooked	inadequate	furious	grim	futile	jealous
forgiving	grand	gallant	put down	incapable	hard-hearted	hopeless	grief	jittery
friendly	gratified	mighty	ridiculed	incompetent	harsh	horrible	helpless	jumpy
generous	great	powerful	shamed	indefensible	heartless	humiliated	hindered	nervous
genuine	happy	robust	slammed	inefficient	hostile	hurt	impaired	on edge
giving	humorous	secure	slandered	inept	hypercritical	in the dumps	impatient	overwhelmed
honest	inspired	self-confident	slighted	inferior	ill-tempered	jilted	imprisoned	panicky
honorable	jovial	self-reliant		insecure	inpatient	kaput	nauseated	restless
hospitable	joyful	sharp		insufficient	inconsiderate	left out	offended	scared
interested	jubilant	spirited		meek	intolerable	lonely	pained	shaky
kind	magnificent	strong		nerveless	intolerant	lonesome	perplexed	shy
kind-	majestic	sure		paralyzed	irritated	miserable	puzzled	strained
hearted	marvelous	tough		powerless	mad	moody	ridiculous	tense
lenient	overjoyed	well equipped		shaken	malicious	mournful	sickened	terrified
lovable	pleased			small	mean	out of sorts	silly	terror-stricken
loving	pleasant			strength less	obstinate	overlooked	skeptical	timid
mellow	proud			trivial	outraged	regretful	speechless	uncomfortable
neighborly	satisfied			unable	perturbed	reprimanded	strained	uneasy
nice	serene			unarmed	pushy	rotten	suspicious	
open	splendid			uncertain	rebellious	run down	swamped	
optimistic	superb			unfit	reckless	stranded	touchy	
patient	terrific			unimportant	spiteful	tearful	ungainly	
peaceful	thrilled			unqualified	stern	terrible	unlucky	
pleasant	tremendous			unsound	stormy	unloved	unpopular	
polite	triumphant			unsubstantiated	unfeeling	worthless	unsatisfied	
receptive	vivacious			useless	unfriendly	wrecked	unsure	
reliable	witty			vulnerable	vicious			
responsible	wonderful			weak	vindictive			
sensitive				weak-hearted				
sympathetic								
sweet								
tender								
thoughtful								
unselfish								

The Lord is My Shepherd
A 12 Step Journey through PSALM 23

DISCOVERY
CHAPTER ONE
†

"The Lord is my Shepherd,"

Step 1 "We admitted that we are powerless over our dependencies – that our lives had become unmanageable."

DISCOVERY

From the author

I was a divorced woman living with a boyfriend in Sacramento. I had a full-time job, working 40 hours a week as a mail carrier for the United States Postal Service. I also spent over 40 hours a week tending to my alcohol and drug activities (craving, obsessing, seeking, finding, waiting, using, defending, rationalizing, recovering, lying, and denying). Over the span of 17 years, my soul continually ached, and my spirit died. My physical desires ruled my life and I was a shell of a person named Marcy. I still had a job and a house so I believed I was okay. It was too painful to notice the broken relationships that I shattered over the years and how isolated I had become from anyone or anything outside my small comfort zone. I was either completely numb or bouncing off the walls… my life was unmanageable. One day while at work the Postmaster called me into his office to put me on "restricted sick-leave." This humiliating experience got my attention. I was embarrassed to see my sick-days plotted out on paper. It meant that I would now need a written doctor's excuse to stay home sick. My embarrassment was quickly replaced with blame, resentment, and of course, denial. Despite my best efforts the day came when I could not make it to work and definitely could not drive across town to see a doctor... In tears, with fears, and from a place of brokenness my words spilled out over the phone to my supervisor, "Charla, I think I have a drinking problem." I'd made many early morning calls to her over the years, but never had I told the truth. And never had I heard a response like the one she gave me that day. "Marcy, do you believe in God? Can I pray for you?" I clung to the phone desperate to hear her every word and heard myself say, "Yes". With a promise to get help I returned to work. I watched Charla after that day and noticed that she took her lunch hour in her car with her Bible. I bet she kept her word about praying for me. I found comfort in that. I was curious about her and felt she genuinely cared about me …***but I couldn't figure out why.*** I wanted to attend a nearby church but I wore my Sunday morning hang-over and necklace of shame and self disgust so I never made it past the church parking lot. Trapped by fear and still strapped in the driver's seat, I listened to the radio telecast of the church service that day alone in my car… afraid, discouraged, and defeated.

Another lost sheep

By this time I had developed many fears, driving was one of them. Weeks ran together in a blur until one day after finishing my first 6-pack I called a hotline number from the phonebook. The volunteer helped me make a plan to drive myself to a women's 12 Step meeting the following evening. To this day, I don't know how I did it. The next thing I know I was slumped at a table, trembling deep inside and panicked that I in the wrong place because the other women gathering around the table were smiling and hugging…and they were **not** like me. The meeting began and I remember hearing two things; "If you are an alcoholic and you continue to drink, IT WILL get worse." I was so tense that I could hardly breathe. I started to feel panicky and was ready to bolt. And then I heard the second thing, "We need God's help." Nothing made sense. I couldn't figure out why a bunch of drunks would be talking about God. I couldn't believe my ears. I heard stories about God helping and loving the other alcoholics in the room. The woman next to me slid a blue book over my way, opening the cover for me to read the entries, "Don't give up before the Miracle. We need you and love you, Love Maria" and "Hang In- from Della" (followed by her phone number). I couldn't look up or begin to make eye contact but when I left I was clutching my new book. It really puzzled me that while I was at my very worst with absolutely nothing to offer, those women bought me a book…. ***and I couldn't figure out why.*** With a glimmer of what must have been hope, I cried out to God with all of my heart asking HIM to please take over my fight with alcohol and drugs. I cried for forgiveness and for the help and love I'd heard about from the women in the meeting. From the driver's seat of my car, alone with God and because of His grace, I accepted Jesus as my Lord and Savior. So it was on September 12, 1986 that I attended my first 12 Step meeting, had my first 24 hours of sobriety, and became a Christian all on the same day. It was the day of all days and one that God had planned for me all along …and ***now I know why.***

The Shepherd came eagerly and quickly, ready to help, to save, and restore. He untangled me from the wired fences made of lies and deceit that had kept me captive and like the Good Shepherd, He moved me to a pasture where things were not quite so comfortable- but for my own good. Oh, the pleasures of being set free from myself and accepted into the arms of ***my Shepherd!***

CHAPTER ONE INTRODUCTION

"The Lord is my Shepherd,"

Without question one of the beautiful features of this poem is its **personal** pronouns; The Lord **(He)** is **my** shepherd!! We establish our personal relationship with the Shepherd at the cross (John 3:16) and enter the sheepfold as His (Psalm 23). The old-timers of the Oxford Group quoted the slogan, "First Things First" to newcomers and referred them to Matthew 6:33 *"But seek first His kingdom and His righteousness, and all these things will be given to you as well."*
In the 10th chapter of John, Jesus assumes the role of the Shepherd of the sheep.

"Truly, truly, I say to you, he who does not enter the sheepfold by the door but climbs in by another way, that man is a thief and a robber; but he who enters by the door is the shepherd of the sheep. To him the gatekeeper opens; the sheep hear his voice, and he calls his own sheep by name and leads them out. When he has brought out all his own, he goes before them, and the sheep follow him, for they know his voice. A stranger they will not follow, but they will flee from him, for they do not know the voice of strangers." (John 10:1-5 ESV)

The Shepherd calls his sheep by name. The relationship is an intimate one. Jesus knows your name and everything about you. David, himself a shepherd and the son of a shepherd stated, "The Lord is my Shepherd." He referred to Jehovah; the Lord God of Israel. We read in Colossians 1:16 *"For by Him all things were created: things in heaven and on earth…"* The first step in *The Lord is My Shepherd: A 12 Step Journey through PSALM 23* reflects on the person of Jesus, on His power and His LOVE FOR US. We establish that we need a shepherd and we declare like David did, **"The Lord is my Shepherd."**

**Step 1 "We admitted that we are powerless over our dependencies –
that our lives had become unmanageable."**

The key principle of this first step is honesty. When life becomes unmanageable we are faced with the fact that we are not self-sufficient. Step 1 asks us to confront the fear of turning loose our control (of self and others) in order to admit our own inability to fix or change people, places and things. In the depths of our dependencies, we are like sheep, "weary and scattered." Our powerlessness and unmanageability, our weariness and despair, allow us to admit the truth about our lives, which never comes without its share of pain and remorse.

Your Shepherd is eager to help because He loves us.
"The Lord is near to all who call on him, to all who call on him in truth." (Psalm 145:18)

There are some important words and concepts to study during this Step 1.			
Unmanageability	**CONTROL**	*denial*	DISEASE OF ADDICTION
HONESTY	**ADMIT**		HOW?... HONEST, OPEN, WILLING
Powerlessness	TRUTH	hitting bottom	surrender

DISCOVERY is where our recovery process begins. We discover our limitations, our need for spiritual strength, and the truth that paves the way to freedom, healing and recovery. **DISCOVERY** contains specific instructions for taking the first three steps in "the solution". The treasure we **DISCOVER** is the Kingdom of God here on earth and we never have to be alone again. Our God is an awesome God!!!!

The Spiritual Principles for STEP 1 are honesty, open-mindedness, willingness, humility and acceptance.

"The Lord is my Shepherd,"

1. Are you able to see yourself as David did…… a sheep in need of a shepherd? Why?

2. Are you recovering from an addiction? _______ Codependency? _______ Pain from your past? _______

3. Are you recovering from a compulsive behavior? (Gambling, spending, eating disorder, work, shopping, sex, love, and/or relationship addiction). You may have more than one. Write them here:

4. What are the losses in your past?

Whatever the circumstances, when we come from a history of LOSS, it is like being first-cousin to the person raised with an addiction. We have been hurt, but recovery with the Good Shepherd promises to bring love and healing.

5. Put a check mark next to each OBSTACLE you have that interferes with hearing the voice of your Shepherd. Now review the column of BELIEFS. Mark the BELIEFS you have in the same way.

OBSTACLES:		BELIEFS:	
Pride		"No matter what I do it's never good enough."	
Fear		"Something bad is going to happen."	
Shame		"It's not OK to ask for help."	
Willpower		"I am in charge of myself."	
Magical thinking		"Things will change if I try harder."	
A misunderstanding of God		"There must be something wrong with me."	
Being obsessed with another person, *reacting* to another person's behavior		"Other people's needs are more important than my own."	

6. Write about the obstacle you battle with most. (What does the voice of the obstacle say to you?)

7. Write about the belief you battle with most.

Ephesians 2:1-6 in The Message reads:
"It wasn't so long ago that you were mired in that old stagnant life of sin. You let the world, which doesn't know the first thing about living, tell you how to live. You filled your lungs with polluted disbelief, and then exhaled disobedience. We all did it, all of us doing what we felt like doing, when we felt like doing it, all of us in the same boat. It's a wonder God didn't lose his temper and do away with the whole lot of us. Instead, immense in mercy and with incredible love, he embraced us. He took our sin-dead lives and made us alive in Christ!"

8. Will you respond to the guiding voice of your Shepherd? (What do you need to hear from Him?)

When we believe what God says and we receive Jesus……. …**eternal life is ours.**
When we renounce our tendency to do things our own way… **true recovery is ours.**

**"We admitted that we are powerless over our dependencies -
that our lives had become unmanageable."**

Take an honest look at your codependency and/or addiction. Give an example of a time when:

1. You lied about your behavior-

2. You embarrassed yourself-

3. You blamed someone else for your problem(s)-

4. You spent a whole day in fear-

THERE IS A SOLUTION

What the AA Big Book says: *"The great fact is just this,* and nothing less: That we have had deep and effective spiritual experiences which have revolutionized our whole attitude toward life, toward our fellows and toward God's universe. *The central fact of our lives today* is the absolute certainty that our creator has entered into our hearts and lives in a way which is indeed miraculous. He has commenced to accomplish those things for which we could never do by ourselves." (p.25, emphasis added)

What the Good Book says: *"And do not be conformed to this world, but be transformed by the renewing of your mind, that you may prove what the will of God is, that which is good and acceptable and perfect."*
 (Romans 12:2 NASB)

The Slogan: "ONE DAY AT A TIME": *"Therefore do not be anxious for tomorrow; for tomorrow will care for itself. Each day has enough trouble of its own."* (Matthew 6:34)

Read Ephesians 4:16 *"From Him the whole body, joined and held together by every supporting ligament, grows and builds itself up in love, as each part does its work"*

5. Name at least two components (or parts) of your solution thus far. What's working?

6. Rate the commitment you will make to either attend a group or work with a PSALM-Partner to establish, renew and strengthen your recovery. (0 is least likely, 10 is most likely): #_______
If you begin this workbook alone begin thinking of a safe person you can share with when you are ready.

Lord is my Shepherd,"
**STEP 1 "We admitted that we are powerless over our dependencies -
that our lives had become unmanageable."**

MATTHEW 5:3

____

____

MATTHEW 9:36

____

____

MATTHEW 11:28-30

____

____

____

MARK 4:38-39 (READ VERSES 35-41)

____

____

MARK 5:26 (READ VERSES 25-34)

____

____

JOHN 1:3 (READ VERSES 1-5)

____

____

____

Rate your physical, psychological, emotional, and spiritual health

- Examine your health in each area of your life. Give each behavior a number from 1-5 (#5 means very well).
- Be HONEST. It's helpful to know the *truth* about your recovery health in order to take care of yourself.
- Circle **one** BEHAVIOR in each area that you are willing to work on daily for the next week.

MY BIOLOGICAL HEALTH (PHYSICAL)

MY RECOVERY DATE:		NUMBER OF CONTINOUS DAYS	
Nutrition- when and what you eat		Physical /dental exams & appointments	
Water		Medications/ daily vitamins	
Identifying/reducing emotional eating		Stress management/keeping it simple	
Sleep/rest (too much, too little)		Eliminating/reducing caffeine	
Exercise (easy does it)		Eliminating/reducing sugar	
Pacing your activities (too much, too little)		Other:	

MY PSYCHOLOGICAL HEALTH (MY THOUGHTS & BEHAVIOR)

Managing denial/ defense mechanisms		Music/art/school work	
Positive vs. Negative thinking		Journaling thoughts & behaviors	
Reducing obsessive thoughts		Making phone calls (sponsor, hotline)	
Daily structure/ being on time		Self-help meetings	
Making amends (promptly admit)		Building self esteem	
Money management		Other:	

MY EMOTIONAL/RELATIONAL HEALTH

Letting go of enabling people		Connecting with family in healthy way	
Managing emotions		Self care	
Spending time with **safe** people		Relaxation exercises	
Setting boundaries		Healthy sexual relations	
Having fun		Journaling feelings/ talking about them	
To Thine Own Self Be True. My "yes" is "yes," and my "no" is "no."		Other:	

MY SPIRITUAL HEALTH

Telling the truth to myself and others		Loving myself/ self-forgiveness	
Service to others		Church / Bible study	
Prayer		Serenity Prayer	
Meditation and/or quiet time with God		Gratitude list, affirmations	
Utilizing the Steps /Spiritual Principles		Enjoying nature	
Balance in everyday life (avoiding extremes)		Seeking/finding my purpose, finding what matters	

- Recognize emotional triggers and <u>change behavior.</u>
- Recognize anxiety and <u>practice relaxation techniques.</u>
- Recognize sleeping / eating habits that are slipping and <u>practice self-care.</u>

"The Lord is my Shepherd,"

Who is this Shepherd we call LORD? Our view of Him is often too small, too human. In Colossians 1:15-17 we see it was He who was directly responsible for the creation of all things.

1. Write the verse here.

Phillip Keller in his book <u>A Shepherd Looks at PSALM 23</u> writes:

God the Father is God the author- the originator of all that exists. It was in His mind, first that all took shape.

God the Son, our Savior, is God the artisan- the artist, the Creator of all that exists. He brought into being all that had been originally formulated in His Father's mind.

God the Holy Spirit is God the agent who presents these facts to both my mind and my spiritual understanding so that they become real and relative to me as an individual.

David, in this poem, is not speaking as a shepherd, but as a sheep. He claims the Lord as his shepherd.

2. What do you know about God's **character** and abilities? He is......

A. ____________________________   D. ____________________________

B. ____________________________   E. ____________________________

C. ____________________________   F. ____________________________

Paul said *"...we have not stopped praying for you and asking God to fill you with the knowledge of His will through all spiritual wisdom and understanding. And we pray this in order that you may live a life worthy of the Lord and may please Him in every way: bearing fruit in every good work, growing in the knowledge of God,"* (Colossians 1:9-10)

3. Why do you need a growing knowledge of God?

4. Read James 3:17. What does this verse say about God's wisdom?

5. List one thing you will do this week to know Him better and better?

6. Write about a time when there was reason to feel helpless, but the Lord, your Shepherd was close at hand and He gave you hope.

**STEP 1 "We admitted that we are powerless over our dependencies -
that our lives had become unmanageable."**

1. You have power in some areas of your life. Name a few here.

A.________________________________   D.________________________________

B.________________________________   E.________________________________

2. When life becomes unmanageable, we are faced with the fact that we are **not** self-sufficient. Read and write JOHN 15:5-6.

3. Have you felt apart from God in terms of your addiction/compulsive behaviors? Have you felt like a branch that is broken off from the vine? What caused the "disconnect?" List a few examples.

4. How has your addiction and/or codependency affected important **relationships** in your life?

5. What efforts have you made to change your dependent/codependent behaviors <u>that have not worked?</u>

6. What efforts <u>have</u> worked?

Pray this Prayer:
"God manage me, because I can't manage myself."

"The Lord is my Shepherd,"
**STEP 1 "We admitted that we are powerless over our dependencies -
that our lives had become unmanageable."**

EPHESIANS 2:1-2

____

____

2 PETER 2:19

____

____

TITUS 3:3 (READ VERSES 3-7)

____

____

PSALM 6:2-4

____

____

____

PSALM 6:6

____

____

PSALM 10:14

____

____

PSALM 12:5

____

____

WEEK TWO WELLNESS CHECK-IN

Rate your physical, psychological, emotional, and spiritual health

- Examine your health in each area of your life. Give each behavior a number from 1-5 (#5 means very well).
- Be HONEST. It's helpful to know the *truth* about your recovery health in order to take care of yourself.
- Circle **one** BEHAVIOR in each area that you are willing to work on daily for the next week.

MY BIOLOGICAL HEALTH (PHYSICAL)

MY RECOVERY DATE:		NUMBER OF CONTINOUS DAYS	
Nutrition- when and what you eat		Physical /dental exams & appointments	
Water		Medications/ daily vitamins	
Identifying/reducing emotional eating		Stress management/keeping it simple	
Sleep/rest (too much, too little)		Eliminating/reducing caffeine	
Exercise (easy does it)		Eliminating/reducing sugar	
Pacing your activities (too much, too little)		Other:	

MY PSYCHOLOGICAL HEALTH (MY THOUGHTS & BEHAVIOR)

Managing denial/ defense mechanisms		Music/art/school work	
Positive vs. Negative thinking		Journaling thoughts & behaviors	
Reducing obsessive thoughts		Making phone calls (sponsor, hotline)	
Daily structure/ being on time		Self-help meetings	
Making amends (promptly admit)		Building self esteem	
Money management		Other:	

MY EMOTIONAL/RELATIONAL HEALTH

Letting go of enabling people		Connecting with family in healthy way	
Managing emotions		Self care	
Spending time with **safe** people		Relaxation exercises	
Setting boundaries		Healthy sexual relations	
Having fun		Journaling feelings/ talking about them	
To Thine Own Self Be True. My "yes" is "yes," and my "no" is "no."		Other:	

MY SPIRITUAL HEALTH

Telling the truth to myself and others		Loving myself/ self-forgiveness	
Service to others		Church / Bible study	
Prayer		Serenity Prayer	
Meditation and/or quiet time with God		Gratitude list, affirmations	
Utilizing the Steps /Spiritual Principles		Enjoying nature	
Balance in everyday life (avoiding extremes)		Seeking/finding my purpose, finding what matters	

- Recognize emotional triggers and <u>change behavior.</u>
- Recognize anxiety and <u>practice relaxation techniques.</u>
- Recognize sleeping / eating habits that are slipping and <u>practice self-care.</u>

"The Lord is my Shepherd,"

Read Luke 15:3-7. *So Jesus used this illustration: "If you had one hundred sheep, and one of them strayed away and was lost in the wilderness, wouldn't you leave the ninety-nine others to go and search for the lost one until you found it?"*

Picture yourself as that lost sheep.

1. How does it feel before, during, and after Your Shepherd comes after you?

   Before... _________________________During... _____________________________After... ___________________________

In life situations ………............ **Keep looking ↑ up.** God wants **His truth** to guide and shepherd your actions.

2. List the beliefs **that lead you astray,**

   Our beliefs can reflect …… **FALSE BELIEFS ← ✝ or → GOD'S TRUTH**. Write them below
      Example: God doesn't care.   God really loves me.

      1.   1.

      2.   2.

      3.   3.

      4.   4.

In our life situations, it's our **BELIEFS** that determine our **THOUGHTS,** and our **THOUGHTS** that determine our **EMOTIONS,** and from there we go into **ACTION,**
(**Ungodly action** versus **Godly action**)

---

3. What behavior in your life has the potential to lead you onto your own path? (i.e. worry, dishonesty, controlling other people, impatience).

4. What is the false belief?

5. Replace the false belief with God's Truth and see how the thoughts, emotions and actions change.

6.What does the Bible say is God's response when He finds you (His lost sheep)?

7. How is it different from a human response?

**STEP 1 "We admitted that we are powerless over our dependencies -
that our lives had become unmanageable."**

Step 1 helps us to see that when we try to control people, places, and things around us, we become exhausted, frustrated and defeated. Yet we keep trying. Step 1 helps loosen our grip on control. Do you believe that there might be another way to live?.

SURRENDER: Read 2 Corinthians 4:7-10

1. How has **open-mindedness** made a difference in your life?

2. What do you need to surrender?

3. What are your **fears** concerning surrender?

4. What would be different in your life if you surrendered to God completely?

5. What are you presently doing to strengthen your recovery? List your **Godly actions.**

Read 2 Corinthians 4:16: *"Therefore we do not lose heart. Though outwardly we are wasting away, yet inwardly we are being renewed day by day."*

HUMILITY: Read Romans 12:2-3

6. Why do you think humility is an important concept?

7. Close your eyes and picture yourself being *humble* (soft and open to the truth about you).
Now picture yourself being prideful. How does **pride** change your stance?

8. How does pride interfere with Step 1?

9. Which Bible verse do you think will help you with your humility? Write it. Who can you share it with? (your group, counselor, Psalm-partner, safe friend)

10. Write about your surrender and humility.

11. Is there something you need to talk about? Write it here.

"The Lord is my Shepherd,"
STEP 1 "We admitted that we are powerless over our dependencies -
that our lives had become unmanageable."

PSALM 31:9-10

____

____

____

PSALM 31:22

____

____

PSALMS 38:3-4

____

____

____

____

PSALM 40:17

____

____

____

PSALM 102:1-2

____

____

____

____

Rate your physical, psychological, emotional, and spiritual health

- Examine your health in each area of your life. Give each behavior a number from 1-5 (#5 means very well).
- Be HONEST. It's helpful to know the *truth* about your recovery health in order to take care of yourself.
- Circle **one** BEHAVIOR in each area that you are willing to work on daily for the next week.

MY BIOLOGICAL HEALTH (PHYSICAL)

MY RECOVERY DATE:		NUMBER OF CONTINOUS DAYS	
Nutrition- when and what you eat		Physical /dental exams & appointments	
Water		Medications/ daily vitamins	
Identifying/reducing emotional eating		Stress management/keeping it simple	
Sleep/rest (too much, too little)		Eliminating/reducing caffeine	
Exercise (easy does it)		Eliminating/reducing sugar	
Pacing your activities (too much, too little)		Other:	

MY PSYCHOLOGICAL HEALTH (MY THOUGHTS & BEHAVIOR)

Managing denial/ defense mechanisms		Music/art/school work	
Positive vs. Negative thinking		Journaling thoughts & behaviors	
Reducing obsessive thoughts		Making phone calls (sponsor, hotline)	
Daily structure/ being on time		Self-help meetings	
Making amends (promptly admit)		Building self esteem	
Money management		Other:	

MY EMOTIONAL/RELATIONAL HEALTH

Letting go of enabling people		Connecting with family in healthy way	
Managing emotions		Self care	
Spending time with **safe** people		Relaxation exercises	
Setting boundaries		Healthy sexual relations	
Having fun		Journaling feelings/ talking about them	
To Thine Own Self Be True. My "yes" is "yes," and my "no" is "no."		Other:	

MY SPIRITUAL HEALTH

Telling the truth to myself and others		Loving myself/ self-forgiveness	
Service to others		Church / Bible study	
Prayer		Serenity Prayer	
Meditation and/or quiet time with God		Gratitude list, affirmations	
Utilizing the Steps /Spiritual Principles		Enjoying nature	
Balance in everyday life (avoiding extremes)		Seeking/finding my purpose, finding what matters	

- Recognize emotional triggers and <u>change behavior.</u>
- Recognize anxiety and <u>practice relaxation techniques.</u>
- Recognize sleeping / eating habits that are slipping and <u>practice self-care</u>.

"The Lord is my Shepherd,"

Sheep have absolutely no means of defending themselves. Sheep can't outrun their enemies and they can't outsmart them either. They can't climb trees and they don't have sharp teeth or claws to fight as a means of defending themselves.

THEIR SHEPHERD IS THEIR ONLY DEFENSE.

1. What behaviors did you use in your childhood to defend yourself?

Use the photo below for the following exercise. The shepherd is standing to the right of the tree. The sheep belong in the flock, behind their shepherd. When we fight our own battles, we move ahead of the Shepherd.

2. What behaviors do you use in your life today to defend yourself?   List them where it says "**your defenses**." Stack the words up like "blocks" to make a wall to defend yourself. anger, blame, denial

God wants <u>you</u> behind HIM   your "EGO" → →   <u>you</u>r defenses ↑   <u>your</u> triggers ↑
                              (makes <u>you</u> race ahead of HIM)   ("blocks" of your WALL)   (threats to your recovery)

3. What are the **temptations or "triggers"** that you want to defend yourself against? List them above. ↑

Example: cravings, peer pressure, someone else's anger, fear, etc.

4. Think about your "EGO" (Edging God Out).
Are you walking **ahead** of your Shepherd and fighting your own battles? When did you do that last?

5. Why do you try to defend yourself? Does it work?

6. ↑ Picture yourself where God wants you, safe behind His care. How does that feel?

7. Read Mark 6:30-32. The Good Shepherd may want to be alone with you for awhile and give you rest. What's your reaction to being still and being relaxed?

**STEP 1 "We admitted that we are powerless over our dependencies -
that our lives had become unmanageable."**

Let's review the qualifying questions of Step 1:

1. Do you have a dependency or codependency problem? (Do you try to control people, places or things you have no control over?) Expand on your answer.

2. Rate the commitment you will make to do something about it and learn how to stay in healthy relationships.
(0 is least likely, 10 is most likely) #________.
3. What are you willing to do?

4. What are you doing that's working?

**Step 1 and the Serenity Prayer help us to stop and THINK.
You must commit yourself to God's TRUTH.**

Review the ways we distort reality.

5. When have you used these techniques? Which do use you most often?

> **Denial:** "I don't have a problem."

> **Minimizing:** "It's not that bad."

> **Hostility**: Becoming angry or making threats when confronted.

> **Rationalization:** Making an excuse, giving a "good" reason.

> **Blaming:** Shifting the responsibility to someone else.

> **Intellectualizing**: Thinking to excess to avoid doing something about the problem (justifying).

> **Diversion:** Bringing up another topic.

Take a piece of paper and write **TRUTH** on it, then tape it to your bathroom mirror. You deserve to live a life of love and truth. You also deserve the love and encouragement of others in recovery.

Oswald Chambers in his book MY UTMOST FOR HIS HIGHEST writes, "We have to realize that we cannot earn or win anything from God through our own effort. We must either receive it as a gift or do without it. The greatest spiritual blessing we receive is when we come to the knowledge that we are destitute. Until we get there, our Lord is powerless. He can do nothing for us as long as we think we are sufficient in and of ourselves. We must enter into His kingdom through the door of destitution. As long as we are "rich," particularly in the area of pride or independence, God can do nothing for us. It is only when we get hungry spiritually that we receive the Holy Spirit. The gift of the essential nature of God is placed and made effective in us by the Holy Spirit. He imparts to us the quickening life of Jesus, making us truly alive. He takes that which was "beyond" us and places it "within" us. And immediately, once "the beyond" has come "within," it rises up to "the above," and we are lifted into the kingdom where Jesus lives and reigns (see John 3:5)." *How's that for TRUTH?*

"The Lord is my Shepherd,"
STEP 1 "We admitted that we are powerless over our dependencies -
that our lives had become unmanageable."

ROMANS 7:15

____

____

ROMANS 7:18, 21

____

____

____

ROMANS 8:7-8

____

____

____

2 CORINTHIANS 1:8-9

____

____

2 CORINTHIANS 4:8-9

____

____

2 CORINTHIANS 12:10

____

____

EPHESIANS 1:7

____

____

WEEK FOUR WELLNESS CHECK-IN

Rate your physical, psychological, emotional, and spiritual health

- Examine your health in each area of your life. Give each behavior a number from 1-5 (#5 means very well).
- Be HONEST. It's helpful to know the *truth* about your recovery health in order to take care of yourself.
- Circle **one** BEHAVIOR in each area that you are willing to work on daily for the next week.

MY BIOLOGICAL HEALTH (PHYSICAL)

MY RECOVERY DATE:		NUMBER OF CONTINOUS DAYS	
Nutrition- when and what you eat		Physical /dental exams & appointments	
Water		Medications/ daily vitamins	
Identifying/reducing emotional eating		Stress management/keeping it simple	
Sleep/rest (too much, too little)		Eliminating/reducing caffeine	
Exercise (easy does it)		Eliminating/reducing sugar	
Pacing your activities (too much, too little)		Other:	

MY PSYCHOLOGICAL HEALTH (MY THOUGHTS & BEHAVIOR)

Managing denial/ defense mechanisms		Music/art/school work	
Positive vs. Negative thinking		Journaling thoughts & behaviors	
Reducing obsessive thoughts		Making phone calls (sponsor, hotline)	
Daily structure/ being on time		Self-help meetings	
Making amends (promptly admit)		Building self esteem	
Money management		Other:	

MY EMOTIONAL/RELATIONAL HEALTH

Letting go of enabling people		Connecting with family in healthy way	
Managing emotions		Self care	
Spending time with **safe** people		Relaxation exercises	
Setting boundaries		Healthy sexual relations	
Having fun		Journaling feelings/ talking about them	
To Thine Own Self Be True. My "yes" is "yes," and my "no" is "no."		Other:	

MY SPIRITUAL HEALTH

Telling the truth to myself and others		Loving myself/ self-forgiveness	
Service to others		Church / Bible study	
Prayer		Serenity Prayer	
Meditation and/or quiet time with God		Gratitude list, affirmations	
Utilizing the Steps /Spiritual Principles		Enjoying nature	
Balance in everyday life (avoiding extremes)		Seeking/finding my purpose, finding what matters	

- Recognize emotional triggers and <u>change behavior.</u>
- Recognize anxiety and <u>practice relaxation techniques.</u>
- Recognize sleeping / eating habits that are slipping and <u>practice self-care</u>.

PSALM 23 "The Lord is my Shepherd."

**STEP 1 "We admitted that we are powerless over our dependencies -
that our lives had become unmanageable."**

COMPLETION

My favorite Scripture for Chapter 1: (write it here)

_______ I understand Chapter 1 and will continue to use it daily.
_______ I completed the Bible study in a ***Psalm 23*** group.
_______ I worked with a PSALM-Partner this month to study Chapter 1.

Psalm Partner NAME: _______________________________________

Psalm Partner Phone # _____________________________________

Today's date ____

My Signature ______________________________ **PSALM-Partner** _________________

BIBLE STUDY AT A GLANCE

Matthew 5:3	Titus 3:3-7	Psalm 42:6
Matthew 9:36	Psalm 6:2-4	Psalm 44:15
Matthew 11:28-30	Psalm 6:6-7	Psalm 55:4-5
Mark 4:35-41	Psalm 10:14	Psalm 69:1-3
Mark 5:25-34	Psalm 12:5	Psalm 69:33
John 1:1-5	Psalm 13:1	Psalm 72:12-13
Romans 7:15	Psalm 16:4	Psalm 88:1-4
Romans 7:18-21	Psalm 18: 6	Psalm 102:1-7
Romans 8:7-8	Psalm 22:1-2	Proverbs 14:12
2 Corinthians 1:8-9	Psalm 25:16-17	Proverbs 18:14
2 Corinthians 4:8-9	Psalm 28:1-2	Proverbs 28:26
2 Corinthians 12:10	Psalm 31:9-10	
Ephesians 1:7	Psalm 31:22	
Ephesians 2:1-2	Psalm 38:1-9	
2 Peter 2:19	Psalm 40:17	

The Lord is My Shepherd
A 12 Step Journey through PSALM 23

DISCOVERY
CHAPTER TWO
†

"I shall not want."

STEP 2 "Came to believe that God could restore us to sanity."

CHAPTER TWO INTRODUCTION

PSALM 23
"I shall not want."

Our Master is flawless and His care for us is certain. As we study the Hebrew names of the Lord, given in the Old Testament, we become familiar with His awesome capabilities towards us as believers. The Lord, our God, is ALL that we need. Consider the essential needs. (refer to page 7)

Tender-Loving Care	Psalm 23:1	He is called "Jehovah-Raah"
Physical Provision	Genesis 22:14	He is called "Jehovah-Jireh"
Heart-Peace	Judges 6:24	His name is "Jehovah-Shalom"
Spiritual Renewal	Exodus 15:26	He is called "Jehovah-Rapha"
Guidance	Jeremiah 23:6	His title is "Jehovah-Tsidkenu"
Companionship	Ezekiel 48:35	His name is "Jehovah-Shammah"
Power over opposition	Exodus 17:15	He is called "Jehovah-Nissi"

Matthew 6:26 "Look at the birds of the air…" Matthew 6:28 "…See how the lilies of the field grow; they do not labor or spin."

Our heavenly Father knows our circumstances, and if we stay focused on Him, instead of our circumstances, we will grow spiritually - just as "the lilies of the field."

STEP 2 "Came to believe that God could restore us to sanity."

Studying the depths of God's character makes it easier to believe that Jesus **could, can, and will** return us to a saner way of living. The Basic Text of AA defines insanity as "repeating the same mistakes and expecting different results." There's another way of doing things and we need help from outside of ourselves to find the answers. When we've acknowledged the powerlessness in Step 1, we'll find the need for hope and faith in order to continue in the recovery process. "Came to believe," suggests a process and a progression of faith over time. AA's sometimes put it like this:

"First, *we came*, that is, we showed up and stumbled in the door.

Second, *we came to*, that is, we sobered up, came to our senses, and began to experience emotional sobriety.

Third, *we came to believe*, we began our real recovery process and our spiritual growth."

From the author… another lost sheep: Even when I felt the pain of my choices and vowed again to stop drinking, I couldn't do it. I couldn't **stay stopped!** I spent years grabbing one thing after another and always needing or wanting MORE. If one drink, one pill, or one whatever was good, then in my thinking, 3 or 4 would be better. I was created with a need for an attachment to God and when I didn't get that connection to HIM, I got connected and wrapped around people and "things" in my desperate attempt to fill that need. This temporary "fix" left me dissatisfied and tangled up. I *came to believe* that Jesus knows what's best for me, and things run smoother when HE is in the driver's seat. Today I am in constant wonder, because I don't know what God is going to do next. The only thing I know is that *God knows what He is doing,* and that "I shall not want." I love it when I have this attitude because it frees me up from worry and builds my confidence in God. God can restore me to sanity when I choose to believe that HE CAN. When we truly believe in God's power to restore us, He will be there, helping us to release our doubt. Let go of control and come "under the influence" of Him.

The Spiritual Principles in STEP 2 are open-mindedness, willingness, faith, trust, and humility.

"I shall not want,"

The welfare of any flock is entirely dependent on the time and care the shepherd gives it. There are differences between belonging to one master or another- to the Good Shepherd or to an imposter.

> ***From the author***... "I never knew a shepherd back in the 1980's, but I knew many dog owners. As a mail carrier I was keenly aware of who owned dogs and I learned which owners were indifferent to their pets. It was to my advantage to make friends with the four-legged beasts. "White-dog," a neglected dog on my route, was given little or no attention and sat along the side of his house in the hot summer and the rainy winter. His master just didn't care. I could hardly bare to see him each day, but he began to recognize the sound of my truck and he looked forward to the time I spent speaking to him, bringing him food and filling his water bowl. In my mind's eye I can still see "White-dog" panting in the Sacramento heat. "Sparky", another dog in Sacramento, had each and every provision met by his master and he had a different destiny. Sparky's master loved the Yellow Lab puppy as much as he loved his master. Sparky was my dog and he grew up with me *one day at a time* in my early recovery.
>
>  He seemed as happy as I was with the arrangement!"

1. There's only one true Shepherd that can meet our needs. Name some imposters.

2. It's not unusual to think that perhaps "the grass is greener on the other side of the fence." What are you letting go of from the other side of the fence? (the agents you sought to meet your deepest needs.... money, career, sex, chemicals, another person, grandiosity...)

   In Philippians 4:19 we read, *"And my God will meet all your needs according to His glorious riches in Christ Jesus."* This is the New Testament echo of this Old Testament statement: *"The Lord is my shepherd; I shall not want."*

   How precious it is to realize that this <u>completeness</u> of the Lord's provision is possible
   because of the <u>completeness</u> of His person!

3. When we come to our senses and turn away from codependent engagement with people, places and things, we turn towards the Shepherd to take care of us and we begin to experience **emotional sobriety**. Have you experienced it yet?

4. What provision(s) do you need right now from your Shepherd?

STEP 2 "Came to believe that God could return us to sanity."

We have experienced problems due to our use or someone else's use of chemicals, other self-destructive behaviors, and/or codependency, ***and we failed to change our behavior***. Sometimes the insanity of living with addiction can cause us to be desperate for help. Jesus says that if we have faith, real faith, it only takes a small amount to make a big difference. Jesus can help with any problem you have.

Check (✓) the problems you currently need help with. Put an (†) on problems already solved. Praise God!!!!

□ *depression*	□ *job loss/problems*	□ *miscarriage*	□ *suicide attempts*
□ *anxiety*	□ *guilt*	□ *sleeplessness*	□ *low self esteem*
□ *loss of credit*	□ *children problems*	□ *STD'S*	□ *embarrassing family members*
□ *incarceration*	□ *victim of abuse*	□ *legal problems*	□ *complaints from family/friends*
□ *isolation*	□ *secrets*	□ *lies*	□ *need to overcompensate*
□ *arrest*	□ *divorce*	□ *self doubt*	□ *changes in physical appearance*
□ *bad reputation*	□ *aggressiveness*	□ *poor decisions*	□ *poor work performance*
□ *loss of trust*	□ *neglect of kids*	□ *emergency room visits*	□ *EGO (Edging God Out)*
□ *self pity*	□ *money problems*	□ *self injury*	□ *driving under the influence*
□ *blackouts*	□ *health problems*	□ *anger/rage*	□ *driving w/ someone who is drunk*

This Step 2 is often referred to as "the HOPE step." Read about the HOPE of FAITH in Hebrews 11:1-10.

1. Describe the religious environment of your childhood. What was it like? What did you learn about God?

2. How did these early experiences influence the beliefs you have today?

3. What experiences have caused you to doubt God?

4. One thing that is sure to rob you of emotional sobriety is …worry. Read Colossians 3:1-4.
How do you deal with worry?

5. Read Philippians 4:6-7. What's Paul's strategy to help guard against troubles?

6. What harmful behaviors do you need to stop in order to increase your chances of recovering your

- Emotional health? ____

____

- Physical health?____

____

- Spiritual health? ____

____

- Psychological health? ____

____

"I shall not want."
STEP 2 "Came to believe that God could return us to sanity."

MATTHEW 9:12-13

MATTHEW 11:29

MARK 5:36

MARK 9:23-24

LUKE 5:31-32

LUKE 11:9-10

LUKE 18:42-43

"I shall not want."
STEP 2 "Came to believe that God could return us to sanity."

Rate your physical, psychological, emotional, and spiritual health

- Examine your health in each area of your life. Give each behavior a number from 1-5 (#5 means very well).
- Be HONEST. It's helpful to know the *truth* about your recovery health in order to take care of yourself.
- Circle **one** BEHAVIOR in each area that you are willing to work on daily for the next week.

MY BIOLOGICAL HEALTH (PHYSICAL)

MY RECOVERY DATE:		NUMBER OF CONTINOUS DAYS	
Nutrition- when and what you eat		Physical /dental exams & appointments	
Water		Medications/ daily vitamins	
Identifying/reducing emotional eating		Stress management/keeping it simple	
Sleep/rest (too much, too little)		Eliminating/reducing caffeine	
Exercise (easy does it)		Eliminating/reducing sugar	
Pacing your activities (too much, too little)		Other:	

MY PSYCHOLOGICAL HEALTH (MY THOUGHTS & BEHAVIOR)

Managing denial/ defense mechanisms		Music/art/school work	
Positive vs. Negative thinking		Journaling thoughts & behaviors	
Reducing obsessive thoughts		Making phone calls (sponsor, hotline)	
Daily structure/ being on time		Self-help meetings	
Making amends (promptly admit)		Building self esteem	
Money management		Other:	

MY EMOTIONAL/RELATIONAL HEALTH

Letting go of enabling people		Connecting with family in healthy way	
Managing emotions		Self care	
Spending time with **safe** people		Relaxation exercises	
Setting boundaries		Healthy sexual relations	
Having fun		Journaling feelings/ talking about them	
To Thine Own Self Be True. My "yes" is "yes," and my "no" is "no."		Other:	

MY SPIRITUAL HEALTH

Telling the truth to myself and others		Loving myself/ self-forgiveness	
Service to others		Church / Bible study	
Prayer		Serenity Prayer	
Meditation and/or quiet time with God		Gratitude list, affirmations	
Utilizing the Steps /Spiritual Principles		Enjoying nature	
Balance in everyday life (avoiding extremes)		Seeking/finding my purpose, finding what matters	

- Recognize emotional triggers and <u>change behavior.</u>
- Recognize anxiety and <u>practice relaxation techniques.</u>
- Recognize sleeping / eating habits that are slipping and <u>practice self-care</u>.

"I shall not want."

Sheep have a poor sense of direction, and they are extremely near-sighted. They can't see the "good" just ahead, or the danger around the corner. Our perception (of people, places and things) is also limited to the close-up.

1. When do you need God's perception most? (parenting, self-esteem, relationships, etc.) Give examples.

2. Is your mind focused on an idol? Is the idol yourself? Is it money, food, clothes, status?

3. Why might you ignore your shepherd?

If your mind is focused on an idol, your ability to see God is blinded. Oswald Chambers, in *My Utmost for His Highest,* writes, "You will be powerless when faced with difficulties and will be forced to endure in darkness." Look to God. Get away from the faces of the idols that are blinding your thinking.

The real test of spiritual focus is being able to bring your thoughts under control.

4, Can you deliberately visualize yourself depending on your Shepherd for all your needs? What can you do to keep your eyes and mind focused on God?

The more we learn about the sheep and shepherd terminology, the better we understand the metaphor of Psalm 23. Our Shepherd watches over all His flock. He sees the big picture. God will provide for you.

5. What have you learned about God from the Bible study so far?

6. What are your prayer requests?

STEP 2 "Came to believe that God could return us to sanity."

It takes honesty and open-mindedness to really understand that we cannot recover alone. We need help.

1. What **fears** get in the way <u>of trusting others?</u>

2. What **fears** get in the way <u>of trusting God?</u>

3. What **fears** get in the way <u>in receiving help?</u>

4. What did you learn from your family about asking for help?

Sometimes we find ourselves so troubled that we can't think straight.

> By working Step 2 we understand:
> **Sanity** as the ability, with God's help, to resist deadly temptation and
> **Insanity** as repeating the same old behavior over and over, knowing (or denying) that the result will always
> be the same (a drunk, a fight, a headache, remorse, a disaster… a relapse!!!!).

5. What does your insanity look like?

6. What does it feel like?

The Second Step is the one that opens the door of understanding and growth. God can return you to sanity when you notice you're repeating an old, ineffective behavior. Maybe you see the old crummy results or you experience the old crummy feelings. That's your cue…. Stop and use Step 2!!!! Remember, it's God who returns you to sanity.

2 Corinthians 12:9: *"But he said to me, "My grace is sufficient for you, for my power is made perfect in weakness."*

"I shall not want."
STEP 2 "Came to believe that God could return us to sanity."

JOHN 10:9

____

JOHN 11:26-27

____

____

____

JOHN 12:46

____

____

JOHN 14:6

____

____

ACTS 3:16

____

____

ACTS 4:12

____

____

PHILIPPIANS 4:19

____

____

____

"I shall not want."
STEP 2 "Came to believe that God could return us to sanity."

Rate your physical, psychological, emotional, and spiritual health

- Examine your health in each area of your life. Give each behavior a number from 1-5 (#5 means very well).
- Be HONEST. It's helpful to know the *truth* about your recovery health in order to take care of yourself.
- Circle **one** BEHAVIOR in each area that you are willing to work on daily for the next week.

MY BIOLOGICAL HEALTH (PHYSICAL)

MY RECOVERY DATE:		NUMBER OF CONTINOUS DAYS	
Nutrition- when and what you eat		Physical /dental exams & appointments	
Water		Medications/ daily vitamins	
Identifying/reducing emotional eating		Stress management/keeping it simple	
Sleep/rest (too much, too little)		Eliminating/reducing caffeine	
Exercise (easy does it)		Eliminating/reducing sugar	
Pacing your activities (too much, too little)		Other:	

MY PSYCHOLOGICAL HEALTH (MY THOUGHTS & BEHAVIOR)

Managing denial/ defense mechanisms		Music/art/school work	
Positive vs. Negative thinking		Journaling thoughts & behaviors	
Reducing obsessive thoughts		Making phone calls (sponsor, hotline)	
Daily structure/ being on time		Self-help meetings	
Making amends (promptly admit)		Building self esteem	
Money management		Other:	

MY EMOTIONAL/RELATIONAL HEALTH

Letting go of enabling people		Connecting with family in healthy way	
Managing emotions		Self care	
Spending time with **safe** people		Relaxation exercises	
Setting boundaries		Healthy sexual relations	
Having fun		Journaling feelings/ talking about them	
To Thine Own Self Be True. My "yes" is "yes," and my "no" is "no."		Other:	

MY SPIRITUAL HEALTH

Telling the truth to myself and others		Loving myself/ self-forgiveness	
Service to others		Church / Bible study	
Prayer		Serenity Prayer	
Meditation and/or quiet time with God		Gratitude list, affirmations	
Utilizing the Steps /Spiritual Principles		Enjoying nature	
Balance in everyday life (avoiding extremes)		Seeking/finding my purpose, finding what matters	

- Recognize emotional triggers and <u>change behavior.</u>
- Recognize anxiety and <u>practice relaxation techniques.</u>
- Recognize sleeping / eating habits that are slipping and <u>practice self-care</u>.

"I shall not want."

Sheep are defenseless (without their shepherd). They can't fight, can't run, can't blend into their surroundings, and they aren't clever in order to outsmart their enemies. We, too, are defenseless (without our shepherd). The Bible makes it clear that Satan is our enemy.

1 Peter 5:8 says *"Be self-controlled and alert. Your enemy the devil prowls around like a roaring lion looking for someone to devour."*

Satan would love to shift our point of view.

Yet we have nothing to fear. God understands and knows every one of His children. His love covers our bad moods, our full-blown disasters, our silent doubts, and our fears. He hears our deafening cries of defeat. He has the tender heart of a shepherd. God tells you the truth. The enemy tells you lies.

1. What are you battling at this time?

What battles do you experience in the following areas?	Look at the Hebrew names of the Lord. (see page 7) What do you need from God?
Physical health? (exercise, nutrition, etc.)	
Your mental health? (negative thinking, isolation, etc.)	
Your emotional health? (ignoring feelings, rage, etc.)	
Your spiritual health? (time with God, lack of faith, etc.)	

2. We don't have to revert to our old hiding places of the past. Name a few of those old places.

King David declared, "The Lord is a refuge for the oppressed, a stronghold in times of trouble. Those who know your name trust in you, for you, Lord, have never forsaken those who seek you" Psalm 9:9-10

3. God is our resting place. He is all we need. Think of a time when GOD was your refuge. Write about gratitude in your prayer to God.

Read & write Matthew 11:28-30.

STEP 2 "Came to believe that God could return us to sanity."

Big Book of Alcoholic Anonymous says:
Page 57: "Even so has God restored us all to our right minds. To this man, the revelation was sudden. Some of us grew into it more slowly. But He has come to all who have honestly sought Him."

The Good Book says:
Hebrews 11:1- *"Now faith is being sure of what we hope for and certain of what we do not see"*.
Hebrews 11:6- *"And without faith it is impossible to please God, because anyone who comes to him must believe that He exists and that he rewards those who earnestly seek Him"*.

1. Step 1 shows us the truth of our powerlessness. What are your vulnerabilities?

2. Step 2 keeps us focused on our recovery, **the solution**. Have you made big troubles out of little ones?

Sometimes it's helpful to stop and ask God for wisdom to discern what's crucial and important and what you can afford to ignore or "put on the shelf" for later.

3. What can you choose to address later in your recovery?

4. The recovery slogans you hear and read about are tools to keep you on track.
Make a list of some of the recovery slogans. Add to your list while in the group as you hear new ones.

5. Which one(s) will help you today?

"I shall not want."
STEP 2 "Came to believe that God could return us to sanity."

PHILIPPIANS 3:20

____

____

COLOSSIANS 2:13

____

____

HEBREWS 2:18

____

____

HEBREWS 7:25

____

____

JAMES 1:18

____

____

I JOHN 4:10

____

____

REVELATION 1:5-6

____

____

____

____

"I shall not want."
STEP 2 "Came to believe that God could return us to sanity."

WEEK THREE WELLNESS CHECK-IN

Rate your physical, psychological, emotional, and spiritual health

- Examine your health in each area of your life. Give each behavior a number from 1-5 (#5 means very well).
- Be HONEST. It's helpful to know the *truth* about your recovery health in order to take care of yourself.
- Circle **one** BEHAVIOR in each area that you are willing to work on daily for the next week.

MY BIOLOGICAL HEALTH (PHYSICAL)

MY RECOVERY DATE:		NUMBER OF CONTINOUS DAYS	
Nutrition- when and what you eat		Physical /dental exams & appointments	
Water		Medications/ daily vitamins	
Identifying/reducing emotional eating		Stress management/keeping it simple	
Sleep/rest (too much, too little)		Eliminating/reducing caffeine	
Exercise (easy does it)		Eliminating/reducing sugar	
Pacing your activities (too much, too little)		Other:	

MY PSYCHOLOGICAL HEALTH (MY THOUGHTS & BEHAVIOR)

Managing denial/ defense mechanisms		Music/art/school work	
Positive vs. Negative thinking		Journaling thoughts & behaviors	
Reducing obsessive thoughts		Making phone calls (sponsor, hotline)	
Daily structure/ being on time		Self-help meetings	
Making amends (promptly admit)		Building self esteem	
Money management		Other:	

MY EMOTIONAL/RELATIONAL HEALTH

Letting go of enabling people		Connecting with family in healthy way	
Managing emotions		Self care	
Spending time with **safe** people		Relaxation exercises	
Setting boundaries		Healthy sexual relations	
Having fun		Journaling feelings/ talking about them	
To Thine Own Self Be True. My "yes" is "yes," and my "no" is "no."		Other:	

MY SPIRITUAL HEALTH

Telling the truth to myself and others		Loving myself/ self-forgiveness	
Service to others		Church / Bible study	
Prayer		Serenity Prayer	
Meditation and/or quiet time with God		Gratitude list, affirmations	
Utilizing the Steps /Spiritual Principles		Enjoying nature	
Balance in everyday life (avoiding extremes)		Seeking/finding my purpose, finding what matters	

- Recognize emotional triggers and <u>change behavior.</u>
- Recognize anxiety and <u>practice relaxation techniques.</u>
- Recognize sleeping / eating habits that are slipping and <u>practice self-care</u>.

"I shall not want."

Another characteristic of sheep is the fact that they cannot cleanse themselves. Other animals wash themselves with their tongues, some roll in sand or dust, and others can bathe in rivers or ponds. Sheep get dirtier and stay that way until their shepherd cleanses them. We cannot clean ourselves *spiritually* any more than sheep can cleanse themselves *physically*. **But we try.** We try by being "religious", through observing "sacraments," and through attempting to be a "good person."

1. Why doesn't it work? What does Scripture teach?

2. We've all failed in one way or another, and we all know what shame feels like. We are ashamed of our past failures and our bad habits. We may grow impatient with ourselves when we continue the same sins over again. This may cause discouragement and fear of relapse.
Do you have trouble forgiving yourself? _______ Expand on your answer here:

3. We no longer have to hide in shame every time we slip. Because of what Jesus has done, we can admit our wrongs, seek HIS will for us and move on. **Rely on His love**….We are living under His power and His love.
Do you see the parallel of what Jesus Christ does for us, and what the shepherd does for his sheep?

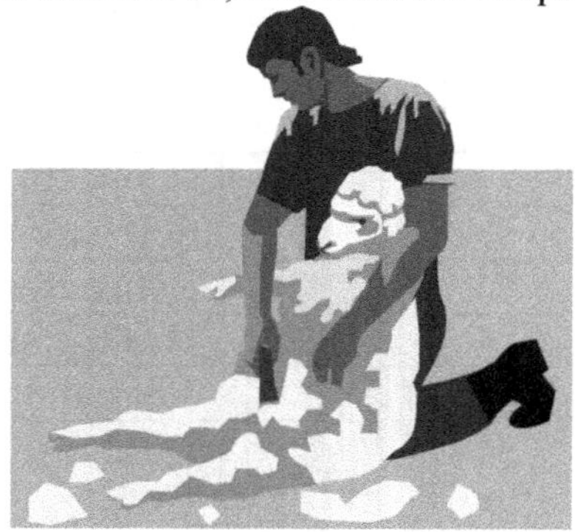

4. When the shepherd shears off the wool (the dirt), it can be used for good (wooly socks).
Are you laying in a bed of shame and self-condemnation, like a sheep in its own dirty wool?
Expand on your answer here:

5. What does God's Word say in Romans 8:28?

6. We need to be patient with ourselves and know that God will never abandon us. Read Romans 8:37-39.
What does it mean to you?

STEP 2 "Came to believe that God could return us to sanity."

The beauty of this step is that we can begin to think about our recovery with the Help, Hope and Power of Jesus Christ by our side.

1. Are you living ***"under the influence"*** of God? What does that mean to you?

2. Insanity is a loss of our perception and our sense of proportion. Is your life out of balance today?

3. Rate your recovery with a number from 1-5 (# 5 is in perfect balance!!)

4. Are you "under the influence" of something other than your Shepherd? (list possible influences below.)
For example: fear, money, other people. Expand on your answer.

Anything you put ABOVE (↑) your recovery, you will lose.
(remember, your recovery is your restored health, your walk with God, …)

The Vine's Expository Dictionary defines the Greek word "hope" like this: "In the New Testament, a favorable and confident expectation." *"May the God of hope fill you with all joy and peace as you trust in him, so that you may overflow with hope by the power of the Holy Spirit."* (Rom. 15:13 NIV)

5. What gives you hope about today?

6. God is working out his good purposes in your life. How hard is it for you to let go of all your questions and trust Him?

7. What does the phrase "came to believe" mean to you?

"I shall not want."
STEP 2 "Came to believe that God could return us to sanity."

ACTS 16:31

ROMANS 8:31

1 CORINTHIANS 1:18

2 CORINTHIANS 1:10

2 CORINTHIANS 5:21

GALATIONS 1:19-20

EPHESIANS 2:4-5

WEEK FOUR WELLNESS CHECK-IN

Rate your physical, psychological, emotional, and spiritual health

- Examine your health in each area of your life. Give each behavior a number from 1-5 (#5 means very well).
- Be HONEST. It's helpful to know the *truth* about your recovery health in order to take care of yourself.
- Circle **one** BEHAVIOR in each area that you are willing to work on daily for the next week.

MY BIOLOGICAL HEALTH (PHYSICAL)

MY RECOVERY DATE:		NUMBER OF CONTINOUS DAYS	
Nutrition- when and what you eat		Physical /dental exams & appointments	
Water		Medications/ daily vitamins	
Identifying/reducing emotional eating		Stress management/keeping it simple	
Sleep/rest (too much, too little)		Eliminating/reducing caffeine	
Exercise (easy does it)		Eliminating/reducing sugar	
Pacing your activities (too much, too little)		Other:	

MY PSYCHOLOGICAL HEALTH (MY THOUGHTS & BEHAVIOR)

Managing denial/ defense mechanisms		Music/art/school work	
Positive vs. Negative thinking		Journaling thoughts & behaviors	
Reducing obsessive thoughts		Making phone calls (sponsor, hotline)	
Daily structure/ being on time		Self-help meetings	
Making amends (promptly admit)		Building self esteem	
Money management		Other:	

MY EMOTIONAL/RELATIONAL HEALTH

Letting go of enabling people		Connecting with family in healthy way	
Managing emotions		Self care	
Spending time with **safe** people		Relaxation exercises	
Setting boundaries		Healthy sexual relations	
Having fun		Journaling feelings/ talking about them	
To Thine Own Self Be True. My "yes" is "yes," and my "no" is "no."		Other:	

MY SPIRITUAL HEALTH

Telling the truth to myself and others		Loving myself/ self-forgiveness	
Service to others		Church / Bible study	
Prayer		Serenity Prayer	
Meditation and/or quiet time with God		Gratitude list, affirmations	
Utilizing the Steps /Spiritual Principles		Enjoying nature	
Balance in everyday life (avoiding extremes)		Seeking/finding my purpose, finding what matters	

- Recognize emotional triggers and <u>change behavior.</u>
- Recognize anxiety and <u>practice relaxation techniques.</u>
- Recognize sleeping / eating habits that are slipping and <u>practice self-care.</u>

PSALM 23   "I shall not want,"

Step 2 "Came to believe that God could return us to sanity."

COMPLETION

My favorite Scripture for Chapter 2: (write it here)

_______ I understand Chapter 2 and will continue to use it daily.
_______ I completed the Bible study in a ***Psalm 23*** group.
_______ I worked with a PSALM-partner this month to study Chapter 2.

Psalm Partner NAME: ____

Psalm Partner Phone # _______________________________________

Today's date ____

My Signature ____________________________ **PSALM-Partner** ________________

BIBLE STUDY AT A GLANCE

Matthew 9:12-13	John 12:46	James 1:18
Matthew 11:29	John 14:6	I John 4:10
Mark 5:35-36	Acts 3:16	Revelation 1:5-6
Mark 9:23-24	Acts 4:12	Psalm 18:3
Luke 1:37	Acts 16:31	Psalm 18: 16-19
Luke 5:31-32	Romans 8:31	Psalm 27:13-14
Luke 11:9-10	1 Corinthians 1:18-25	Psalm 33:20-21
Luke 18:42-43	2 Corinthians 1:10	Psalm 34:10
John 3:15-18	2 Corinthians 5:21	Psalm 34:18
John 6:29	Galatians 1:19-20	Psalm 119:153-154
John 6:63	Ephesians 2:4-5	Psalm 119:166
John 6:68-69	Philippians 3:20	Psalm 121:7-8
John 7:37-38	Philippians 4:19	Psalm 130:1-5
John 8:12	Colossians 2:13	Psalm 142:6
John 10:9	Hebrews 2:14-18	Psalm 145:15-16
John 11:25-27	Hebrews 7:24-25	Proverbs 1:7
		Proverbs 2:1-5

The Lord is My Shepherd
A 12 Step Journey through PSALM 23

DISCOVERY
CHAPTER THREE
†

Psalm 23
"He makes me lie down in green pastures;"

STEP 3 "Made a decision to turn our will and
our lives over to the care of God"

CHAPTER THREE INTRODUCTION

PSALM 23
"He makes me lie down in green pastures;"

A good shepherd knows what makes his sheep healthy, content, and safe. He painstakingly searches out green pastures and quiet waters for his flock, defends them against attack, cares for those that are injured and carries the young of the flock in his arms. He tends to them all day and under the stars at night. Sheep are timid and fearful and they must have things just right to be calm enough to lie down. A good shepherd can meet the requirements, but it's not easy work. Sheep need freedom from **fear**, freedom from **tension**, freedom from the torment of parasites and insects **(aggravations),** and freedom from **hunger**. Their physical, earthly needs must be met. We, as humans, have many of these same needs that keep us from lying down in green pastures too. At all times we would be wise to walk a little closer to Jesus, our Lord and Shepherd.

Our Good Shepherd not only meets our physical needs
but we get spiritual nourishment from the Word of God!!!

STEP 3 "Made a decision to turn our will and our lives over to the care of God"

We may have to "make the decision" over and over again and practice giving up control to our Shepherd. It's so easy to take it (the control) back into our own hands. Use <u>AA's Third Step Prayer</u> as you practice letting go.
"God, I offer myself to Thee- to build with me and to do with me as Thou wilt. Relieve me of the bondage of self, that I may better do thy will. Take away my difficulties, that victory over them may bear witness to those I would help in Thy power, Thy love, and Thy way of life. May I do Thy will always!" (Alcoholics Anonymous, p. 63)

In Chapter 1 we admitted that we are not the Shepherd, that our lives are out of control and that we are powerless to change things on our own. **(HONESTY)**	**"I CAN'T"**
In Chapter 2 we came to believe that God could help us out of our pain, chaos and troubled thinking. Because Jesus is our Shepherd, "we shall not want" for anything. **(HOPE)**	**"GOD CAN"**
Now in Chapter 3 we ask God to assume control over every aspect of our lives. **(FAITH)** God makes a way for us to lie down in His green pastures and invites us to get out of the center of our universe. We make a decision to hand that place back to HIM. Then God said, **"Never will I leave you; never will I forsake you"** (Hebrews 13:5)	**"I THINK I' LL LET HIM"**

It is critical to stop running on self-will.

Trust comes into play after faith has been applied. We can practice the spiritual principle of commitment by reaffirming our decision on a regular basis and by continuing to take action. Keep going to recovery groups and learning about Jesus. Our Shepherd has it all planned out. When we actually lie down, we can make a healthy decision to turn our will and our lives over to the only one who is worthy of being trusted. The Bible tells us, *"God is not a man, that He should lie, nor a son of man, that he should change His mind."*   (Numbers 23:19)

"Be still and know that I am God; I will be exalted among the nations. I will be exalted in the earth." (Psalm 46:10)
The Spiritual Principles for STEP 3 are surrender, willingness, faith, trust, and commitment.

"He makes me lie down in green pastures;"

It is the Good Shepherd who makes it possible for his sheep to lie down, to rest, to relax, to be content and quiet. The flock that is restless, discontented, always agitated and disturbed **will not** flourish. Restless sheep will not lie down. They remain standing just in case they need to flee. Like sheep, we need Christ's presence to dispel fear and panic.

1. What are you like when you are **anxious**?

2. What **fears** do you have that prevent you from lying down? (relaxing in the Lord).

3. Describe a time when anxiety and fear prevented you from flourishing?

4. **How often** does fear of the unknown worry you?

5. Describe a time when the awareness of the presence of the Shepherd helped calm a difficult situation.

---

2 Timothy 1:7 *"For God did not give us the spirit of timidity, but a spirit of power, of love, and of self-discipline.*
"

STEP 3 "Made a decision to turn our will and our lives over to the care of God."

"Made a decision"- Some of us haven't made a decision in a long time. We've had our decisions made for us by our addiction, codependency, or by default because of procrastination, fear, or depression.

1. What has prevented you from making decisions in the past?

Page 62 of The Big Book says:

> We had to have God's help. This is the how and why of it. First of all, we had to quit playing God. It didn't work. Next, we decided that hereafter in this drama of life; God was going to be our director. He is the Principal; we are His agents. He is the Father and we are His children. Most good ideas are simple and this concept was the keystone of the new and triumphant arch through which we passed to freedom.

2. What areas of your life are difficult for you to turn over to God?

3. What do you fear might happen if you do?

4. Why is it important to turn them over anyway?

5. What **action** can you take to help make your decision stick?

> THE GOOD SHEPHERD HAS PERFECT VISION OF THE PRESENT AND THE FUTURE.
> He's the director. Only He can view "the end from the beginning." Read Isaiah 46:10.

6. As one of His sheep, we have the benefit of His perfect perspective.
How does this help you with your walk in recovery (living "under the influence" of GOD)?

"He makes me lie down in green pastures;"
STEP 3 "Made a decision to turn our will and our lives over to the care of God."

MATTHEW 6:33-34

MATTHEW 9:36

MATTHEW 10:38-39

MATTHEW 11:28-30

MATTHEW 16:24-25

ACTS 2:21

Rate your physical, psychological, emotional, and spiritual health

- Examine your health in each area of your life. Give each behavior a number from 1-5 (#5 means very well).
- Be HONEST. It's helpful to know the *truth* about your recovery health in order to take care of yourself.
- Circle **one** BEHAVIOR in each area that you are willing to work on daily for the next week.

MY BIOLOGICAL HEALTH (PHYSICAL)

MY RECOVERY DATE:		NUMBER OF CONTINOUS DAYS	
Nutrition- when and what you eat		Physical /dental exams & appointments	
Water		Medications/ daily vitamins	
Identifying/reducing emotional eating		Stress management/keeping it simple	
Sleep/rest (too much, too little)		Eliminating/reducing caffeine	
Exercise (easy does it)		Eliminating/reducing sugar	
Pacing your activities (too much, too little)		Other:	

MY PSYCHOLOGICAL HEALTH (MY THOUGHTS & BEHAVIOR)

Managing denial/ defense mechanisms		Music/art/school work	
Positive vs. Negative thinking		Journaling thoughts & behaviors	
Reducing obsessive thoughts		Making phone calls (sponsor, hotline)	
Daily structure/ being on time		Self-help meetings	
Making amends (promptly admit)		Building self esteem	
Money management		Other:	

MY EMOTIONAL/RELATIONAL HEALTH

Letting go of enabling people		Connecting with family in healthy way	
Managing emotions		Self care	
Spending time with **safe** people		Relaxation exercises	
Setting boundaries		Healthy sexual relations	
Having fun		Journaling feelings/ talking about them	
To Thine Own Self Be True. My "yes" is "yes," and my "no" is "no."		Other:	

MY SPIRITUAL HEALTH

Telling the truth to myself and others		Loving myself/ self-forgiveness	
Service to others		Church / Bible study	
Prayer		Serenity Prayer	
Meditation and/or quiet time with God		Gratitude list, affirmations	
Utilizing the Steps /Spiritual Principles		Enjoying nature	
Balance in everyday life (avoiding extremes)		Seeking/finding my purpose, finding what matters	

- Recognize emotional triggers and <u>change behavior.</u>
- Recognize anxiety and <u>practice relaxation techniques.</u>
- Recognize sleeping / eating habits that are slipping and <u>practice self-care</u>.

"He makes me lie down in green pastures;"

Sheep have an order of dominance or status within the group referred to as the "butting order." Generally, an old domineering ewe butts her way to the top to claim the best grazing spots or favorite bedding grounds. The other sheep use the same tactics to maintain their position often causing such rivalry and competition that they *remain standing* to drive off the intruder. Continuous conflict causes the sheep to become edgy, tense, discontented, restless and irritable.

1. When has jealousy or competition made you restless?

2. Do you worry about what others are thinking about you? Write about your worry.

3. Have you lost sleep or rest?

4. When have you been hurt by competition in your….
FAMILY?

WORK?

SCHOOL?

GROUPS?

A few LESSONS we can learn from the sheep:
1. The less aggressive sheep are often far more contented, quiet and restful.
2. All of the friction stops when the shepherd comes into view. The shepherd's presence makes all the difference in their behavior. When our eyes are on our Master they are not on those around us.

Matthew 5:7 "Blessed are the merciful, for they will be shown mercy."

5. Can either of the lessons above help you with a current situation? Write about it here.

STEP 3 "Made a decision to turn our will and our lives over to the care of God."

Reflections from the Old-timers in A.A.:
"We submit ourselves to the care of God to become different **on the inside** (our will) and **on the outside** (our lives). And that is a life changing experience!"

1. What's the difference between your will and God's will?

Self-will – look for (dishonesty, resentment, selfish, and fear)	versus	God's will- notice (honesty, purity, unselfishness, and love)
1		
2		
3		
4		
5		
6		
7		

2. What were your *motives* THE LAST TIME you acted on self-will?

EGO
E (Edging) **G** (God) **O** (Out)

---

3. When we try to get our way at all costs, we ignore the feelings or needs of others.
Who has your ego hurt?

God's will is unconditional and always waiting for us. Turning our lives over to God allows His love to fill up Our hearts. Filling up on God's love helps us to avoid relapses and overcome our most powerful insecurities.

Insecurities on the inside; Your Will   **Insecurities on the outside; Your Life**

"He makes me lie down in green pastures;"
STEP 3 "Made a decision to turn our will and our lives over to the care of God."

ROMANS 3:21-24

ROMANS 4:20-21

ROMANS 5:1-2

ROMANS 5:8-9

ROMANS 8:1-4

Rate your physical, psychological, emotional, and spiritual health

- Examine your health in each area of your life. Give each behavior a number from 1-5 (#5 means very well).
- Be HONEST. It's helpful to know the *truth* about your recovery health in order to take care of yourself.
- Circle **one** BEHAVIOR in each area that you are willing to work on daily for the next week.

MY BIOLOGICAL HEALTH (PHYSICAL)

MY RECOVERY DATE:		NUMBER OF CONTINOUS DAYS	
Nutrition- when and what you eat		Physical /dental exams & appointments	
Water		Medications/ daily vitamins	
Identifying/reducing emotional eating		Stress management/keeping it simple	
Sleep/rest (too much, too little)		Eliminating/reducing caffeine	
Exercise (easy does it)		Eliminating/reducing sugar	
Pacing your activities (too much, too little)		Other:	

MY PSYCHOLOGICAL HEALTH (MY THOUGHTS & BEHAVIOR)

Managing denial/ defense mechanisms		Music/art/school work	
Positive vs. Negative thinking		Journaling thoughts & behaviors	
Reducing obsessive thoughts		Making phone calls (sponsor, hotline)	
Daily structure/ being on time		Self-help meetings	
Making amends (promptly admit)		Building self esteem	
Money management		Other:	

MY EMOTIONAL/RELATIONAL HEALTH

Letting go of enabling people		Connecting with family in healthy way	
Managing emotions		Self care	
Spending time with **safe** people		Relaxation exercises	
Setting boundaries		Healthy sexual relations	
Having fun		Journaling feelings/ talking about them	
To Thine Own Self Be True. My "yes" is "yes," and my "no" is "no."		Other:	

MY SPIRITUAL HEALTH

Telling the truth to myself and others		Loving myself/ self-forgiveness	
Service to others		Church / Bible study	
Prayer		Serenity Prayer	
Meditation and/or quiet time with God		Gratitude list, affirmations	
Utilizing the Steps /Spiritual Principles		Enjoying nature	
Balance in everyday life (avoiding extremes)		Seeking/finding my purpose, finding what matters	

- Recognize emotional triggers and <u>change behavior.</u>
- Recognize anxiety and <u>practice relaxation techniques.</u>
- Recognize sleeping / eating habits that are slipping and <u>practice self-care</u>.

"He makes me lie down in green pastures;"

From early dawn until late at night the sheep owner is alert to the welfare of his flock. His sharp eye detects whether they are ill or if a sheep or lamb requires special care. The flock becomes discontent and distracted when parasites and insects such as nasal flies, warble flies and ticks torment them. They are completely defenseless without their shepherd. He applies insect repellent and has his sheep dipped to clear their fleeces of ticks BECAUSE he loves his sheep, each and every one. We often have our own little irritations, frustrations and pet peeves.

1. What bugs you?

2. Do you have a *re-occurring* annoyance?

> The Holy Spirit brings <u>healing, comfort</u> and <u>calmness</u> in the face of the abrasive aspects of life.
> When we turn and expose the problem we can then ask for help (I can't cope, please take over!)

3. How hard is it for you to do this? WHY?

4. Read Matthew 13:22-23.
What "cares of the world" enter into your life?

5. Do you believe they can *choke out the Word* and prevent you from bearing fruit? Why?

> Receive the Holy Spirit. No matter what ***changes*** God has performed in you, never rely on them.
> Build only on the Person of Jesus Christ, and on the Spirit He gives.

6. What does this mean to you?

STEP 3 "Made a decision to turn our will and our lives over to the care of God."

THIRD STEP PRAYER

Dear God,
I come to you in the name of Jesus. I'm sorry about the mess I've made in my life. I want to turn away from all the wrong things I've ever done. Please forgive me for it all.
I know you have the power to change my life and can turn me into a winner. Thank You Lord for getting my attention long enough to interest me in trying it Your way.
God, please take over the management of my life, my affairs, and everything about me. I am making this conscious decision to turn my will and my life over to Your care and I'm asking You to please take over all parts of my life. I surrender my will to Your will and ask you to take over the decision-making for me, because I haven't done too well on my own. Thank You, Jesus, for understanding how hard it is for me to give myself up.
Please, God, move into my heart, through Jesus Your Son, the one who died for me and whom You raised from the dead. However You do it, is Your business, but make Yourself real inside me and fill my awful emptiness. Fill me with Your love and Holy Spirit and make me know Your will for me. And now Lord, help Yourself to me and keep on doing it. I'm not sure I want You to, but do it anyhow.
I rejoice that I am now part of Your people; that my uncertainty is gone forever and that You have control of my will and life. Thank You for saying in Your Word that You'll never leave me or forsake me.
      Praise Your Name!

1. Make this prayer your own. Underline the parts that have special meaning for you.

2. How can you turn a situation over to God and let go of the results?

3. What can you do when your friends or loved ones make decisions you don't like?

4. What can you do to try to see others as God sees them?

5. How can you express God's will in your actions and words towards others?

Remember, it is not what we do that determines who we are,
it is who we are and what we believe that determines what we do.
WE WALK BY FAITH

"He makes me lie down in green pastures;"
Step 3 "Made a decision to turn our will and our lives over to the care of God."

1 PETER 1:3-4

1 PETER 2:24-25

1 PETER 4:11

2 TIMOTHY 4:22

HEBREWS 4:16

HEBREWS 11:1-2

PSALM 3:8

Rate your physical, psychological, emotional, and spiritual health

- Examine your health in each area of your life. Give each behavior a number from 1-5 (#5 means very well).
- Be HONEST. It's helpful to know the *truth* about your recovery health in order to take care of yourself.
- Circle **one** BEHAVIOR in each area that you are willing to work on daily for the next week.

MY BIOLOGICAL HEALTH (PHYSICAL)

MY RECOVERY DATE:		NUMBER OF CONTINOUS DAYS	
Nutrition- when and what you eat		Physical /dental exams & appointments	
Water		Medications/ daily vitamins	
Identifying/reducing emotional eating		Stress management/keeping it simple	
Sleep/rest (too much, too little)		Eliminating/reducing caffeine	
Exercise (easy does it)		Eliminating/reducing sugar	
Pacing your activities (too much, too little)		Other:	

MY PSYCHOLOGICAL HEALTH (MY THOUGHTS & BEHAVIOR)

Managing denial/ defense mechanisms		Music/art/school work	
Positive vs. Negative thinking		Journaling thoughts & behaviors	
Reducing obsessive thoughts		Making phone calls (sponsor, hotline)	
Daily structure/ being on time		Self-help meetings	
Making amends (promptly admit)		Building self esteem	
Money management		Other:	

MY EMOTIONAL/RELATIONAL HEALTH

Letting go of enabling people		Connecting with family in healthy way	
Managing emotions		Self care	
Spending time with **safe** people		Relaxation exercises	
Setting boundaries		Healthy sexual relations	
Having fun		Journaling feelings/ talking about them	
To Thine Own Self Be True. My "yes" is "yes," and my "no" is "no."		Other:	

MY SPIRITUAL HEALTH

Telling the truth to myself and others		Loving myself/ self-forgiveness	
Service to others		Church / Bible study	
Prayer		Serenity Prayer	
Meditation and/or quiet time with God		Gratitude list, affirmations	
Utilizing the Steps /Spiritual Principles		Enjoying nature	
Balance in everyday life (avoiding extremes)		Seeking/finding my purpose, finding what matters	

- Recognize emotional triggers and <u>change behavior.</u>
- Recognize anxiety and <u>practice relaxation techniques.</u>
- Recognize sleeping / eating habits that are slipping and <u>practice self-care</u>.

"He makes me lie down in green pastures;"

There's still another aspect of the shepherd's job that is crucial to the contentment of his flock. There must be the freedom from the *fear of hunger*. Green pastures are the result of tremendous toil by the skillful shepherd. He clears rocky land, plows, plants, and irrigates the brown barren hills. His goal is to supply such an ample amount that his sheep can not only eat their fill, but can even lie down **in the abundance.** The Good Shepherd has prepared green pastures for you.

1. How much of your time are you spending in God's green pastures?

2. God doesn't force us to feed on his Word. It is our option.
Have you left the Good Shepherd's provisions for something else? Where are you spending your time?

3. Read John 6:36-40. The words we read and study point to GOD. Describe your relationship with God.

4. Read John 6:56-57. When we "feed" on God we will see our lives transformed.
What can you do to keep up your spiritual nutrition?

5. With healthy boundaries you can choose to say yes or no to people- do you need to work on your **boundaries** to keep yourself on track? Make a list of the obstacles to your spiritual nutrition.

STEP 3 "Made a decision to turn our will and our lives over to the care of God."

We don't have to be "good enough" to turn our lives over to God, only willing. He will be with us, to help us change, as we take the action steps in our recovery.

1. How does your faith build on the surrender you developed in Chapter One and Chapter Two??

2. Rate how comfortable you are giving up the responsibility of running everything?
 (Rate with a number from 1 to10, 10 is high, very comfortable) Why?

3. Have you had a bad experience in a relationship where you trusted someone who was untrustworthy?

4. Read Matthew 7:7-8 (*ask, seek, knock*)
How does this relate to turning your will and life over to Jesus?

5. You may have to "turn it over" even when doing so doesn't seem to be having any positive effect.
What should you do then?

6. Read James 1. Your Notes:

7. What happens if you don't like His will for you and it doesn't fit into your plans?

8. How do you feel about *trusting* Him anyway?

9. Which verse from the Bible helps you to "Let go, Let God"?
You may like it better like this, "Let God, Let go!"
Read Matthew 7:24-27.

"He makes me lie down in green pastures;"
STEP 3 "Made a decision to turn our will and our lives over to the care of God."

LUKE 11:2-4

JOHN 1:12

JOHN 5:24

JOHN 6:35

JOHN 8:12

JOHN 12:26

JOHN 17:3

WEEK FOUR WELLNESS CHECK-IN

Rate your physical, psychological, emotional, and spiritual health

- Examine your health in each area of your life. Give each behavior a number from 1-5 (#5 means very well).
- Be HONEST. It's helpful to know the *truth* about your recovery health in order to take care of yourself.
- Circle **one** BEHAVIOR in each area that you are willing to work on daily for the next week.

MY BIOLOGICAL HEALTH (PHYSICAL)

MY RECOVERY DATE:		NUMBER OF CONTINOUS DAYS	
Nutrition- when and what you eat		Physical /dental exams & appointments	
Water		Medications/ daily vitamins	
Identifying/reducing emotional eating		Stress management/keeping it simple	
Sleep/rest (too much, too little)		Eliminating/reducing caffeine	
Exercise (easy does it)		Eliminating/reducing sugar	
Pacing your activities (too much, too little)		Other:	

MY PSYCHOLOGICAL HEALTH (MY THOUGHTS & BEHAVIOR)

Managing denial/ defense mechanisms		Music/art/school work	
Positive vs. Negative thinking		Journaling thoughts & behaviors	
Reducing obsessive thoughts		Making phone calls (sponsor, hotline)	
Daily structure/ being on time		Self-help meetings	
Making amends (promptly admit)		Building self esteem	
Money management		Other:	

MY EMOTIONAL/RELATIONAL HEALTH

Letting go of enabling people		Connecting with family in healthy way	
Managing emotions		Self care	
Spending time with **safe** people		Relaxation exercises	
Setting boundaries		Healthy sexual relations	
Having fun		Journaling feelings/ talking about them	
To Thine Own Self Be True. My "yes" is "yes," and my "no" is "no."		Other:	

MY SPIRITUAL HEALTH

Telling the truth to myself and others		Loving myself/ self-forgiveness	
Service to others		Church / Bible study	
Prayer		Serenity Prayer	
Meditation and/or quiet time with God		Gratitude list, affirmations	
Utilizing the Steps /Spiritual Principles		Enjoying nature	
Balance in everyday life (avoiding extremes)		Seeking/finding my purpose, finding what matters	

- Recognize emotional triggers and <u>change behavior.</u>
- Recognize anxiety and <u>practice relaxation techniques.</u>
- Recognize sleeping / eating habits that are slipping and <u>practice self-care.</u>

PSALM 23 "He makes me lie down in green pastures;"

STEP 3 "Made a decision to turn our will and our lives over to the care of God."

COMPLETION

My favorite Scripture for Chapter 3: (write it here)

_______ I understand Chapter 3 and will continue to use it daily.
_______ I completed the Bible study in a ***PSALM 23*** group.
_______ I worked with a PSALM-Partner this month to study Chapter 3.

PSALM-Partner NAME: ____

PSALM-Partner Phone # _______________________________________

Today's date ____

My Signature ___________________________ **PSALM-Partner** _______________

BIBLE STUDY AT A GLANCE

Matthew 6:31-34	Acts 2:21	Psalm 3:8	Psalm 113:7-8
Matthew 9:36	Romans 3:21-24	Psalm 7:1	Psalm 116:1-4
Matthew 10:37-39	Romans 4:20-25	Psalm 9:9-10	Psalm 142:5-6
Matthew 11:28-30	Romans 5:1	Psalm 17:6-8	Psalm 147:11
Matthew 16:24-26	Romans 5:8-11	Psalm 23:2	Proverbs 3:5-6
Luke 9:57-62	Romans 8:1	Psalm 30:1-3	Proverbs 16:9
Luke 11:2-4	Romans 10:9-13	Psalm 31:14-16	
Luke 24:46-47	2 Corinthians 1:3-5	Psalm 56:3-4	
John 1:12-13	Ephesians 1:3-11	Psalm 61:1-4	
John 5:24	Ephesians 1:11-14	Psalm 62:5-7	
John 6:35-40	Ephesians 2:8-9	Psalm 68:19-20	
John 8:12	Hebrews 4:1-2	Psalm 86:11-13	
John 12:26	I Peter 1:3-5	Psalm 91:1-4	
John 17:3	I Peter 2:24-25	Psalm 94:17-19	

The Lord is My Shepherd
A 12 Step Journey through PSALM 23

DECISION
CHAPTER FOUR
✝

PSALM 23
"He leads me beside the quiet waters."

STEP 4
"Made a searching and fearless moral inventory
of ourselves."

DECISION

FROM THE AUTHOR

I had avoided my family during my alcohol and drug using years. I moved back to my hometown and closer to my family towards the end my first year of recovery. I was able to make this move because God opened the door for a job transfer with the United States Post Office. In retrospect I see that God handpicked the specific Post Office and time of that move, but back in 1987, I was a beginner in my spiritual walk, so I stepped through the door that opened and hoped for the best. I was pretty beat up physically, emotionally, mentally and spiritually. God made me lay down in the green pastures and boy did I need the rest. In my DECISION to follow my Shepherd, He led me to quiet waters and had me really take an honest look at myself.

I realized I had a thinking problem. My thinking centered around my need to be liked and accepted, to get my own way *at any cost* and to be "in control." Automatic behaviors reflected my self-centered motives whether I picked up a drink or not! My personality was riddled with secrets, lies, and denial (minimizing, manipulating, blaming).

ANOTHER LOST SHEEP

These traits and behaviors were like dirty rocks and stones hidden out of my sight and tucked away in my "backpack". Under their weight along with boulders of quilt, shame, fear, and resentment my reflection in the quiet waters mirrored a face lined with physical, mental, emotional and spiritual stress. The Good Shepherd led this lost and broken sheep to the quiet waters and there I sat with Jesus by my side. He helped me unload the stones into the quiet waters. They fell to the bottom, disappearing out of sight leaving only a ring of ripples at the entry site. Some of the heavy stones made a "kerplunk" and a splash back into my face, bringing refreshment and relief. How could this be happening… refreshment at a time of such deep regret? My reflection over time began changing and God began restoring my soul.

By making the DECISION to unload my old ways of thinking and behaving, in exchange for God's ways, I am experiencing God's faithfulness to do for me what I can't do for myself. He walks with me through the valleys of life while his rod and his staff comfort me. David's words and the order of each line in his poem demonstrate the heart of a shepherd that knows what's best for his sheep.

"Humble yourselves before the Lord, and he will lift you up." James 4:10

CHAPTER FOUR INTRODUCTION

PSALM 23
"He leads me beside the quiet waters."

The shepherd plans ahead and has watering places already prepared for the arrival of his flocks. This is not easy for a shepherd in dry seasons, or in arid regions. Only through his sweat, energy, and strength will his sheep be satisfied. The three main sources of water for his sheep are: 1) dew on the grass, 2) deep wells, and 3) springs and streams. The flock of the good shepherd has clean and fresh water abundantly provided for them.

A poorly managed flock will set out on their own in search of water and may end up finding polluted potholes where the water is filthy and contaminated with parasite eggs and insects. Jesus knows that we have thirsty souls that can only be fully satisfied and fully quenched by His "Living Water" that overflows of Himself. In MATTHEW 5:6, He said, *"Blessed are they which do hunger and thirst after righteousness; for they shall be filled (satisfied)."* He gently leads us beside the quiet waters. He doesn't "drive" us there. **We must allow Jesus, our Good Shepherd, to lead us.** Having made the **DECISION** to continue on our quest for recovery and optimal health, we commit to letting The Good Shepherd lead us forward. We'll take a long hard look at ourselves and unload anything that doesn't fit into God's will.

STEP 4 "Made a searching and fearless moral inventory of ourselves."

The Transition Phase: Now we identify the defects of character that have kept us in bondage. Clarence Snyder, an old-timer from AA, states, "This is the most misunderstood Step. We are talking about the 'nature' of our wrongs - not necessarily all the details of each act we have done. Steps 4 through Step 7 talk about our moral inventory; the nature of our wrongs, defects in character, and shortcomings. They do not say we are to make a list of all the dirt, scum, etc. The Steps are to remove the NATURE of our wrongs or character defects, (for example: selfishness, conceit, jealousy, carelessness)

God created us with INSTINCTS. These instincts are 1) **desire for material security,** 2) **emotional security,** 3) **sexual desire**, and 4) **desire for community/companionship**.

If these instincts become misdirected, *they can drive us, dominate us, and insist on ruling our lives.*

Writing out our inventory drops us right down in the **middle** of our recovery path. We'll look at our resentments, self-pity, and unwarranted pride. We will drop the word "blame" from our vocabulary where other people are concerned. Keep in mind the truth, hope, and faith found in the **beginning** chapters of this workbook. There we made the **DISCOVERY** about our need for the Good Shepherd and His ability and desire to love and guide us. We discovered the "treasure" of the Kingdom of God. Now we get into action, clean out the cobwebs of the past, and decide to keep moving forward. Identifying patterns will be helpful as we look at our past. When the middle seems tough, peek at the **end** of David's poem. The **DESIRES** of our hearts will come to pass, *"And I will dwell in the house of the Lord forever."* It will make the **DECISION** to "sell out" for Jesus a "NO-BRAINER."

The Spiritual Principles are courage, trust, faith, honesty, and willingness

"He leads me beside the quiet waters."

Did you know that sheep can go months without actually drinking water? In the early hours of the quiet morning, the vegetation is drenched with dew. The diligent shepherd makes sure his sheep are out early grazing on the droplets of dew hanging heavy on the grass and leaves of their surroundings. He rises early to call out his beloved sheep at a slow and leisurely pace. The scene is one of tranquility, satisfaction, and rest. Read JOHN 10:3-4. *"...He calls his own sheep by name and leads them out. When he has brought out all his own, he goes on ahead of them, and his sheep follow him because they know his voice."* God makes the first move. God calls us, seeking us to seek Him, and we do because <u>we were made for God</u>. Without His love we ache in loneliness and emptiness. **God calls and waits for an answer.** (BE QUIET, LISTEN, ANSWER, BE REFRESHED)

1. **BE QUIET:** You too, can be satisfied in the morning. Read and write ISAIAH 50:4

2. How do you get solitude in order to *graze on the Lord* and *drink Him in?*

3. **LISTEN:** The bible is the *mind* of the Lord. Meditate on His words until His thoughts begin to take shape in your mind. There's something to be said for meeting Almighty God before your busy day begins.
If you're not hearing God's thoughts early in the morning, whose thoughts might you be hearing?

4. Sit at His feet and let Him feed you. That's the place to be. (LUKE10:38-42)
What have you heard from God lately?

5. **ANSWER:** "go into your room," Jesus said, "close your door and pray to your father, who is unseen" (MATTHEW 6:6). Prayer is our response to the revelation and unfolding of God's heart.
Do you have a special prayer today?

BE REFRESHED: Our Shepherd delights to know your soul and spirit have been refreshed and satisfied.

6. Begin writing your story. *We will be using MUSIC as our theme for this exercise.* ♪♪

 Divide your life into 8-9 parts, or *"movements."* For example: early childhood, grade school, junior high, senior high, college, first job, graduate school, marriage, kids, etc. Use one music sheet per *"movement."* Use the worksheets in Appendix A. Take your first *movement* and note the critical events. Illustrate on the music sheet what your life looked and sounded like. Place the high notes ♫ (good events) on the top set of rows (treble) and low notes (hard or bad events) on the second set of rows (bass). Draw the note as a circle on the line or space along with a word or two indicating the specific event. Notes on the top row are, Very Good, 2nd row Good, 3rd row pretty Good, and 4th row "just OK." Do the same for the low notes as you begin to remember the rhythm of your song. You'll notice you experienced high, positive notes ♪ at the same time as the low, negative notes ♪. Take it easy, drink from the quiet waters while working on this exercise.

7. Psalm 33:1 David speaks of singing to God a new song; a song of praise. This is an idea to suggest that the "song of Lord" in our life is indeed His, and not our own. Think about this day. Are you "in tune" with the LORD?

STEP 4 "Made a searching and fearless moral inventory of ourselves."

In this Step you will take a look at what problems your dependent and codependent behaviors have caused. It is an opportunity to take an honest look at yourself and identify both positive and negative aspects of your personality. It is a mechanism for relieving resentment, anger, and guilt. Listing your resentments will help to let go of old anger and will help you identify the ways you set yourself up to be disappointed in others, especially when your expectations were too high. It will reveal patterns that might keep you trapped in self pity or anger.

Use this prompt list to help you make your RESENTMENT INVENTORY. You may add to the list provided as the Holy Spirit leads you in this process.

1. Make a check (√) on the list if you recognize something you feel resentment towards, cannot forgive, cannot let go of, or can't seem to ignore and forget no matter how hard you try.

People			Institutions		Principles	
Spouse		(Ex)	Marriage		Original Sin (Adam & Eve)	
Son	Daughter	(Step)	12 Step programs		God / Deity	
Father	Mother	(Step)	Priest		Forgiveness	
Sister(s)	Brother(s)	(Step)	Bible		Ten Commandments	
Aunts	Uncles		Church	Religion	Jesus Christ	
Cousins	In-laws		Law	Races	Satan	
Clergy	Police		Authority	War	Death	
Lawyers	Judges		Government		Life After Death	
Employers	Employees		Educational System		Heaven	
Co-workers	Creditors		Correctional System		Hell	
Childhood friends	Teachers		Mental Health System		Sin	Retribution
School friends	Best friends		Nationalities		Adultery	The 12 Steps
Acquaintances	AA Friends		Philosophies		Golden Rule	
Girlfriends	Boyfriends		Military Service			
Parole officers	Self					

2. Use the Resentment Inventory Worksheet in Appendix B to outline your resentments. Example:

I'm resentful at	The Cause	Affects on me "The wound"	Character Defects (Traits used for protection)
1. Brother	Didn't invite me	Sad, mad, left out	Emotionally distant Perfectionism, entitlement.
2. Death	My grandma died when I was 8 years old.	Abandoned, mad	Minimization, Isolation

3. Next, write about each resentment in more detail on Appendix C Worksheet.

4. Make a second check (√√) on the list after you have written about it.

5. What are your feelings about working this part of Step 4?_______________________________________

6. Do you have pages (experiences) from "the story of your life" you would like to *tear out*? _______________

HELPFUL HINT:

Instead of *tearing pages* out of your story, **look at the impact** your difficult "valley experiences" had on your view of yourself, God and others. We keep secrets and hide our emotions because we don't want to face difficult experiences. We have all kinds of fears of being found-out, judged, ridiculed, and abandoned. We tend to bury valley experiences or deny that they really hurt or even exist. STEP 4 HELPS US LOOK AT WHAT WE LOST IN THE VALLEY.

7. Have you **invited God** into your difficult places? Do that right now. Date: _______________

---

8. **Are you ready** to be released from crippling bitterness, shame, guilt and all that other "stuff" that seemingly controls your choices? Why?

9. **When** can you carve out time this month to do the necessary writing for Step 4?

"He leads me beside the quiet waters."
STEP 4 "Made a searching and fearless moral inventory of ourselves."

MATTHEW 5:29

____

____

MATTHEW 6:23

____

____

MATTHEW 26:75

____

____

LUKE 11:35

____

____

____

LUKE 16:15

____

____

ACTS 3:19

____

____

ROMANS 7:15

____

____

WEEK ONE WELLNESS CHECK-IN

Rate your physical, psychological, emotional, and spiritual health

- Examine your health in each area of your life. Give each behavior a number from 1-5 (#5 means very well).
- Be HONEST. It's helpful to know the *truth* about your recovery health in order to take care of yourself.
- Circle **one** BEHAVIOR in each area that you are willing to work on daily for the next week.

MY BIOLOGICAL HEALTH (PHYSICAL)

MY RECOVERY DATE:		NUMBER OF CONTINOUS DAYS	
Nutrition- when and what you eat		Physical /dental exams & appointments	
Water		Medications/ daily vitamins	
Identifying/reducing emotional eating		Stress management/keeping it simple	
Sleep/rest (too much, too little)		Eliminating/reducing caffeine	
Exercise (easy does it)		Eliminating/reducing sugar	
Pacing your activities (too much, too little)		Other:	

MY PSYCHOLOGICAL HEALTH (MY THOUGHTS & BEHAVIOR)

Managing denial/ defense mechanisms		Music/art/school work	
Positive vs. Negative thinking		Journaling thoughts & behaviors	
Reducing obsessive thoughts		Making phone calls (sponsor, hotline)	
Daily structure/ being on time		Self-help meetings	
Making amends (promptly admit)		Building self esteem	
Money management		Other:	

MY EMOTIONAL/RELATIONAL HEALTH

Letting go of enabling people		Connecting with family in healthy way	
Managing emotions		Self care	
Spending time with **safe** people		Relaxation exercises	
Setting boundaries		Healthy sexual relations	
Having fun		Journaling feelings/ talking about them	
To Thine Own Self Be True. My "yes" is "yes," and my "no" is "no."		Other:	

MY SPIRITUAL HEALTH

Telling the truth to myself and others		Loving myself/ self-forgiveness	
Service to others		Church / Bible study	
Prayer		Serenity Prayer	
Meditation and/or quiet time with God		Gratitude list, affirmations	
Utilizing the Steps /Spiritual Principles		Enjoying nature	
Balance in everyday life (avoiding extremes)		Seeking/finding my purpose, finding what matters	

- Recognize emotional triggers and <u>change behavior.</u>
- Recognize anxiety and <u>practice relaxation techniques.</u>
- Recognize sleeping / eating habits that are slipping and <u>practice self-care.</u>

"He leads me beside the quiet waters."

The experienced shepherd prepares his own deep watering wells to satisfy his flock. He hand-chisels room like caverns in the sandstone along sandy rivers and then prepares smooth ramps that lead down into the dark wells where cool, clear, and clean water awaits his thirsty sheep. Their shepherd is with them. Many of the places we are **led** into will appear to us as dark and deep and downright scary, but we must remember that *God is with us* and following Him is bound to produce a benefit for us. READ Isaiah 42:16.

1. Write about a time in your life when God was leading you … but you were afraid of the unknown.

2. Have you tried drinking deeply from the **wells of the world**? Name them here. How do you *feel* about those experiences?

Proverbs 23:31-32 states, "Do not gaze at wine when it is red, when it sparkles in the cup, when it goes down smoothly! In the end it bites like a snake and poisons like a viper."

3. What's the difference between the *beginning* (verse 31) and in the *end* (verse 32)?

 4. What might "the sparkle" represent to you? (the lure such as alcohol, food, money, pleasing others, enabling others, seeking perfection)

5. What are the "bites and stings" at the end for you?

FAMILY INFLUENCE: Our family of origin has had an influence on who we are today. It's alright to admit what brought us into bondage. We have the right to hold others accountable and grieve over the negative effects their actions have had on our lives.
None of us set out to become addicted to something. None of us set out to be controlled by our instincts.
We were seeking ways to escape from pain or make up for our brokenness and loss.

6. Read and write Proverbs 3:21-23.

7. Continue reading Proverbs 3:24-26.

The Lord will be our confidence. We can reach out to others in recovery, become mature in the safety of the flock and let it grace our necks like an ornament that testifies of God's Amazing Grace.
Comments:

STEP 4 "Made a searching and fearless moral inventory of ourselves."

RELATIONSHIPS:
We need to write about our relationships so we can find out where our choices, beliefs and actions have resulted in unhealthy or destructive behaviors. You may have completed some of this work in the previous week. Expand on your yes or no answers. Use the worksheets in Appendix C.

1. Do you have a hard time maintaining friendships?

2. Write about your friendships

* make a list here of **past** relationships you will write about.

* make a list here of **present** relationships you will write about.

3. Have you compulsively sought relationships? Give examples.

4. Do you have problems making commitments? Write about what comes to your mind.

5. Whose feelings are more important to you? Write about your answer.
_____yours?
_____the other persons feelings?
_____are they equally important?
6. Do others take advantage of you? Write about your answer.

7. Do you take advantage of others? Write about your answer.

Easy does it. In early recovery we often postpone working on the area of "abuse." It is painful work. You are not to blame. Getting the truth out begins a process that can lead to the relief of pain. Discuss and pray about this decision with someone you trust.

---

8. Has abuse (physical, emotional, sexual) affected your relationships with others?

9. Are there any secrets that you haven't written about yet?

10. Who is a safe person that you could talk to when you are ready?

"He leads me beside the quiet waters."
STEP 4 "Made a searching and fearless moral inventory of ourselves."

ROMANS 13:12-13

____

____

____

____

1 CORINTHIANS 3:3

____

____

2 CORINTHIANS 7:1

____

____

____

GALATIANS 5:19-21

____

____

____

EPHESIANS 5:3

____

____

COLOSSIANS 3:5

____

____

____

WEEK TWO WELLNESS CHECK-IN

Rate your physical, psychological, emotional, and spiritual health

- Examine your health in each area of your life. Give each behavior a number from 1-5 (#5 means very well).
- Be HONEST. It's helpful to know the *truth* about your recovery health in order to take care of yourself.
- Circle **one** BEHAVIOR in each area that you are willing to work on daily for the next week.

MY BIOLOGICAL HEALTH (PHYSICAL)

MY RECOVERY DATE:		NUMBER OF CONTINOUS DAYS	
Nutrition- when and what you eat		Physical /dental exams & appointments	
Water		Medications/ daily vitamins	
Identifying/reducing emotional eating		Stress management/keeping it simple	
Sleep/rest (too much, too little)		Eliminating/reducing caffeine	
Exercise (easy does it)		Eliminating/reducing sugar	
Pacing your activities (too much, too little)		Other:	

MY PSYCHOLOGICAL HEALTH (MY THOUGHTS & BEHAVIOR)

Managing denial/ defense mechanisms		Music/art/school work	
Positive vs. Negative thinking		Journaling thoughts & behaviors	
Reducing obsessive thoughts		Making phone calls (sponsor, hotline)	
Daily structure/ being on time		Self-help meetings	
Making amends (promptly admit)		Building self esteem	
Money management		Other:	

MY EMOTIONAL/RELATIONAL HEALTH

Letting go of enabling people		Connecting with family in healthy way	
Managing emotions		Self care	
Spending time with **safe** people		Relaxation exercises	
Setting boundaries		Healthy sexual relations	
Having fun		Journaling feelings/ talking about them	
To Thine Own Self Be True. My "yes" is "yes," and my "no" is "no."		Other:	

MY SPIRITUAL HEALTH

Telling the truth to myself and others		Loving myself/ self-forgiveness	
Service to others		Church / Bible study	
Prayer		Serenity Prayer	
Meditation and/or quiet time with God		Gratitude list, affirmations	
Utilizing the Steps /Spiritual Principles		Enjoying nature	
Balance in everyday life (avoiding extremes)		Seeking/finding my purpose, finding what matters	

- Recognize emotional triggers and <u>change behavior.</u>
- Recognize anxiety and <u>practice relaxation techniques.</u>
- Recognize sleeping / eating habits that are slipping and <u>practice self-care</u>.

"He leads me beside the quiet waters."

David, the author of PSALM 23, was a shepherd in the desert (1 Samuel 17:28). He knew the dedication of a good shepherd. The shepherd makes provision not only for his flock's thirst, but also for its **fears.** Sheep are afraid to drink from turbulent water. Not only are they afraid of the noise made by the swift and churning rivers but of being swept away by the water. If they fell in, their heavy wool would fast become water-logged and they would drown. The dedicated shepherd digs a small ditch leading out from the stream, makes a dam to form a small pool, and leads his sheep to the quiet waters. It satisfies their thirst and gives them peace in place of **fear.**

As we recover from our addiction, codependency, and compulsive behaviors we may feel afraid and discouraged because the old desires <u>still tempt us.</u> *We may fear that we will fall back into a turbulent lifestyle.*

1. What are your **feelings** in your turbulent lifestyle:
My feelings:

2. Describe your old/ present turbulent lifestyle:

3. What do you miss about the turbulent lifestyle? Think hard and be honest.

4. What do you do to protect yourself from getting too close to your old ways?

We may feel fear, lack of confidence, deep anguish, or a host of other emotions that threaten to stop us in our tracks. But we can look up to our beloved shepherd and be confident that He will give us the strength we need for the next step.

Romans 6:12-14: Paul gives us this warning, "…don't give in." Immerse yourself in healthy actions, thoughts, and relationships. Continue to focus on relapse prevention.
Romans 13:12-14… "let us behave decently…"

5. What are your **feelings** at the pool of clear, clean water? Don't be afraid to admit it takes some "getting used to." All this quiet water calmness may feel boring, unfamiliar, or odd.

6. Do the quiet waters quench your thirst?

We have God's free gifts waiting for us. He has prepared quiet waters filled with Himself. There we find His forgiveness, acceptance, and powerful support. It's from here we approach Step 4 and our commitment to recovery.

STEP 4 "Made a searching and fearless moral inventory of ourselves."

Self-centered fear lies just below our addictive and compulsive behaviors.
This prompt list may be helpful in your **resentment inventory**: Please add to the list if you need to.

Fear of God	Fear of unemployment	Fear of emotional pain
Fear of dying	Fear of employment	Fear of military service
Fear of insanity	Fear of getting old	Fear of drowning
Fear of rejection	Fear of losing a spouse	Fear of (other) men
Fear of loneliness	Fear of losing a child	Fear of (other) women
Fear of diseases	Fear of relationships	Fear of being alone
Fear of alcohol	Fear of violence	Fear of other people
Fear of drugs	Fear of police	Fear of crying
Fear of relapse	Fear of stealing	Fear of poverty
Fear of sex	Fear of creditors	Fear of other races
Fear of sin	Fear of being found out	Fear of the unknown
Fear of self-expression	Fear of change	Fear of jail
Fear of authority	Fear of failure	Fear of going outdoors
Fear of heights	Fear of responsibility	Fear of wealthy people
Fear of abandonment	Fear of hospitals	Fear of guns
Fear of intimacy	Fear of your feelings	Fear of homosexuals/lesbians
Fear of disapproval	Fear of parents	Fear of success
Fear of confrontation	Fear of having a child	Fear of fear
Fear of sobriety	Fear of writing this inventory	Fear of being hurt

1. Make a check (√) on the list if you recognize something you fear.
2. Write about each fear on the Step 4 Resentment Worksheets (see Appendix C at the end of the book).
3. Make a second check (√√) after you have written about it.

4. Draw a picture of one of your fears.

5. Write out the words you need or needed to hear *(but didn't hear)* when you were afraid.
Example: "I needed to hear my Mother tell me 'It's OK ask for help."

6. Is there someone to can tell what you need and feel safe about it?

"He leads me beside the quiet waters."
STEP 4 "Made a searching and fearless moral inventory of ourselves."

1 THESSALONIANS 5:6-7

____

____

____

1 TIMOTHY 5:24

____

____

JAMES 2:12-13

____

____

PSALM 66:18

____

____

PSALM 73:21-22

____

____

PSALM 90:8

____

____

PROVERBS 5:3-6

____

____

____

WEEK THREE WELLNESS CHECK-IN

Rate your physical, psychological, emotional, and spiritual health

- Examine your health in each area of your life. Give each behavior a number from 1-5 (#5 means very well).
- Be HONEST. It's helpful to know the *truth* about your recovery health in order to take care of yourself.
- Circle **one** BEHAVIOR in each area that you are willing to work on daily for the next week.

MY BIOLOGICAL HEALTH (PHYSICAL)

MY RECOVERY DATE:		NUMBER OF CONTINOUS DAYS	
Nutrition- when and what you eat		Physical /dental exams & appointments	
Water		Medications/ daily vitamins	
Identifying/reducing emotional eating		Stress management/keeping it simple	
Sleep/rest (too much, too little)		Eliminating/reducing caffeine	
Exercise (easy does it)		Eliminating/reducing sugar	
Pacing your activities (too much, too little)		Other:	

MY PSYCHOLOGICAL HEALTH (MY THOUGHTS & BEHAVIOR)

Managing denial/ defense mechanisms		Music/art/school work	
Positive vs. Negative thinking		Journaling thoughts & behaviors	
Reducing obsessive thoughts		Making phone calls (sponsor, hotline)	
Daily structure/ being on time		Self-help meetings	
Making amends (promptly admit)		Building self esteem	
Money management		Other:	

MY EMOTIONAL/RELATIONAL HEALTH

Letting go of enabling people		Connecting with family in healthy way	
Managing emotions		Self care	
Spending time with **safe** people		Relaxation exercises	
Setting boundaries		Healthy sexual relations	
Having fun		Journaling feelings/ talking about them	
To Thine Own Self Be True. My "yes" is "yes," and my "no" is "no."		Other:	

MY SPIRITUAL HEALTH

Telling the truth to myself and others		Loving myself/ self-forgiveness	
Service to others		Church / Bible study	
Prayer		Serenity Prayer	
Meditation and/or quiet time with God		Gratitude list, affirmations	
Utilizing the Steps /Spiritual Principles		Enjoying nature	
Balance in everyday life (avoiding extremes)		Seeking/finding my purpose, finding what matters	

- Recognize emotional triggers and <u>change behavior.</u>
- Recognize anxiety and <u>practice relaxation techniques.</u>
- Recognize sleeping and eating habits that are slipping and <u>practice self-care.</u>

"He leads me beside the quiet waters."

Step 4 can bring up many emotions. We have God's free gifts waiting for us. He's prepared quiet waters.

1. What threatens you and your recovery work today? Make a list of your emotional "triggers." While sitting at the quiet waters, list the positive actions you can take for each trigger.

My emotional "triggers."	My healthy action(s)
1.	1.
2.	2.
3.	3.
4.	4.
5.	5.

Why do you need a recovery plan? To be in recovery, you need to be MOVING FORWARD. If you stop moving forward, the old patterns are waiting to take over again, ready to grab the steering wheel.

**We can look up to our Beloved Shepherd and be confident that
He will give us the strength we need for the next step**

PSALM 23:1 "The Lord is my shepherd; I shall not want."

PSALM 28:9 "Save your people and bless your inheritance; be their shepherd and carry them forever."

PSALM 95:7 "for He is our God and we are the people of his pasture, the flock under his care"

PSALM 100:3 "Know that the LORD is God. It is he who made us, and we are his."

ISAIAH 40:11 "He tends his flock like a shepherd: He gathers the lambs in his arms and carries them close to his heart; he gently leads those that have young."

EZEKIEL 34:31 "You my sheep, the sheep of my pasture, are people, and I am your God," declares the Sovereign LORD."

MARK 6:34 "When Jesus landed and saw a large crowd, he had compassion on them, because they were like sheep without a shepherd. So he began teaching them many things."

1 PETER 2:25 "For you were like sheep going astray, but now you have returned to the Shepherd and Overseer of your souls."

REVELATION 7:17 "For the Lamb at the center of the throne will be their shepherd; he will lead them to springs of living water. And God will wipe away every tear from their eyes."

WEEK FOUR STEP 4

STEP 4 "Made a searching and fearless moral inventory of ourselves."
Put an "X" on the line between Liability and Asset to indicate your position (most of the time) between the two behaviors.
Review the introduction to Step 4. Which of the 4 instincts is driving your behavior when it is negative? Put the number next to the X.
Your NEED for (1) physical security,   (2) emotional security,   (3) sexual desires, and/or   (4) need for community?

Liability (Negative))	**Asset (Positive)**
Example: Resentment_______________X (2)__________	Forgiveness
Resentment____	Forgiveness
Hanging on to injury or anger.	
Fear____	Courage
Holds us back from doing worthwhile things.	*Healthy fear helps avoid danger. Courage is fear that has said its prayers.*
Self-Pity ____	Self-Forgetfulness
Thinking like a victim-"poor me."	
Self-Justification ____	Humility
Defending ourselves rather than admitting our faults	
Self-Importance (Egotism) _________________________________	Modesty
Putting ourselves first, self-centeredness.	
Self-Condemnation (Guilt) _________________________________	Self-Validation
Putting ourselves down. Bad self talk.	
Dishonesty____	Honesty
Pretending -to ourselves and others.	
Impatience ____	Patience
Wanting what I want, when I want it.	
Hate____	Love
Continued anger, murderous feelings toward someone.	
Laziness ____	Activity
Unwilling to work. Undisciplined. Proverbs 26:13-15.	
Procrastination ____	Promptness
Putting things off; leaves burdens on others. (Energy drain).	
Insincerity ____	Straight Forwardness
Putting up a false front; people pleasing. Acting like we care when we don't.	
Negative Thinking ______________________________________	Positive Thinking
Dwelling on why things can't work. Discouraging others.	
Immoral Thinking_______________________________________	Spiritual/Clean Thinking
Lust, use of pornography, dirty jokes	
Intolerance (Perfectionism)_______________________________	Tolerance
Never being satisfied with a result. (not good enough) Expecting too much of self and others.	
Criticizing and Gossip___________________________________	Praise For Others
A fault-finding attitude. Malicious or careless gossip	
Greed (Gluttony)_______________________________________	Generosity
Wanting more than our share. We can deceive ourselves into thinking we are doing a service for others, but we are doing it for ourselves.	
Jealousy ____	Trust
Fear of losing someone or something. (Related to fear.)	
Envy ____	Satisfaction
Wanting what someone else has. Related to greed.	

"He leads me beside the quiet waters."
STEP 4 "Made a searching and fearless moral inventory of ourselves."

MATTHEW 12:36-37

LUKE 6:45

ACTS 3:19

ROMANS 7:15

1 CORINTHIANS 15:34

2 CORINTHIANS 13:5

GALATIANS 5:19-21

Rate your physical, psychological, emotional, and spiritual health

- Examine your health in each area of your life. Give each behavior a number from 1-5 (#5 means very well).
- Be HONEST. It's helpful to know the *truth* about your recovery health in order to take care of yourself.
- Circle **one** BEHAVIOR in each area that you are willing to work on daily for the next week.

MY BIOLOGICAL HEALTH (PHYSICAL)

MY RECOVERY DATE:		NUMBER OF CONTINOUS DAYS	
Nutrition- when and what you eat		Physical /dental exams & appointments	
Water		Medications/ daily vitamins	
Identifying/reducing emotional eating		Stress management/keeping it simple	
Sleep/rest (too much, too little)		Eliminating/reducing caffeine	
Exercise (easy does it)		Eliminating/reducing sugar	
Pacing your activities (too much, too little)		Other:	

MY PSYCHOLOGICAL HEALTH (MY THOUGHTS & BEHAVIOR)

Managing denial/ defense mechanisms		Music/art/school work	
Positive vs. Negative thinking		Journaling thoughts & behaviors	
Reducing obsessive thoughts		Making phone calls (sponsor, hotline)	
Daily structure/ being on time		Self-help meetings	
Making amends (promptly admit)		Building self esteem	
Money management		Other:	

MY EMOTIONAL/RELATIONAL HEALTH

Letting go of enabling people		Connecting with family in healthy way	
Managing emotions		Self care	
Spending time with **safe** people		Relaxation exercises	
Setting boundaries		Healthy sexual relations	
Having fun		Journaling feelings/ talking about them	
To Thine Own Self Be True. My "yes" is "yes," and my "no" is "no."		Other:	

MY SPIRITUAL HEALTH

Telling the truth to myself and others		Loving myself/ self-forgiveness	
Service to others		Church / Bible study	
Prayer		Serenity Prayer	
Meditation and/or quiet time with God		Gratitude list, affirmations	
Utilizing the Steps /Spiritual Principles		Enjoying nature	
Balance in everyday life (avoiding extremes)		Seeking/finding my purpose, finding what matters	

- Recognize emotional triggers and <u>change behavior.</u>
- Recognize anxiety and <u>practice relaxation techniques.</u>
- Recognize sleeping and eating habits that are slipping and <u>practice self-care.</u>

PSALM 23 **"He leads me beside the quiet waters."**

STEP 4 "Made a searching and fearless moral inventory of ourselves."

COMPLETION

My favorite Scripture for Chapter 4: (write it here)

______ I understand Chapter 4 and will continue to use it daily.
______ I studied and completed the Bible study in a *Psalm 23* group.
______ I worked with a PSALM-Partner this month to study Chapter 4.

PSALM-Partner NAME: ______________________________________

PSALM-Partner Phone # __________________________________

Today's date _____________________________________

My Signature __________________________ **PSALM-Partner** _______________________

BIBLE STUDY AT A GLANCE

MATTHEW 5:27-32	1 CORINTHIANS 3:1-3	1 THESSALONIANS 5:6-7	PROVERBS 20:19-20
MATTHEW 6:23	1 CORINTHIANS 4:5	1 TIMOTHY 5:24	PROVERBS 21:9
MATTHEW 12:36-37	1 CORINTHIANS 7:3-16	JAMES 2:8-13	PROVERBS 22:24-25
MATTHEW 15:11	1 CORINTHIANS 11:27-32	PSALM 66:18	PROVERBS 23:27
MATTHEW 23:23-28	1 CORINTHIANS 15:34	PSALM 73:21-22	PROVERBS 23:29-35
MATTHEW 26:75	2 CORINTHIANS 10:12	PSALM 90:8	PROVERBS 25:28
LUKE 6:45	2 CORINTHIANS 13:5	PROVERBS 5:3-6	PROVERBS 26:20-22
LUKE 11:33-36	2 CORINTHIANS 16:14-7	PROVERBS 10:17	PROVERBS 29:1
LUKE 12:1-6	GALATIANS 5:19-21	PROVERBS 13:13	PROVERBS 29:11
LUKE 12:15	GALATIANS 6:3-5	PROVERBS 14:14-15	PROVERBS 29:20
LUKE 16:14-15	EPHESIANS 5:3-7	PROVERBS 15:11	PROVERBS 29:22-23
LUKE 17:3-6	EPHESIANS 5:18	PROVERBS 15:31-33	PROVERBS 30:11-12
ACTS 3:19	EPHESIANS 5:22-23	PROVERBS 16:2-3	
ROMANS 7:15-18	EPHESIANS 6:1-4	PROVERBS 19:19	
ROMANS 13:11-14	COLOSSIANS 3:5-8	PROVERBS 20:1	

The Lord is My Shepherd
A 12 Step Journey through PSALM 23

DECISION
CHAPTER FIVE

PSALM 23
"He restores my soul;"

STEP 5
"Admitted to God, to ourselves, and another human being
the exact nature of our wrongs."

CHAPTER FIVE INTRODUCTION

PSALM 23

"He restores my soul;"

David knew what it was like to be cast down. He felt the frustration of falling into temptation. He was brought face-to-face with his corruption in 2 Samuel 12:7-9. He confessed in 2 Samuel 12:13 "I have sinned against the Lord." And Nathan said, "Yes, but the Lord has forgiven you, and you won't die for this sin." David received God's amazing grace in that instant because of the healing experience of God's love. God has never yet despised a broken and contrite heart (Psalm 51:17). Sheep desperately need to be restored when they are "cast down." As a shepherd, David was in the business of restoring cast sheep, sometimes on a daily basis. And Jesus restores our hope when we stumble again and again into bad judgment, by giving us His loving presence.

And He has promised to stay! (Matthew 28:20)

Let's look at what it means to be cast down and how sheep and believers are restored.

What does it mean to be "cast down?" Any cast down sheep is helpless, close to death and vulnerable to attack because it is lying on its back with its feet in the air. It has no way to stand up *on its own*.

How does a sheep become "cast down?" Sheep, when resting can roll over into a depression in the ground causing a shift in body weight resulting in being cast. Sometimes the cause may be too much wool or excess fat.

Application: Our spiritual bankruptcy (jealousy, self-defensiveness, self-pity, self-indulgence, etc.) is seldom a blowout. It's more like a slow leak that we hardly even notice at first........until it has drained us of everything. When we find ourselves "cast," empty and numb, it's OUR SHEPHERD'S LOVE that can restore our souls. His love in the face of our sin causes us to long for His righteousness. When we acknowledge and confess our sin it only works for good.

STEP 5 "Admitted to God, to ourselves, and another human being the exact nature of our wrongs."

The work you've accomplished in Step 4 will provide the foundation for Step 5 through Step 7. Step 5 takes action on our part, which when completed, will mean we have admitted to God, to ourselves, and to another human being the exact nature of our defects. **We use God's Word as our measuring stick.** We've put our finger on the weak items in our personal inventory. This is perhaps difficult- especially the part about admitting our defects to another person. Revealing ourselves to another person stirs up fear of being publicly exposed. Look at what Jesus has to say in John 8:3-11. When we find a safe person, we can expose our secrets and see they will be written in dust- not etched in stone. A sin often does not appear in all its sinfulness until it is brought into the light. On the other hand, it almost always seems more unforgivable when it remains unshared. Shame has kept us in hiding, but the TRUTH will set us free! You may find that you are motivated to continue the process of recovery in *The Lord is My Shepherd: A 12 Step Journey through PSALM 23* because of your desire and DECISION for more recovery.

JAMES 5:16   MATTHEW 18:20   "When can we meet?"

The Spiritual Principles are trust, courage, self-honesty, and commitment.

"He restores my soul;"

What does it mean to be "cast down?" A "cast" sheep has turned over on its back. It struggles to try to get back on its feet without success. It is a pathetic sight. Sheep are helpless in this situation. The "cast" sheep has only a matter of hours when the temperature is hot and a few days when it is cool before it succumbs to the build-up of stomach gasses.   The sheep's blood circulation is eventually cut off to the extremities of the body, especially the legs. Buzzards, vultures and other predators have their eyes on "cast" sheep knowing they are easy prey and near death. Another sheep can be of *no help* to the cast sheep. Without the protection of the shepherd, the bystander becomes yet another target for predators. The experienced shepherd is always alert for a missing sheep and circling vultures. He is in the business of restoring his sheep. God's children also repeatedly wander away from The Good Shepherd. We stumble and get hurt physically, emotionally and spiritually.

What does it mean to be "cast down?" *It means to be cut off from the Shepherd.*

1. When was the last time you felt cast down?

2. What are your biggest temptations right now?

3. Can you name your predators circling above?

4. Have you felt the numbness caused by being cast down?

GOD HEARS OUR PRAYERS.

JEREMIAH 29:12 "Then you will call upon me and come and pray to me and I will listen to you."

PSALM 66:19-20 "But God has surely listened and heard my voice in prayer. Praise be to God, who has not rejected my prayer or withheld his love from me!"

PSALM 34:17 "The righteous cry out, and the LORD hears them; he delivers them from all their troubles."

ROMANS 8:26 "In the same way, the Spirit helps us in our weakness. We do not know what we ought to pray for, but the Spirit himself intercedes for us with groans that words cannot express."

JAMES 5:13 "Is any one of you in trouble? He should pray. Is anyone happy? Let him sing songs of praise."

5. How does it feel when your Shepherd appears to restore you?

6. Read and write Psalm 41:4.

STEP 5 "Admitted to God, to ourselves, and another human being the exact nature of our wrongs."

God and His Word, *not the opinions of others,* are the standards for our behavior. His Word is the spiritual "plumb line." When things don't measure up it's time to admit there is a problem and start rebuilding. The purpose of Scripture is to bring people into a vital relationship with the grace of God. God sent his Word to us so that we may receive forgiveness. We don't need to not earn it but receive it.

1. "Admitted to God" …… that means no more cover-ups, no more over-compensating. It's time to be honest before Jesus. How hard is it for you to admit your mistakes?

2."It is not the healthy who need a doctor, but the sick. But go and learn what this means: 'I desire mercy, not sacrifice.' For I have not come to call the righteous, but sinners." Matthew 9:12

 One of the most remarkable features of the human condition is our capacity to pretend that we are healthy when our lives are in total chaos. Have you ever fooled yourself into thinking you were spiritually right with God when you weren't?

3. How do you cover up your shortcomings?

4. What are your *motives* when you stay in denial about your problems?

5. How can admitting your faults to God help you?

6. Write about how you *feel* after you have "Admitted to God."   What is today's date? _____________.

Romans 2:4 "God's kindness leads you toward repentance."
When we confess our sins, we will find internal peace and be restored.

"He restores my soul;"
STEP 5 "Admitted to God, to ourselves, and another human being the exact nature of our wrongs."

MATTHEW 23:12

____

____

LUKE 11:35-36

____

____

____

LUKE 15:18-19

____

____

____

JOHN 8:7

____

____

ACTS 19:18

____

____

ACTS 24:16

____

____

ROMANS 8:1-2

____

____

____

WEEK ONE WELLNESS CHECK-IN

Rate your physical, psychological, emotional, and spiritual health

- Examine your health in each area of your life. Give each behavior a number from 1-5 (#5 means very well).
- Be HONEST. It's helpful to know the *truth* about your recovery health in order to take care of yourself.
- Circle **one** BEHAVIOR in each area that you are willing to work on daily for the next week.

MY BIOLOGICAL HEALTH (PHYSICAL)

MY RECOVERY DATE:		NUMBER OF CONTINOUS DAYS	
Nutrition- when and what you eat		Physical /dental exams & appointments	
Water		Medications/ daily vitamins	
Identifying/reducing emotional eating		Stress management/keeping it simple	
Sleep/rest (too much, too little)		Eliminating/reducing caffeine	
Exercise (easy does it)		Eliminating/reducing sugar	
Pacing your activities (too much, too little)		Other:	

MY PSYCHOLOGICAL HEALTH (MY THOUGHTS & BEHAVIOR)

Managing denial/ defense mechanisms		Music/art/school work	
Positive vs. Negative thinking		Journaling thoughts & behaviors	
Reducing obsessive thoughts		Making phone calls (sponsor, hotline)	
Daily structure/ being on time		Self-help meetings	
Making amends (promptly admit)		Building self esteem	
Money management		Other:	

MY EMOTIONAL/RELATIONAL HEALTH

Letting go of enabling people		Connecting with family in healthy way	
Managing emotions		Self care	
Spending time with **safe** people		Relaxation exercises	
Setting boundaries		Healthy sexual relations	
Having fun		Journaling feelings/ talking about them	
To Thine Own Self Be True. My "yes" is "yes," and my "no" is "no."		Other:	

MY SPIRITUAL HEALTH

Telling the truth to myself and others		Loving myself/ self-forgiveness	
Service to others		Church / Bible study	
Prayer		Serenity Prayer	
Meditation and/or quiet time with God		Gratitude list, affirmations	
Utilizing the Steps /Spiritual Principles		Enjoying nature	
Balance in everyday life (avoiding extremes)		Seeking/finding my purpose, finding what matters	

- Recognize emotional triggers and <u>change behavior.</u>
- Recognize anxiety and <u>practice relaxation techniques.</u>
- Recognize sleeping and eating habits that are slipping and <u>practice self-care.</u>

He restores my soul.

How does a sheep become "cast down?" Sheep look for the softest, coziest, most comfortable spot to lie down. It's the slight depressions in the ground that cause a sheep to become cast. The sheep rolls on its side to stretch out and relax, and suddenly the center of gravity in its body shifts. It turns so far on its back that the feet no longer touch the ground. Now the sheep is cast. If it is an ewe with unborn lambs, they all perish. If she has suckling young lambs, they become orphans.

Some of us may set out for the easy life, the one where there's no demand upon self-discipline. In the movie "Annie" there is a reference to "easy-street." A plan is made by a couple of the characters in the movie to find the "easy way" and they decide to get ahead by lying. We may know what we want but set out to get it in our own way.
1. What problems have resulted from your lack of self-discipline?

When we face the horrible experience of being found out after making a poor choice, at first we might deny, blame others and become defensive.
2. What feelings will that produce in you?

3. How have others responded to your mistakes in the past?

Use the promise in 1 John 1:9: "If we confess our sins, he is faithful and just to forgive us our sins and to cleanse us from all unrighteousness." (NASB)

Read Luke 15:18-20. The prodigal son, in a well-practiced speech stated, "…I am no longer worthy."
4. Have you felt unworthy for something you have done or said?

5. Have you felt unworthy for no particular reason?

If you hear about being unworthy often enough, especially in childhood, you may begin to believe it and think of yourself in unhealthy ways. You can ask for God to help you see yourself the way He sees you.

6. How did the father respond to his prodigal?

7. What does this verse teach you about the way God thinks and feels about you?

8. Are you able to see yourself as worthy to be loved?

STEP 5 "Admitted to God, to ourselves, and another human being the exact nature of our wrongs."

Step 5 says good-bye to self-deception. When we get specific about every wrong, we will no longer be able to fool ourselves. The lying that kept our problems a secret is no longer necessary when we choose to face reality. God promises to bless all humanity through His son, Jesus Christ. In Christ we are dead to sin and alive to God. Knowing that our God loves us enough to pay for our sins can help us be more "fear-less" with our moral inventory.

1. What fears, if any, are you having about working this Step?

2. How will this admission to yourself help you in your recovery?

3. Without excusing our behavior, we try to recognize what basic need or fear was operating when we acted the way we did. Look at your resentment chart in the Appendix and review the last column. The Spiritual Principles on Page 6 will help you with this chart.

Character defects (traits used to protect myself)	**Spiritual Principles/ healthy behaviors** to help me let go of past resentments and future "wounds"/ hurts.
Example: Emotionally distant, perfectionism, entitlement	Example: **Honesty**- speak up, ask questions, **acceptance**- admitting powerlessness over other people, **humility**- not everything is about me

4. What are you learning about yourself?

Nobody is served by beating ourselves up for the past. This Step is about acknowledging the patterns of behavior that no longer serve us and trusting God to determine the best results of this Step for us.

5. Can you trust God to determine the best results of this Step for you?

"He restores my soul;"
STEP 5 "Admitted to God, to ourselves, and another human being the exact nature of our wrongs."

1 CORINTHIANS 11:31-32

____

____

____

2 CORINTHIANS 8:21

____

____

GALATIONS 6:8

____

____

EPHESIANS 4:22-24

____

____

____

COLOSSIANS 3:7

____

____

JAMES 4:7-8

____

____

1 JOHN 1:8-9

____

____

Rate your physical, psychological, emotional, and spiritual health

- Examine your health in each area of your life. Give each behavior a number from 1-5 (#5 means very well).
- Be HONEST. It's helpful to know the *truth* about your recovery health in order to take care of yourself.
- Circle **one** BEHAVIOR in each area that you are willing to work on daily for the next week.

MY BIOLOGICAL HEALTH (PHYSICAL)

MY RECOVERY DATE:		NUMBER OF CONTINOUS DAYS	
Nutrition- when and what you eat		Physical /dental exams & appointments	
Water		Medications/ daily vitamins	
Identifying/reducing emotional eating		Stress management/keeping it simple	
Sleep/rest (too much, too little)		Eliminating/reducing caffeine	
Exercise (easy does it)		Eliminating/reducing sugar	
Pacing your activities (too much, too little)		Other:	

MY PSYCHOLOGICAL HEALTH (MY THOUGHTS & BEHAVIOR)

Managing denial/ defense mechanisms		Music/art/school work	
Positive vs. Negative thinking		Journaling thoughts & behaviors	
Reducing obsessive thoughts		Making phone calls (sponsor, hotline)	
Daily structure/ being on time		Self-help meetings	
Making amends (promptly admit)		Building self esteem	
Money management		Other:	

MY EMOTIONAL/RELATIONAL HEALTH

Letting go of enabling people		Connecting with family in healthy way	
Managing emotions		Self care	
Spending time with **safe** people		Relaxation exercises	
Setting boundaries		Healthy sexual relations	
Having fun		Journaling feelings/ talking about them	
To Thine Own Self Be True. My "yes" is "yes," and my "no" is "no."		Other:	

MY SPIRITUAL HEALTH

Telling the truth to myself and others		Loving myself/ self-forgiveness	
Service to others		Church / Bible study	
Prayer		Serenity Prayer	
Meditation and/or quiet time with God		Gratitude list, affirmations	
Utilizing the Steps /Spiritual Principles		Enjoying nature	
Balance in everyday life (avoiding extremes)		Seeking/finding my purpose, finding what matters	

- Recognize emotional triggers and <u>change behavior.</u>
- Recognize anxiety and <u>practice relaxation techniques.</u>
- Recognize sleeping and eating habits that are slipping and <u>practice self-care.</u>

"He restores my soul;"

Sometimes a sheep is cast because its fleece is too long and heavy. When the shepherd notices an ewe in possible danger, he does what he must by shearing and cleaning the "not so happy" sheep. The shepherd loves her despite her filthy fleece full of manure, ticks and clumps of mud. He wants her safe, clean and restored. Actually, both shepherd and sheep are relieved when it's all over.

1. What similarities do you see between sheep and people?

Wool depicts the old-life in Scripture. It spoke of self, pride, and personal aspirations.

2. What are you clinging to that may weigh you down? (i.e. worldly ideas, possessions, etc.)

3. When was the last time you wanted to "do your own thing" or "act on self-will?" It helps to check your motives when thinking about your behavior.

It only makes it worse when we beat ourselves up with our negative self-talk. **Automatic Negative Thoughts (ANTS) can be exterminated! Learn what they are and how to detect when they are in your head**. Look for "always/never" thinking, fortune-telling (predicting the worst possible outcome), mind reading (believing you know what others are thinking), labeling, personalizing, and blaming.

ANTS- AUTOMATIC NEGATIVE THOUGHTS ARE AUTOMATIC! Be Aware!

4. How often do you speak lies to yourself and "should" yourself? (I "should" feel happy, grateful, etc. or I "should have" known….). Give some examples of what you say to yourself.

5. Read Galatians 6:8-9. 

Don't give up. Long to please God's Spirit and ask for His help. Self-effort doesn't work. "<u>He</u> restores my soul".

6. Write your thoughts:

OUR SINS ARE ALREADY FORGIVEN
When we confess our sins to God, He will set us free from their destructive nature.

STEP 5 "Admitted to God, to ourselves, and another human being the exact nature of our wrongs."

God allows us to have a part in what He does. When we work a recovery program to improve our emotional, physical, and spiritual health, God can use our small resources (time, talents, gifts, or possessions) to work a miracle of recovery for others and us.

Read Mark 8:1-10. Jesus uses **small resources** to complete His plan. Our maturity and recovery health occur only when we begin following God's will.

1. What are your resources/ personal assets? Name at least 5 of your strengths.

2. What can slow down your maturity process?

3. One of the best ways to protect yourself from self-sufficiency is to be accountable to others. How much does the opinion of others matter to you? Expand on your answer.

4. How will this Step 5 help your spiritual growth?

The third part of Step 5 is sharing your 4th Step with another person.
The *Psalm 23* bible study groups can use 15 minutes of group time on Week Four to share and listen to inventories by breaking into pairs. If you have not completed Step 4 you can share something that comes to your mind after listening to your partner. If you are not in a group, share Step 5 with someone you trust.

5. What is your plan?

6. How do you *feel* about your plan?

"He restores my soul;"
STEP 5 "Admitted to God, to ourselves, and another human being the exact nature of our wrongs."

HOSEA 10:2

____

____

PSALM 32:5

____

____

PSALM 38:17-18

____

____

____

PSALM 40:12

____

____

PSALM 41:4

____

____

PSALM 51:3-4

____

____

____

PSALM 62:8

____

____

WEEK THREE WELLNESS CHECK-IN
Rate your physical, psychological, emotional, and spiritual health

- Examine your health in each area of your life. Give each behavior a number from 1-5 (#5 means very well).
- Be HONEST. It's helpful to know the *truth* about your recovery health in order to take care of yourself.
- Circle **one** BEHAVIOR in each area that you are willing to work on daily for the next week.

MY BIOLOGICAL HEALTH (PHYSICAL)

MY RECOVERY DATE:		NUMBER OF CONTINOUS DAYS	
Nutrition- when and what you eat		Physical /dental exams & appointments	
Water		Medications/ daily vitamins	
Identifying/reducing emotional eating		Stress management/keeping it simple	
Sleep/rest (too much, too little)		Eliminating/reducing caffeine	
Exercise (easy does it)		Eliminating/reducing sugar	
Pacing your activities (too much, too little)		Other:	

MY PSYCHOLOGICAL HEALTH (MY THOUGHTS & BEHAVIOR)

Managing denial/ defense mechanisms		Music/art/school work	
Positive vs. Negative thinking		Journaling thoughts & behaviors	
Reducing obsessive thoughts		Making phone calls (sponsor, hotline)	
Daily structure/ being on time		Self-help meetings	
Making amends (promptly admit)		Building self esteem	
Money management		Other:	

MY EMOTIONAL/RELATIONAL HEALTH

Letting go of enabling people		Connecting with family in healthy way	
Managing emotions		Self care	
Spending time with **safe** people		Relaxation exercises	
Setting boundaries		Healthy sexual relations	
Having fun		Journaling feelings/ talking about them	
To Thine Own Self Be True. My "yes" is "yes," and my "no" is "no."		Other:	

MY SPIRITUAL HEALTH

Telling the truth to myself and others		Loving myself/ self-forgiveness	
Service to others		Church / Bible study	
Prayer		Serenity Prayer	
Meditation and/or quiet time with God		Gratitude list, affirmations	
Utilizing the Steps /Spiritual Principles		Enjoying nature	
Balance in everyday life (avoiding extremes)		Seeking/finding my purpose, finding what matters	

- Recognize emotional triggers and <u>change behavior.</u>
- Recognize anxiety and <u>practice relaxation techniques.</u>
- Recognize sleeping and eating habits that are slipping and <u>practice self-care.</u>

"He restores my soul;"

Over-weight sheep are not only unhealthy and less productive but are at very high risk of becoming cast down. When the shepherd notices this, he makes **long-range plans** to correct the problem. The ewes will get less grain and will be watched closely. It's definitely the fattest sheep that becomes cast and in danger of an early death. This type of loss to the shepherd is avoided at all costs so the wise shepherd makes sure every sheep is fit and strong and able to be on its feet.

1. How does this relate to your life today? Is God making *long-range* plans to correct a problem?

Jesus sees past the exterior of our material life and is concerned about the health of our souls.

2. Why does your Shepherd care about you so much?

When the shepherd finds one of his cast sheep he is filled with fear and relief. He worries that he may be too late. The frightened sheep hears its master's soft voice as he gently reassures her. He immediately rolls it to the side to relieve the pressure of gasses in the stomach. He massages the legs to bring the circulation back. Straddling the sheep, the shepherd lifts and holds it securely erect. The shepherd has come to the rescue and restores his beloved sheep.

Picture yourself recuperating while hanging over the shoulders of the Good Shepherd.

3. How would that feel?

4. The other sheep also welcome the lost sheep back into the fold. How sweet it is to see the flock gather around one of its own. Do you have a flock to return to?

5. Write about a time when God restored your soul. Give the details.

STEP 5 "Admitted to God, to ourselves, and another human being the exact nature of our wrongs."

Humility will protect us from the devastation of a relapse. It allows us to see our vulnerability so that we can seek support and help. God restores our souls and we learn we can serve others. We do this by sharing our "story," listening to others in recovery (Step 5), feeling their pain, sharing their joy, and standing by them in the tough times. As we support others in the recovery process, we will be strengthened as we continue on our recovery path.

ROMANS 12:11-13 "Never be lacking in zeal, but keep your spiritual fervor, serving the LORD. Be joyful in hope, patient in affliction, faithful in prayer. Share with God's people who are in need. Practice hospitality."

1 PETER 5:2 "Be shepherds of God's flock that is under your care, serving as overseers- not because you must, but because you are willing, as God wants you to be; not greedy for money, but eager to serve."

COLOSSIANS 3:23-24 "Whatever you do, work at it with all your heart, as working for the LORD, not for men, since you know that you will receive an inheritance from the LORD as a reward. It is the LORD Christ you are serving."

1. How do you feel **before** you share with another person?

Sit with a PSALM–Partner, counselor, pastor or friend and begin working Step 5.
A PSALM- Partner is someone from the group you can meet with to discuss your answers, Bible verses, or reflections from the work you've completed.
2. What was it like to share your inventory?

3. What are you learning about yourself?

4. What is it like for you when you listen to another person share honestly about themselves?

"He restores my soul;"
STEP 5 "Admitted to God, to ourselves, and another human being the exact nature of our wrongs."

LUKE 5:31

____

____

ACTS 26:18

____

____

ROMANS 2:8

____

____

ROMANS 14:12

____

____

EPHESIANS 4:31

____

____

HEBREWS 4:12-13

____

____

____

____

JAMES 5:16

____

____

____

WEEK FOUR WELLNESS CHECK-IN

Rate your physical, psychological, emotional, and spiritual health

- Examine your health in each area of your life. Give each behavior a number from 1-5 (#5 means very well).
- Be HONEST. It's helpful to know the *truth* about your recovery health in order to take care of yourself.
- Circle **one** BEHAVIOR in each area that you are willing to work on daily for the next week.

MY BIOLOGICAL HEALTH (PHYSICAL)

MY RECOVERY DATE:		NUMBER OF CONTINOUS DAYS	
Nutrition- when and what you eat		Physical /dental exams & appointments	
Water		Medications/ daily vitamins	
Identifying/reducing emotional eating		Stress management/keeping it simple	
Sleep/rest (too much, too little)		Eliminating/reducing caffeine	
Exercise (easy does it)		Eliminating/reducing sugar	
Pacing your activities (too much, too little)		Other:	

MY PSYCHOLOGICAL HEALTH (MY THOUGHTS & BEHAVIOR)

Managing denial/ defense mechanisms		Music/art/school work	
Positive vs. Negative thinking		Journaling thoughts & behaviors	
Reducing obsessive thoughts		Making phone calls (sponsor, hotline)	
Daily structure/ being on time		Self-help meetings	
Making amends (promptly admit)		Building self esteem	
Money management		Other:	

MY EMOTIONAL/RELATIONAL HEALTH

Letting go of enabling people		Connecting with family in healthy way	
Managing emotions		Self care	
Spending time with **safe** people		Relaxation exercises	
Setting boundaries		Healthy sexual relations	
Having fun		Journaling feelings/ talking about them	
To Thine Own Self Be True. My "yes" is "yes," and my "no" is "no."		Other:	

MY SPIRITUAL HEALTH

Telling the truth to myself and others		Loving myself/ self-forgiveness	
Service to others		Church / Bible study	
Prayer		Serenity Prayer	
Meditation and/or quiet time with God		Gratitude list, affirmations	
Utilizing the Steps /Spiritual Principles		Enjoying nature	
Balance in everyday life (avoiding extremes)		Seeking/finding my purpose, finding what matters	

- Recognize emotional triggers and <u>change behavior.</u>
- Recognize anxiety and <u>practice relaxation techniques.</u>
- Recognize sleeping and eating habits that are slipping and <u>practice self-care.</u>

PSALM 23 "He restores my soul;"

STEP 5 "Admitted to God, to ourselves, and another human being the exact nature of our wrongs."

COMPLETION

My favorite Scripture for Chapter 5: (write it here)

_______ I understand Chapter 5 and will continue to use it daily.
_______ I studied and completed the Bible study in a *PSALM 23* group.
_______ I worked with a PSALM-Partner this month to study Chapter 5.

PSALM-Partner NAME: ____

PSALM-Partner Phone # ____

Today's date ____

My Signature _______________________________ **PSALM-PARTNER** _______________________________

BIBLE STUDY AT A GLANCE

MATTHEW 23:12	2 CORINTHIANS 8:21	PSALM 32:3-5	
LUKE 5:31	GALATIANS 6:7-10	PSALM 38:17-18	
LUKE 11:35-36	EPHESIANS 4:22-25	PSALM 40:11-13	
LUKE 15:17-20	EPHESIANS 4:31	PSALM 41:4	
JOHN 8:3-11	COLOSSIANS 3:7-10	PSALM 51:3-4	
ACTS 19:18	HEBREWS 4:12-16	PSALM 62:8	
ACTS 24:16	JAMES 4:7-8	PSALM 69:5	
ACTS 26:12-18	JAMES 5:16	PSALM 119:66-67	
ROMANS 2:8	1 JOHN 1:8-9	PROVERBS 16:18	
ROMANS 2:12-15	1 JOHN 2:1-2	PROVERBS 21:2	
ROMANS 8:1-2	GENESIS 38:1-30	PROVERBS 27:17	
ROMANS 14:12-13	HOSEA 10:2	PROVERBS 28:13-14	
ROMANS 14:22	AMOS 7:7-8	PROVERBS 30:32	
1 CORINTHIANS 6:11			
1 CORINTHIANS 11:27-32			

The Lord is My Shepherd
A 12 Step Journey through PSALM 23

DECISION
CHAPTER SIX

†

PSALM 23
"He guides me in the paths of righteousness for
His name's sake."

STEP 6
"We were entirely ready to have God remove
all of these defects of character."

CHAPTER SIX INTRODUCTION

PSALM 23
"He guides me in the paths of righteousness for His name's sake."

Sheep need to be under the meticulous control of their shepherd. No other class of livestock requires more intelligent handling and direction than sheep do. If left to themselves, sheep will gnaw productive grasslands down to the root leaving sheep ranges ruined beyond repair. Familiar trails become ruts until they are corrupt with disease and parasites.

The attentive owner not only manages his flock 24 hours a day but also has intimate knowledge of his pastures. As he leads, he directs with his *voice*. He keeps his sheep on the move leading his flock along a route that he himself has already prepared and experienced.

God always wants to give us new things. He wants to make **you** new. Every day The Good Shepherd leads us in the right paths, choices, and decisions for His name's sake. Read 2 Corinthians 6:17-18.

STEP 6 "We were entirely ready to have God remove all of these defects of character."

The Twelve Steps and the Twelve Traditions (page 65) says, "Since most of us are born with an abundance of natural desires, it isn't strange that we often let these far exceed their intended purpose. When they drive us blindly, or we willfully demand that they supply us with more satisfactions or pleasures than are possible or due us, that is the point at which we depart from the degree of perfection that God wishes for us here on earth. That is the measure of our character defects, or if you wish, for our sins."

Becoming **entirely ready** won't happen all at once. It is a process. Many of us will want some of them to be gone, the sooner the better! We might have a few that we're not ready to give up on the spot. There may be an element of fear and uncertainty about changing. Then for some we'll say, "I won't, I can't, or I don't want to give this up yet. I'll suppress it myself." Be aware of your thoughts and struggles in this Step. It is God's free gift of forgiveness and the power to live a new life that will release us from the bondage of the past. Look for recurring patterns in your relationships and boundaries that hint at a character defect. Each individual character defect requires specific changes with the help of God. Without HIM we are doomed to cycles of painful failure.

The secret to *becoming ready* and *following Him* is our LOVE for the Shepherd who is leading us.

It's important that we make a beginning in Step 6 and keep trying. Practice open-mindedness and faith every day.
The Good Shepherd leads us in right paths, right choices, and right decisions.
Can you hear His precious rhythm?

The Spiritual Principles are commitment and perseverance, willingness, faith, trust, and self-acceptance.

"He guides me in the paths of righteousness for His name's sake."

Sheep are creatures of *habit*. If left to themselves sheep will gnaw grass down to the root. Our behavior and habits are similar to sheep. Look at what Scripture says in Isaiah 53:6.

1. What are your bad habits?

2. Are you clinging to a habit that you have seen ruin the lives of others who practice the same habit?

3. We are reminded everywhere of the ruin and remorse of men and women who have gone astray. How does this make you feel?

4. What habit(s) have you changed already?

5. How can pride keep you from letting Jesus guide you?

Through the power of God's Holy Spirit, we have all the power necessary for complete transformation *in every area of our life*.

6. Jot down a few destructive habits in each area:

PHYSICAL ____

EMOTIONAL ____

PSYCHOLOGICAL (THINKING AND BEHAVING) ____________________________________

SPIRITUAL ____

God is strong.
PSALM 73:26 "My flesh and my heart may fail, but God is the strength of my heart and my portion forever."
PROVERBS 18:10 "The name of the LORD is a strong tower; the righteous run to it and are safe."
HABAKKUK 3:19 "The Sovereign LORD is my strength; he makes my feet like the feet of a deer; he enables me to go on the heights."

STEP 6 "We were entirely ready to have God remove all of these defects of character."

On page 58 of the Big Book (AA) it states: "Some of us have tried to hold on to our old ideas and the result was nil until we let go absolutely." And on page 59 it says: "Half measures availed us nothing."

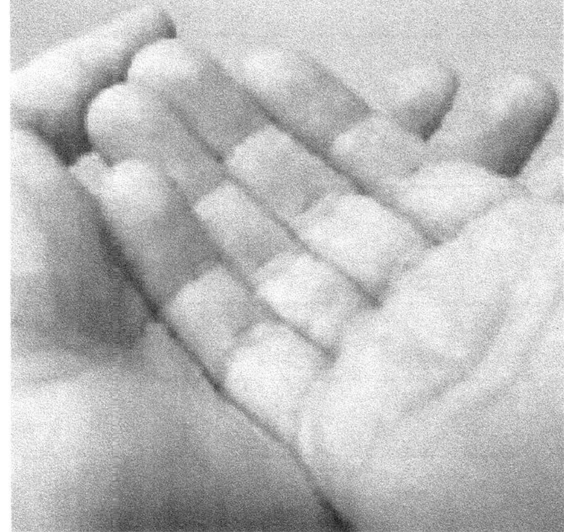

How do we get "entirely ready?" Amid all the doubts, fear, and confusion, Christ the Good Shepherd wants us to follow Him. Read Mark 8:34. This Step is where the <u>rubber meets the road</u>. A Christian either "goes on" with God or he "goes back" from following God.

1. Do you believe you can change?

2. Have you tried to change while still holding on to your own ways? What happened?

3. Do you have any defects that you think cannot be removed? What are they?

4. Please read and write Matthew 5:4.

God wants us to mourn over our sins and admit our brokenness.

"He guides me in the paths of righteousness for His name's sake."
STEP 6 "We were entirely ready to have God remove all of these defects of character."

MATTHEW 5:3

____

____

ROMANS 6:1-2

____

____

ROMANS 12:2

____

____

1 CORINTHIANS 15:57

____

____

2 CORINTHIANS 7:9-10

____

____

GALATIANS 5:16-17

____

____

EPHESIANS 5:8-10

____

____

____

WEEK ONE WELLNESS CHECK-IN

Rate your physical, psychological, emotional, and spiritual health

- Examine your health in each area of your life. Give each behavior a number from 1-5 (#5 means very well).
- Be HONEST. It's helpful to know the *truth* about your recovery health in order to take care of yourself.
- Circle **one** BEHAVIOR in each area that you are willing to work on daily for the next week.

MY BIOLOGICAL HEALTH (PHYSICAL)

MY RECOVERY DATE:		NUMBER OF CONTINOUS DAYS	
Nutrition- when and what you eat		Physical /dental exams & appointments	
Water		Medications/ daily vitamins	
Identifying/reducing emotional eating		Stress management/keeping it simple	
Sleep/rest (too much, too little)		Eliminating/reducing caffeine	
Exercise (easy does it)		Eliminating/reducing sugar	
Pacing your activities (too much, too little)		Other:	

MY PSYCHOLOGICAL HEALTH (MY THOUGHTS & BEHAVIOR)

Managing denial/ defense mechanisms		Music/art/school work	
Positive vs. Negative thinking		Journaling thoughts & behaviors	
Reducing obsessive thoughts		Making phone calls (sponsor, hotline)	
Daily structure/ being on time		Self-help meetings	
Making amends (promptly admit)		Building self esteem	
Money management		Other:	

MY EMOTIONAL/RELATIONAL HEALTH

Letting go of enabling people		Connecting with family in healthy way	
Managing emotions		Self care	
Spending time with **safe** people		Relaxation exercises	
Setting boundaries		Healthy sexual relations	
Having fun		Journaling feelings/ talking about them	
To Thine Own Self Be True. My "yes" is "yes," and my "no" is "no."		Other:	

MY SPIRITUAL HEALTH

Telling the truth to myself and others		Loving myself/ self-forgiveness	
Service to others		Church / Bible study	
Prayer		Serenity Prayer	
Meditation and/or quiet time with God		Gratitude list, affirmations	
Utilizing the Steps /Spiritual Principles		Enjoying nature	
Balance in everyday life (avoiding extremes)		Seeking/finding my purpose, finding what matters	

- Recognize emotional triggers and <u>change behavior.</u>
- Recognize anxiety and <u>practice relaxation techniques.</u>
- Recognize sleeping and eating habits that are slipping and <u>practice self-care.</u>

Sheep huddle together on their favored spots and when they follow the same worn path, the area becomes infested with parasites. Read Proverbs 14:12 and 16:25. The Shepherd guides his flock off the infested ground before the organisms complete their life cycles. David knew the precise action plan of shepherding. God has a pre-determined plan of action and His sound management will guide us towards right decisions. There is no lack in His leading... but there can be great lack in following.

1. What character traits or habits did you learn from your childhood *family*?

2. What character traits or habits did you learn from your childhood *friends*?

3. Some friends might be **uncomfortable** with our changes to improve our health. What are some of the reasons this might happen?

4. We may become embarrassed among old friends and succumb to the pressure to turn away from our commitment to the truth about our need for recovery. How could this happen?

5. Do you need to put any of your codependent relationships "on hold" for a time, or even permanently so that you aren't triggered to fall back and away from the recovery God desires for you?

6. Who is your support in recovery?

7. Is there anything holding you back from getting a PSALM-Partner? (someone you can review your answers and thoughts with while working in you're ***The Lord is My Shepherd: 12 Step Journey through Psalm 23*** workbook)

STEP 6 "We were entirely ready to have God remove all of these defects of character."

God has a journey of recovery planned for us. He wants to give us MORE. Read Isaiah 54:2.

Think of the word **change.**
1. What did change mean for you **in the past**?

2. Name your feelings as you think about changing **now**?

3. Reflect on the following questions:

       a. Do you assume responsibility for other's feelings or behaviors?

       b. Do you have difficulty identifying and then expressing your feelings?

       c. Are you afraid of being hurt or rejected by others?

       d. Does your fear of other people's feelings determine how you respond or react?

       e. Do you judge everything you do as "not good enough?"

       f. Are you steadfastly loyal- even when the loyalty is unjustified?

       g. Do you tend to minimize, alter, or even deny the truth about how you feel?

4. Did you identify with some of the codependent behaviors listed above? Expand on your answer here and in your journal notes in the Appendix.

5. Are some of your perceptions and beliefs going to be barriers in your personal growth and healing?

6. Have you totally committed to the *process of recovery*? Write what this means **to you.**

7. Rate your motivation for this Step   1 - 2 - 3 - 4 - 5   (#5 indicates being highly motivated).

"He guides me in the paths of righteousness for His name's sake."
STEP 6 "We were entirely ready to have God remove all of these defects of character."

1 THESSALONIANS 4:3-4

TITUS 2:12

HEBREWS 6:12

HEBREWS 12:1-2

JAMES 1:5

1PETER 1:13

1JOHN 2:28

WEEK TWO WELLNESS CHECK-IN

Rate your physical, psychological, emotional, and spiritual health

- Examine your health in each area of your life. Give each behavior a number from 1-5 (#5 means very well).
- Be HONEST. It's helpful to know the *truth* about your recovery health in order to take care of yourself.
- Circle **one** BEHAVIOR in each area that you are willing to work on daily for the next week.

MY BIOLOGICAL HEALTH (PHYSICAL)

MY RECOVERY DATE:		NUMBER OF CONTINOUS DAYS	
Nutrition- when and what you eat		Physical /dental exams & appointments	
Water		Medications/ daily vitamins	
Identifying/reducing emotional eating		Stress management/keeping it simple	
Sleep/rest (too much, too little)		Eliminating/reducing caffeine	
Exercise (easy does it)		Eliminating/reducing sugar	
Pacing your activities (too much, too little)		Other:	

MY PSYCHOLOGICAL HEALTH (MY THOUGHTS & BEHAVIOR)

Managing denial/ defense mechanisms		Music/art/school work	
Positive vs. Negative thinking		Journaling thoughts & behaviors	
Reducing obsessive thoughts		Making phone calls (sponsor, hotline)	
Daily structure/ being on time		Self-help meetings	
Making amends (promptly admit)		Building self esteem	
Money management		Other:	

MY EMOTIONAL/RELATIONAL HEALTH

Letting go of enabling people		Connecting with family in healthy way	
Managing emotions		Self care	
Spending time with **safe** people		Relaxation exercises	
Setting boundaries		Healthy sexual relations	
Having fun		Journaling feelings/ talking about them	
To Thine Own Self Be True. My "yes" is "yes," and my "no" is "no."		Other:	

MY SPIRITUAL HEALTH

Telling the truth to myself and others		Loving myself/ self-forgiveness	
Service to others		Church / Bible study	
Prayer		Serenity Prayer	
Meditation and/or quiet time with God		Gratitude list, affirmations	
Utilizing the Steps /Spiritual Principles		Enjoying nature	
Balance in everyday life (avoiding extremes)		Seeking/finding my purpose, finding what matters	

- Recognize emotional triggers and <u>change behavior.</u>
- Recognize anxiety and <u>practice relaxation techniques.</u>
- Recognize sleeping and eating habits that are slipping and <u>practice self-care.</u>

WEEK THREE PSALM 23

"He guides me in the paths of righteousness for His name's sake."

The shepherd keeps his flock moving over the land in the pattern of grazing he has worked out in advance, looking for the maximum benefit for both sheep and land. The Lord, our Shepherd promises to move us into maturity and deliver us from evil. Read 2 Corinthians 3:18.

For some of us it's much easier to start something than to finish it. Everything worthwhile takes time, **but time is on our side**.
1. How is time on our side?

2. Many of us encounter problems of procrastination. Is this one of your problems? If so, how long has it been a problem?

3. In recovery we learn that time is a good thing. It's a gift from God. Do you struggle with the concept of time? (there's not enough time, too much time, etc.)

4. What will you need to do to prevent yourself from "running out of gas" while recovering your health? Read Hebrews 6:11-12

5. Relapse prevention planning helps us work through the recovery process. Have you slipped backwards in any area and out of God's timing? Your Weekly Wellness Check-in will help you stay in tune.

Physical Health:____

Psychological Health:____

Emotional Health:____

Spiritual Health:____

5. What do you need to change to stay in God's timing?

6. Read Galatians 6:8-9. When have you seen the consequences of sinful desires?

7. When have you seen the consequences of pleasing the Spirit?

Recovery depends on accepting the fact that following our own desires is destructive.
God is in the business of preparing our soul for restoration.

STEP 6 "We were entirely ready to have God remove all of these defects of character."

"to have God remove…" This Step makes it clear that we cannot remove our own shortcomings. God loves you. He wants to see you mature in His love. Because you are a child of God, you have direct access to God through the Spirit (Ephesians 2:18).

1. Read and write the following verses:

ROMANS 8:1 ____

____

1 CORINTHIANS 2:12 ____

____

EPHESIANS 1:3 ____

____

EPHESIANS 1:7-8 ____

____

____

HEBREWS 4:16 ____

____

By the grace of God, you have been firmly rooted in Christ and now you are being built up in Him. (Col. 2:7)

2. What defects of character do you need God to "weed out"? List them below.

2 Timothy 1:7 "For God has not given us a spirit of fear and timidity,
but of power, love, and self-discipline."

(NLT version)

3. Do you have a different translation? Write it here.

"He guides me in the paths of righteousness for His name's sake."
STEP 6 "We were entirely ready to have God remove all of these defects of character."

PSALM 32:5

____

____

____

PSALM 119:10-11

____

____

____

PSALM 119:36-37

____

____

____

PROVERBS 13:18

____

____

____

ROMANS 4:6-8

____

____

____

PHILIPPIANS 3:12-14

____

____

EPHESIANS 3:17-18

____

____

____

WEEK THREE WELLNESS CHECK-IN

Rate your physical, psychological, emotional, and spiritual health

- Examine your health in each area of your life. Give each behavior a number from 1-5 (#5 means very well).
- Be HONEST. It's helpful to know the *truth* about your recovery health in order to take care of yourself.
- Circle **one** BEHAVIOR in each area that you are willing to work on daily for the next week.

MY BIOLOGICAL HEALTH (PHYSICAL)

MY RECOVERY DATE:		NUMBER OF CONTINOUS DAYS	
Nutrition- when and what you eat		Physical /dental exams & appointments	
Water		Medications/ daily vitamins	
Identifying/reducing emotional eating		Stress management/keeping it simple	
Sleep/rest (too much, too little)		Eliminating/reducing caffeine	
Exercise (easy does it)		Eliminating/reducing sugar	
Pacing your activities (too much, too little)		Other:	

MY PSYCHOLOGICAL HEALTH (MY THOUGHTS & BEHAVIOR)

Managing denial/ defense mechanisms		Music/art/school work	
Positive vs. Negative thinking		Journaling thoughts & behaviors	
Reducing obsessive thoughts		Making phone calls (sponsor, hotline)	
Daily structure/ being on time		Self-help meetings	
Making amends (promptly admit)		Building self esteem	
Money management		Other:	

MY EMOTIONAL/RELATIONAL HEALTH

Letting go of enabling people		Connecting with family in healthy way	
Managing emotions		Self care	
Spending time with **safe** people		Relaxation exercises	
Setting boundaries		Healthy sexual relations	
Having fun		Journaling feelings/ talking about them	
To Thine Own Self Be True. My "yes" is "yes," and my "no" is "no."		Other:	

MY SPIRITUAL HEALTH

Telling the truth to myself and others		Loving myself/ self-forgiveness	
Service to others		Church / Bible study	
Prayer		Serenity Prayer	
Meditation and/or quiet time with God		Gratitude list, affirmations	
Utilizing the Steps /Spiritual Principles		Enjoying nature	
Balance in everyday life (avoiding extremes)		Seeking/finding my purpose, finding what matters	

- Recognize emotional triggers and <u>change behavior.</u>
- Recognize anxiety and <u>practice relaxation techniques.</u>
- Recognize sleeping and eating habits that are slipping and <u>practice self-care.</u>

"He guides me in the paths of righteousness for His name's sake."

It will be easier to follow The Good Shepherd when we release our attitudes, faults, and lifestyles. Jesus asked the invalid by the pool, "Do you want to get well?" (John 5:1-8)

1. How did the invalid respond?

2. Ask yourself that same question. "Do I want to get well? Do I really want to get healthy?"

3. God's ultimate intent is to rid us of ungodliness. Read Titus 2:11-12. What does this mean to you?

4. What does "recovery" mean to you?

5. Can you picture yourself being personally guided by the Shepherd? Does the Shepherd fit into your present lifestyle?

6. Is it hard for you to accept things from others? Expand on your answers.

Gifts:

Compliments:

Help:

7. Can you accept the grace, mercy and forgiveness God offers to you? Why or why not?

STEP 6 "We were entirely ready to have God remove all of these defects of character."

The character defects (liabilities) from the Step 4 inventory are basic human traits that have been distorted by self-centeredness and misdirected instincts that drive us, dominate us, and insist on ruling our lives.

1. Take the list of character defects and rewrite them below.	How does it affect my life? How does it affect others?	What are my feelings when I practice it?

2. Rewrite the list again.	What spiritual principle can I apply instead?	What are my feelings when I practice the spiritual principle?

SPIRITUAL PRINCIPLES from Steps 1-6

Step 6 Spiritual Principles are **commitment, perseverance, willingness, faith, trust,** and **self-acceptance.**

Step 5 Spiritual Principles are **trust, courage, self-honesty,** and **commitment.**

Step 4 Spiritual Principles are **courage, trust, faith, honesty,** and **willingness**.

Step 3 Spiritual Principles are **surrender, willingness, faith, trust,** and **commitment**.

Step 2 Spiritual Principles **are open-mindedness, willingness, faith, trust,** and **humility.**

Step 1 Spiritual Principles are **honesty, open-mindedness, willingness, humility,** and **acceptance.**

3. Write you response to this exercise

"He guides me in the paths of righteousness for His name's sake."
STEP 6 "We were entirely ready to have God remove all of these defects of character."

2 CORINTHIANS 5:17

GALATIANS 5:16-17

EPHESIANS 4:17-23

PHILIPPIANS 4:13

COLOSSIANS 3:5-8

TITUS 2:12

HEBREWS 6:12

WEEK FOUR WELLNESS CHECK-IN

Rate your physical, psychological, emotional, and spiritual health

- Examine your health in each area of your life. Give each behavior a number from 1-5 (#5 means very well).
- Be HONEST. It's helpful to know the *truth* about your recovery health in order to take care of yourself.
- Circle **one** BEHAVIOR in each area that you are willing to work on daily for the next week.

MY BIOLOGICAL HEALTH (PHYSICAL)

MY RECOVERY DATE:		NUMBER OF CONTINOUS DAYS	
Nutrition- when and what you eat		Physical /dental exams & appointments	
Water		Medications/ daily vitamins	
Identifying/reducing emotional eating		Stress management/keeping it simple	
Sleep/rest (too much, too little)		Eliminating/reducing caffeine	
Exercise (easy does it)		Eliminating/reducing sugar	
Pacing your activities (too much, too little)		Other:	

MY PSYCHOLOGICAL HEALTH (MY THOUGHTS & BEHAVIOR)

Managing denial/ defense mechanisms		Music/art/school work	
Positive vs. Negative thinking		Journaling thoughts & behaviors	
Reducing obsessive thoughts		Making phone calls (sponsor, hotline)	
Daily structure/ being on time		Self-help meetings	
Making amends (promptly admit)		Building self esteem	
Money management		Other:	

MY EMOTIONAL/RELATIONAL HEALTH

Letting go of enabling people		Connecting with family in healthy way	
Managing emotions		Self care	
Spending time with **safe** people		Relaxation exercises	
Setting boundaries		Healthy sexual relations	
Having fun		Journaling feelings/ talking about them	
To Thine Own Self Be True. My "yes" is "yes," and my "no" is "no."		Other:	

MY SPIRITUAL HEALTH

Telling the truth to myself and others		Loving myself/ self-forgiveness	
Service to others		Church / Bible study	
Prayer		Serenity Prayer	
Meditation and/or quiet time with God		Gratitude list, affirmations	
Utilizing the Steps /Spiritual Principles		Enjoying nature	
Balance in everyday life (avoiding extremes)		Seeking/finding my purpose, finding what matters	

- Recognize emotional triggers and <u>change behavior.</u>
- Recognize anxiety and <u>practice relaxation techniques.</u>
- Recognize sleeping and eating habits that are slipping and <u>practice self-care.</u>

PSALM 23 **"He guides me in the paths of righteousness for His name sake."**

STEP 6 "We were entirely ready to have God remove all these defects of character."

COMPLETION

My favorite Scripture for Chapter 6: (write it here)

______ I understand Chapter 6 and will continue to use it daily.
______ I studied and completed the Bible study in *Psalm 23* group.
______ I worked with a PSALM-Partner this month to study Chapter 6.

PSALM-Partner NAME: _____________________________________

PSALM-Partner Phone # _________________________________

Today's date _____________________________________

My Signature ________________________ **PSALM-PARTNER** ____________________

BIBLE STUDY AT A GLANCE

MATTHEW 3:8	COLOSSIANS 3:5-8	PSALM 4:4-5	
MATTHEW 5:3	I THESSALONIANS 4:3-8	PSALM 16:7-11	
MATTHEW 9:17	TITUS 2:11-14	PSALM 19:12-13	
ROMANS 6:1-4	HEBREWS 6:11-12	PSALM 32:1-5	
ROMANS 6:11-12	HEBREWS 12:1-2	PSALM 94:12-13A	
ROMANS 12:2	JAMES 1:5-6	PSALM 119:10-12	
1 CORINTHIANS 15:57	JAMES 1:21	PSALM 119:27-40	
2 CORINTHIANS 5:17	I PETER 1:13-16	PSALM 139:23-24	
2 CORINTHIANS 7:9-10	I PETER 2:1-2	PSALM 141:3-4	
GALATIANS 5:16-17	I JOHN 2:28-3:3	PROVERBS 3:11-12	
EPHESIANS 4:17-23	I JOHN 4:18	PROVERBS 13:18	
EPHESIANS 5:8-10	REVELATION 3:19-20	PROVERBS 17:10	
PHILIPPIANS 4:13			

The Lord is My Shepherd
A 12 Step Journey through PSALM 23

DECISION
CHAPTER SEVEN
†

PSALM 23
*"Even though I walk through the valley of the shadow
of death, I fear no evil; for Thou art with me."*

STEP 7
"Humbly asked God to remove our shortcomings."

CHAPTER SEVEN INTRODUCTION

PSALM 23

"Even though I walk through the valley of the shadow of death, I fear no evil; for Thou art with me."

The Good Shepherd guides *his* sheep from the "home" ranch into the hill country for the summer. It requires preparation, commitment, and a desire for what's best for the flock. The long trek onto the distant summer range is a time when the flock is entirely alone with their shepherd. The shepherd knows his sheep and calls them by name. **Each face has a story.**

Notice how the grammar shifts at this time in David's poem from speaking of God in the third person, *He*, to the second person, *Thou* or *You*. This makes sense because the walk through the valley is an intimate time for both sheep (us) and shepherd (JESUS). We use these comforting words of David's Twenty Third Psalm to console us at funerals and memorial services of our loved ones. Death is a door to a higher place with the Lord. And for those of us here on earth, we use David's words to <u>discover the ways of God</u> and His everlasting faithfulness even in the midst of life's battles. From our valley experience we can trust God to take us to a higher place. David knew exactly why he took his flock through the valleys in his route to the high country;
1) It is the gentlest way to the mountaintop. 2) It is the best watered route. 3) It has the best and richest feed.
Be still. Be alone with the Shepherd.
He cares and wants to see your face.

STEP 7 "Humbly asked God to remove our shortcomings."

This Step will explore our attitudes, humility, and living at peace with ourselves and others.
Seventh Step Prayer, from <u>Our A.A. Legacy to the Faith Community</u>, compiled and edited by Dick B.

Dear God,
We come to you in the name of Jesus. Thank you for taking complete control of my life in Step Three, and thank you for this opportunity to wipe my slate clean and start my life over anew. I am coming to you on my knees in all humility to humbly ask you to forgive all my past wrongs and remove all my shortcomings.
I acknowledge that my past was sinful, and I ask you now, God, to please forgive all my past sins. I am so thankful that you have promised to do this and that you have the power to do it if I ask. I want to start a new life today, and I ask you to help me do so and to keep helping if I keep asking.
In Step Three I turned my will and my life over to your care. In Steps Four, Five, and Six, I have completed my moral inventory and admitted to myself and another person the exact nature of my wrongs. I now admit these wrongs to you, Lord, and I am entirely ready to have you remove all my defects of character.
I am entirely ready and ask and pray that you remove from me every single defect of character. Specifically, I ask you to remove the following defects of character listed in my Fourth Step Inventory. (Read aloud those defects you listed.) Thank you, God, for removing all my defects of character. Please help me learn how to keep them out of my life through the effective use of Step Ten. Thank you, God, for this opportunity for a new beginning in my life and a chance to be a part of the solution in life instead of the problem. Please grant me wisdom, knowledge, and strength as I go from here to do your work and live the victorious life you designed for me. Thank you, Jesus, for these Twelve Steps which will make your plan for my life clear to me. Thank You and Praise Your Name. Amen.

For the next 30 days keep thanking God for removing your shortcomings.

The Spiritual Principles are surrender, trust, faith, patience, and humility.

"Even though I walk through the valley of the shadow of death, I fear no evil; for Thou art with me."

The shepherd leads his sheep into the wild country where they were faced with ***difficulties, dangers,*** and ***delights***. The sudden change in weather such as rain or hail is a threat the shepherd is always aware of. A soaked and chilled sheep can become ***dangerously*** sick with respiratory complications. The shepherd is always prepared and he is always there with his sheep.

From the author: "The last 5 years of my mother's life was filled with new and changing mental and physical complications. She and my father drove to doctor appointments nearly every day. Sometimes Mom spent months at a time in the hospital with Dad always by her side. We were exposed to the storms and adversities of life and Jesus stood close to me through it all. One of my mother's surgeries had a surprising result. The doctor came to the family stating that when he got in there, the mass on her lung was completely gone! We experienced ***difficulties, dangers and delights.***
God sustained us all through the darkest hours of my mother's illnesses. The nursing staff warned us that after a long stay in a hospital room, patients can become mentally confused and it can be *dangerous*. The dim shadows of *difficulty* multiplied and darkened before we *delighted* in wheeling mom home for another Christmas.
2004-2005: My valleys were roads to a higher, more intimate relationship with God. My family grew closer to each other, closer to Mom and I grew closer to God. We really needed and loved each other. When my mother died on that February morning, she passed on to a higher place where she has the Lord's *perfect peace* because she has the Lord's *certain presence*. Thank you Jesus!" -Marcy Hawkins

The valley of the shadow of death is usually associated with the end of living and is most often read at funerals. David placed the valleys in the **middle** of his Psalm because he faced hardships and valleys intermittently through his life. God's presence was David's comfort.

1. Do you need to talk to someone about your grief over the death or illness of a loved one?

2. When, over the last year have you experienced ***difficulties***?

3. When, over the last year have you experienced ***dangers***?

4. How did you feel towards God through your difficulties and dangers?

5. When, over the last year have you experienced ***delights*** while in the valley?

STEP 7 "Humbly asked God to remove our shortcomings."

Lets look at the word Humility. (excerpt from "The Twelve Steps and The Twelve Traditions" of Alcoholics Anonymous.)

"Humility, as a word and as an ideal, has a very bad time of it in our world. Not only is the idea misunderstood; the word itself is often intensely disliked. Many people haven't even a nodding acquaintance with humility as a way of life. Much of the everyday talk we hear, and a great deal of what we read, highlights man's pride in his own achievements.

With great intelligence, men of science have been forcing nature to disclose her secrets. The immense resources now being harnessed promise such quantity of material blessings that many have come to believe that a man-made millennium lies just ahead. Poverty will disappear, and there will be such abundance that everybody can have all the security and personal satisfactions he desires. The theory seems to be that once everybody's primary instincts are satisfied, there won't be much left to quarrel about. The world will become happy and be free to concentrate on culture and character. Solely by their own intelligence and labor, men will have shaped their own destiny.

Certainly, no alcoholic, and surely no member of A.A., wants to deprecate material achievement. Nor do we enter into debate with the many who still so passionately cling to the belief that to satisfy our basic natural desires is the main objective in life. But we are sure that no class of people in the world ever made a worse mess of trying to live by this formula than alcoholics. For thousands of years we have been demanding more than our share of security, prestige, and romance. When we seemed to be succeeding, we drank to dream still greater dreams. When we were frustrated, even in part, we drank to oblivion. Never was there enough of what we thought we wanted.

In all these strivings, so many of them well-intentioned, our crippling handicap has been our lack of humility. We lacked the perspective to see that character-building and spiritual values had to come first, and that material satisfactions were not the purpose of living...."

1. Underline the words or lines that pertain to your personal recovery.

2. What does the word humility mean to you?

3. Do you work compulsively to get things to work out *the way you want them to*?

4. Do you become afraid and upset when your way is threatened?

Without humility, we are often on the edge of being out of control, frustrated, lonely, depressed and angry. Step 7 helps us to release control back to God. Read Philippians 2:1-18

5. Are you willing to work on this? What are you willing to do?

Isaiah 26:3 "You will keep in perfect peace him whose mind is steadfast, because he trusts in you."
Psalm 46:10 "BE STILL AND KNOW THAT I AM GOD."

**"Even though I walk through the valley of the shadow of death, I fear no evil; for Thou art with me."
STEP 7 "Humbly asked God to remove our shortcomings."**

MATTHEW 7:7-8

MATTHEW 26:41

LUKE 18:14

ACTS 3:19

PHILIPPIANS 4:19

HEBREWS 4:16

HEBREWS 8:12

Rate your physical, psychological, emotional, and spiritual health

- Examine your health in each area of your life. Give each behavior a number from 1-5 (#5 means very well).
- Be HONEST. It's helpful to know the *truth* about your recovery health in order to take care of yourself.
- Circle **one** BEHAVIOR in each area that you are willing to work on daily for the next week.

MY BIOLOGICAL HEALTH (PHYSICAL)

MY RECOVERY DATE:		NUMBER OF CONTINOUS DAYS	
Nutrition- when and what you eat		Physical /dental exams & appointments	
Water		Medications/ daily vitamins	
Identifying/reducing emotional eating		Stress management/keeping it simple	
Sleep/rest (too much, too little)		Eliminating/reducing caffeine	
Exercise (easy does it)		Eliminating/reducing sugar	
Pacing your activities (too much, too little)		Other:	

MY PSYCHOLOGICAL HEALTH (MY THOUGHTS & BEHAVIOR)

Managing denial/ defense mechanisms		Music/art/school work	
Positive vs. Negative thinking		Journaling thoughts & behaviors	
Reducing obsessive thoughts		Making phone calls (sponsor, hotline)	
Daily structure/ being on time		Self-help meetings	
Making amends (promptly admit)		Building self esteem	
Money management		Other:	

MY EMOTIONAL/RELATIONAL HEALTH

Letting go of enabling people		Connecting with family in healthy way	
Managing emotions		Self care	
Spending time with **safe** people		Relaxation exercises	
Setting boundaries		Healthy sexual relations	
Having fun		Journaling feelings/ talking about them	
To Thine Own Self Be True. My "yes" is "yes," and my "no" is "no."		Other:	

MY SPIRITUAL HEALTH

Telling the truth to myself and others		Loving myself/ self-forgiveness	
Service to others		Church / Bible study	
Prayer		Serenity Prayer	
Meditation and/or quiet time with God		Gratitude list, affirmations	
Utilizing the Steps /Spiritual Principles		Enjoying nature	
Balance in everyday life (avoiding extremes)		Seeking/finding my purpose, finding what matters	

- Recognize emotional triggers and <u>change behavior.</u>
- Recognize anxiety and <u>practice relaxation techniques.</u>
- Recognize sleeping and eating habits that are slipping and <u>practice self-care.</u>

"Even though I walk through the valley of the shadow of death, I fear no evil; for Thou art with me."

One of the reasons the shepherd takes his flock into the high country by way of the valleys is because it really is the gentlest way to the mountaintop. It is the shepherd's long-range plan for his beloved sheep.

1. How do you react to life's battles?

2. Have you ever felt alone in the valley? What were your thoughts and feelings?

3. Which Spiritual Principles will help you in your valleys? Why do you think they will help you?

Remember: The valley is the gentlest way to the mountaintop.
4. What does *"keep it simple"* mean to you? Do you like this slogan?

5. What Scripture or slogan helps you in your recovery in the good times? How about in the bad times?

Deuteronomy 31:8 "The Lord himself goes before you and will be with you; he will never leave you nor forsake you. Do not be afraid; do not be discouraged."

6. What is the biggest obstacle blocking your walk through the valleys <u>with your Shepherd</u>? Please consider dumping your defects of character while in the valley…..it'll lighten your load while walking through and out of the valley.

STEP 7 "Humbly asked God to remove our shortcomings."

Perhaps Step 7 will be a good exercise for your neck muscles as you confront long established patterns of *looking down* at your problems by relying on people and things to function as little <u>gods</u> in your life. GOD (with a capital G) wants to see your face when you *look up* to ask Him to remove your shortcomings or defects of character. When you look up in a spirit of humility you will encounter His sustaining love **moment by moment**. Your Shepherd is happy to see your face. Keep looking UP!

"Prayer unites the soul to God"- Julian of Norwich

1. Which shortcoming is causing you the **most** trouble right now? Name it out loud with God's help.

2. What benefits do you get from it?

3. What problems does it cause?

4. What other shortcoming is also causing you trouble right now? Name it out loud with God's help.

5. What benefits do you get from it?

6. What problems does it cause?

Ephesians 6:12 "For our struggle is not against flesh and blood, but against the rulers, against the authorities, against the powers of this dark world and against spiritual forces of evil in the heavenly realms."

Hebrews 12:3 "Consider him who endured such opposition from sinful men, so that you will not grow weary and lose heart."

2 Corinthians 3:18 "And we, who with unveiled faces all reflect the Lord's glory, are being transformed into His likeness with ever-increasing glory, which comes from the Lord, who is the Spirit."

It is important to remember that recovery is a process and all of our shortcomings will probably not disappear immediately. We will always fall short of perfection.

7. Is the slogan *"progress not perfection"* hard for you to accept? Explain your answer.

8. How compassionate are you towards yourself?

9. What "self-care" activity will you commit to this week?

10. Do you have a PSALM-Partner to talk with? A close friend?

1 John 2:1 "My dear children, I write this to you so that you will not sin. But if anybody does sin, we have one who speaks to the Father in our defense- Jesus Christ, the Righteous One."

Romans 6:14 "For sin shall not be your master, because you are not under law, but under grace."

"Even though I walk through the valley of the shadow of death, I fear no evil; for Thou art with me."
STEP 7 "Humbly asked God to remove our shortcomings."

JAMES 4:7

____

____

1 PETER 2:4

____

____

1 PETER 5:6-7

____

____

1 JOHN 1:9

____

____

1 JOHN 3:22

____

____

PSALM 10:17

____

____

PSALM 25:8-9

____

____

____

WEEK TWO WELLNESS CHECK-IN

Rate your physical, psychological, emotional, and spiritual health

- Examine your health in each area of your life. Give each behavior a number from 1-5 (#5 means very well).
- Be HONEST. It's helpful to know the *truth* about your recovery health in order to take care of yourself.
- Circle **one** BEHAVIOR in each area that you are willing to work on daily for the next week.

MY BIOLOGICAL HEALTH (PHYSICAL)

MY RECOVERY DATE:		NUMBER OF CONTINOUS DAYS	
Nutrition- when and what you eat		Physical /dental exams & appointments	
Water		Medications/ daily vitamins	
Identifying/reducing emotional eating		Stress management/keeping it simple	
Sleep/rest (too much, too little)		Eliminating/reducing caffeine	
Exercise (easy does it)		Eliminating/reducing sugar	
Pacing your activities (too much, too little)		Other:	

MY PSYCHOLOGICAL HEALTH (MY THOUGHTS & BEHAVIOR)

Managing denial/ defense mechanisms		Music/art/school work	
Positive vs. Negative thinking		Journaling thoughts & behaviors	
Reducing obsessive thoughts		Making phone calls (sponsor, hotline)	
Daily structure/ being on time		Self-help meetings	
Making amends (promptly admit)		Building self esteem	
Money management		Other:	

MY EMOTIONAL/RELATIONAL HEALTH

Letting go of enabling people		Connecting with family in healthy way	
Managing emotions		Self care	
Spending time with **safe** people		Relaxation exercises	
Setting boundaries		Healthy sexual relations	
Having fun		Journaling feelings/ talking about them	
To Thine Own Self Be True. My "yes" is "yes," and my "no" is "no."		Other:	

MY SPIRITUAL HEALTH

Telling the truth to myself and others		Loving myself/ self-forgiveness	
Service to others		Church / Bible study	
Prayer		Serenity Prayer	
Meditation and/or quiet time with God		Gratitude list, affirmations	
Utilizing the Steps /Spiritual Principles		Enjoying nature	
Balance in everyday life (avoiding extremes)		Seeking/finding my purpose, finding what matters	

- Recognize emotional triggers and <u>change behavior.</u>
- Recognize anxiety and <u>practice relaxation techniques.</u>
- Recognize sleeping and eating habits that are slipping and <u>practice self-care.</u>

"Even though I walk through the valley of the shadow of death, I fear no evil; for Thou art with me."

The Good Shepherd is prepared for the long "drives" into the distant summer ranges. The sheep move slowly along the pre-determined and best-watered route. The sheep get hot and thirsty and are happy to be guided to the rivers, streams and quiet pools. Sometimes the valleys we find ourselves in are very deep and long. Our Shepherd can lead us to a *place of refreshment* in the midst of our difficulties.

1. When have you felt refreshed and restored despite desperate circumstances?

2. What is it like for you to watch someone else walk through one of their valleys?

3. Define courage.

4. Read and write Psalm 56:3-4

5. Read Hebrews 12:1-2. Keep looking up!

6. Read Genesis 28:15. "I will not leave you."

7. Where is the Lord and where is the refreshment when you are facing unemployment?

8. Where is the Lord and where is the refreshment when you have a sick child?

9. Where is the Lord and where is the refreshment when you are in debt?

10. Where is the Lord and where is the refreshment when you are betrayed by a friend?

11. Where is the Lord and where is the refreshment when you are ________________________?
Your present difficulty

You are not alone. The Lord is with you.

STEP 7 "Humbly asked God to remove our shortcomings."

Perhaps you were consistently refused, rejected, ignored, or disappointed by your family of origin so you decided to never need anything from anybody. This type of coping mechanism can cause continued hurt by holding us back from asking for and accepting God's help. Maybe you received positive reinforcement and praise for high achievement, and you were put up on a pedestal. This can also keep us from allowing Jesus to shepherd us.

1. What role did self-sufficiency have in your early childhood?

2. What role did self-sufficiency have in your teen years?

3. What is the difference between humility and humiliation?

4. Read and write Isaiah 64:8-9

5. Complete this Prayer in your own words.

Dear Lord, I feel you smoothing out my rough edges…….

"Even though I walk through the valley of the shadow of death, I fear no evil; for Thou art with me."
STEP 7 "Humbly asked God to remove our shortcomings."

PSALM 37:4-6

PSALM 51:1-2

PSALM 51:10

JEREMIAH 29:11

JOHN 12:46

1 CORINTHIANS 4:5

EPHESIANS 1:7

WEEK THREE WELLNESS CHECK-IN

Rate your physical, psychological, emotional, and spiritual health

- Examine your health in each area of your life. Give each behavior a number from 1-5 (#5 means very well).
- Be HONEST. It's helpful to know the *truth* about your recovery health in order to take care of yourself.
- Circle **one** BEHAVIOR in each area that you are willing to work on daily for the next week.

MY BIOLOGICAL HEALTH (PHYSICAL)

MY RECOVERY DATE:		NUMBER OF CONTINOUS DAYS	
Nutrition- when and what you eat		Physical /dental exams & appointments	
Water		Medications/ daily vitamins	
Identifying/reducing emotional eating		Stress management/keeping it simple	
Sleep/rest (too much, too little)		Eliminating/reducing caffeine	
Exercise (easy does it)		Eliminating/reducing sugar	
Pacing your activities (too much, too little)		Other:	

MY PSYCHOLOGICAL HEALTH (MY THOUGHTS & BEHAVIOR)

Managing denial/ defense mechanisms		Music/art/school work	
Positive vs. Negative thinking		Journaling thoughts & behaviors	
Reducing obsessive thoughts		Making phone calls (sponsor, hotline)	
Daily structure/ being on time		Self-help meetings	
Making amends (promptly admit)		Building self esteem	
Money management		Other:	

MY EMOTIONAL/RELATIONAL HEALTH

Letting go of enabling people		Connecting with family in healthy way	
Managing emotions		Self care	
Spending time with **safe** people		Relaxation exercises	
Setting boundaries		Healthy sexual relations	
Having fun		Journaling feelings/ talking about them	
To Thine Own Self Be True. My "yes" is "yes," and my "no" is "no."		Other:	

MY SPIRITUAL HEALTH

Telling the truth to myself and others		Loving myself/ self-forgiveness	
Service to others		Church / Bible study	
Prayer		Serenity Prayer	
Meditation and/or quiet time with God		Gratitude list, affirmations	
Utilizing the Steps /Spiritual Principles		Enjoying nature	
Balance in everyday life (avoiding extremes)		Seeking/finding my purpose, finding what matters	

- Recognize emotional triggers and <u>change behavior.</u>
- Recognize anxiety and <u>practice relaxation techniques.</u>
- Recognize sleeping and eating habits that are slipping and <u>practice self-care.</u>

"Even though I walk through the valley of the shadow of death, I fear no evil; for Thou art with me."

The good shepherd knows that if his sheep fend for themselves, they will be dissatisfied and miss the benefits of the best and richest food the valleys have to offer. He knows how deep in the valleys to go and which poisonous plants could harm his precious flock. Coyotes, bears, wolves and wild cats are another threat, but the shepherd takes his flock through the valleys again and again in spite of the hazards. When we allow our Good Shepherd to lead us through the valleys and depend on his strength and courage for every step, we become less and less fearful and more at peace with the freedom we find in the valleys.

1. When were you most dissatisfied with your life?

2. What did you fill your hunger and thirst with during that time?

3. What problem do you have today that needs the mercy and grace of the Lord?

4. Read Isaiah 49:9-11. Can you let God nourish the hunger in your soul?

The shepherd takes his flock through the valleys again and again in spite of the hazards.
5. What are some benefits of the valley experience? Name at least 5 benefits or *delights*.

Matthew 13:44 "The kingdom of heaven is like treasure hidden in a field. When a man found it, he hid it again, and then in his joy went and sold all he had and bought that field."

To make it out of your valley experiences you may need to let go of your heavy burdens.

---

6. Are you clutching on to old coping mechanisms of the past?

7. What are you ready to let go of?

8. Will you sell out for Jesus? In Matthew 13:14, the man sold all he had.

STEP 7 "Humbly asked God to remove our shortcomings."

Step 7 represents a turning point in our recovery. It is the bridge between the work completed in Steps 1-6 and Steps 8-12 where we make changes in our behavior.

1. Do you see how your shortcomings get in the way of your relationship with God? Read Isaiah 59:2.

2. What have you learned about yourself this month?

3. What behaviors are you asking God to help you leave in the valley?

4. Why do you want to continue working the Steps?

5. The bible study through the remaining verses in *PSALM 23* promises to bless us. We will look at our relationships with others in order to learn, heal and grow in our ongoing recovery. We hope to experience the DESIRES of our hearts as the result of our hard work. Which verse of *PSALM 23* are you looking forward to studying?

**Even though I walk through the valley of the shadow of death, I fear no evil; for Thou art with me."
STEP 7 "Humbly asked God to remove our shortcomings."**

ACTS 3:19

____

____

PHILIPPIANS 4:19

____

____

HEBREWS 4:12-13

____

____

HEBREWS 4:16

____

____

JAMES 4:6

____

____

JAMES 5:15

____

____

1 PETER 2:2

____

____

Rate your physical, psychological, emotional, and spiritual health

- Examine your health in each area of your life. Give each behavior a number from 1-5 (#5 means very well).
- Be HONEST. It's helpful to know the *truth* about your recovery health in order to take care of yourself.
- Circle **one** BEHAVIOR in each area that you are willing to work on daily for the next week.

MY BIOLOGICAL HEALTH (PHYSICAL)

MY RECOVERY DATE:		NUMBER OF CONTINOUS DAYS	
Nutrition- when and what you eat		Physical /dental exams & appointments	
Water		Medications/ daily vitamins	
Identifying/reducing emotional eating		Stress management/keeping it simple	
Sleep/rest (too much, too little)		Eliminating/reducing caffeine	
Exercise (easy does it)		Eliminating/reducing sugar	
Pacing your activities (too much, too little)		Other:	

MY PSYCHOLOGICAL HEALTH (MY THOUGHTS & BEHAVIOR)

Managing denial/ defense mechanisms		Music/art/school work	
Positive vs. Negative thinking		Journaling thoughts & behaviors	
Reducing obsessive thoughts		Making phone calls (sponsor, hotline)	
Daily structure/ being on time		Self-help meetings	
Making amends (promptly admit)		Building self esteem	
Money management		Other:	

MY EMOTIONAL/RELATIONAL HEALTH

Letting go of enabling people		Connecting with family in healthy way	
Managing emotions		Self care	
Spending time with **safe** people		Relaxation exercises	
Setting boundaries		Healthy sexual relations	
Having fun		Journaling feelings/ talking about them	
To Thine Own Self Be True. My "yes" is "yes," and my "no" is "no."		Other:	

MY SPIRITUAL HEALTH

Telling the truth to myself and others		Loving myself/ self-forgiveness	
Service to others		Church / Bible study	
Prayer		Serenity Prayer	
Meditation and/or quiet time with God		Gratitude list, affirmations	
Utilizing the Steps /Spiritual Principles		Enjoying nature	
Balance in everyday life (avoiding extremes)		Seeking/finding my purpose, finding what matters	

- Recognize emotional triggers and <u>change behavior.</u>
- Recognize anxiety and <u>practice relaxation techniques.</u>
- Recognize sleeping and eating habits that are slipping and <u>practice self-care.</u>

PSALM 23
"Even though I walk through the valley of the shadow of death, I fear no evil; for Thou art with me."

STEP 7 "Humbly asked God to remove our shortcomings."

COMPLETION

My favorite Scripture for Chapter 7: (write it here)

______ I understand Chapter 7 and will continue to use it daily.
______ I studied and completed the Bible study in **PSALM 23** group.
______ I worked with a PSALM-Partner this month to study Chapter 7.

PSALM-Partner NAME: _______________________________________

PSALM-Partner Phone # __________________________________

Today's date ____

My Signature _________________________ **PSALM-Partner** ______________________

BIBLE STUDY AT A GLANCE

MATTHEW 7:7-11	HEBREWS 8:12	PSALM 10:17	PSALM 51:10
MATTHEW 15:22-28	HEBREWS 9:14	PSALM 25:8-11	PSALM 79:9
MATTHEW 18:19-20	JAMES 4:6	PSALM 32:1	PSALM 91:14-16
MATTHEW 21:21-22	JAMES 5:15	PSALM 32:6-8	PSALM 103:2-5
MATTHEW 26:41	1 PETER 2:2	PSALM 34:4-6	PSALM 119:133
LUKE 18:9-14	1 PETER 5:6-7	PSALM 34:15	PROVERBS 18:12
ACTS 3:19	1 JOHN 1:9	PSALM 37:4-6	PROVERBS 22:4
PHILIPPIANS 4:19	1 JOHN 3:4-9	PSALM 37:23-24	
HEBREWS 4:12-13	1 JOHN 3:22-24	PSALM 39:7-8	
HEBREWS 4:16	1 JOHN 5:14-15	PSALM 51:1-2	

The Lord is My Shepherd
A 12 Step Journey through PSALM 23

DESIRES
CHAPTER EIGHT
†

PSALM 23
"Thy rod and thy staff, they comfort me."

STEP 8
"We made a list of all the persons we had harmed and became willing to make amends to them all."

DESIRES

FROM THE AUTHOR ....

Before my recovery began, my ability to nurture and maintain relationships was compromised by my addiction. Relationships with friends and family were shallow, stressed, and fake. I had become crafty at living a double life, all the while keeping those persons at a distance. After all, I had many secrets and much to hide. If I lost a friend along the way, I chalked it up to the changing times or geographical distance. People that I once cared about became ignored and even avoided. This surprised my family, as I had been a friendly and popular child, as well as very active in high school relationships with cheerleading and sports. My parents did not know what was wrong with me, but they did know that I had changed. My sister and mother would talk about my situation together but felt powerless to do or say anything. Apparently, I became defensive when questioned about such matters. I suppose my family was in as much denial about the severity of my problems as I was.

Even though my relationships with those near me went array, I held strong to my relationship with mood-altering substances in order to "feel good." The one relationship I had grown to trust was that which I developed with alcohol. For many years I had control of my usage and it seemed to assist me in my relationships with others. I felt I was more relaxed, more fun, and more spontaneous. Yet in a blink of an eye, in the time it took to look back, this special friend of mine named "Bud," as in Budweiser beer, had me under the influence of its spell for most of my days. This relationship with alcohol was complicated by an eating disorder and became the only thing that truly mattered to me. I would spend years alone or with others, feeling isolated in either instance, with a disconnection from the world and relationships around me.

ANOTHER LOST SHEEP…

I had been hanging on to two core beliefs that fueled my drinking; firstly, "I do not have an addiction," and secondly, "I have control over my drinking." I made little rules for myself like, "I'll drink a 7-up between beers" or "I'll only drink good red wine" or anything I could think of that proved I had control and was a normal drinker. I now know that the control was long gone and replaced by a very high tolerance for alcohol. My body was depending on my daily dose to feel normal. It was now a biological fact. I didn't know that then, so I thought I had to try harder. Failing proved I was weak or bad, or both! But the truth is I was sick.

In recovery, I slowly developed relationships with other people, rather than with an object such as a beer or mood- altering drug. I remember reading stories in the Big Book of AA that described thoughts and behaviors that were JUST LIKE MINE! I couldn't believe what I was reading. I thought I was the only one that thought and behaved the way I did. Hearing the truth awakened the DESIRE deep inside me that had been drowning in a sea of lies. *The* DESIRES *of my heart* was to be honest, open and truly myself in my relationships. I was a beginner and just like a baby bird hunkered down in its nest my world would remain small and focused on my recovery while I got the feathers I would need to take flight. I was dependent on my new relationships to be "fed". My "nest" kept me safe and was made up of family, church, 12-step meetings, exercise, and much needed good nutrition. And I learned about self-care as I lined my nest with things and behaviors that would comfort and soothe. It was all so new but so much easier now that I was no longer poisoning my brain with alcohol. Amazingly my heightened anxiety began dissipating as my health improved. God restored my soul and then carried me close to His heart throughout my first year of sobriety. It was in my third year that God brought me a therapist to help me heal from some deeper issues that got buried along the way. She was perfect for me and I trusted her. Towards the end of that relationship I soured like an eagle with a grateful heart for what time and healthy relationships had given me. One day she told me that in her opinion I would make a great therapist someday. I kept that in mind when I left the US Postal Service at age thirty-nine to prepare my life for my first child. With a new-born at home I began my coursework to work in the field of Addiction Studies.

This little sheep still has the DESIRE to connect with others in a healthy way. I have fallen in love with The Good Shepherd and I stand in awe of how much He loves me. It is the assurance in my salvation that brings heart-felt joy, an awareness of a purpose-filled life, and a grateful heart for how continuously *He Restores My Soul.*

CHAPTER ONE INTRODUCTION

PSALM 23
"Thy rod and Thy staff, they comfort me."

The long trek into the high country and up to the mountain meadows began in the last workbook in Step 7. The sheep cannot make it through the valleys without developing an intimate relationship with their master. They find comfort in seeing their shepherd with his rod. It's an extension of his right arm and is used for examination, protection, and discipline. We can find our direction, comfort and discipline in God's Word. **The Scriptures are God's rod**. The written Word is the extension of God's mind to us.

Every shepherd has a staff and this unique instrument is used only in the care and benefit of sheep. The shepherd's staff is carefully selected, smoothed and shaped with a hook on one end. The staff is used to draw the sheep together, to reach out and hook a wandering sheep, and to guide the sheep gently along paths and through gates. The Spirit of God is for the benefit and comfort of His children. **The Spirit of God is God's staff**. The Holy Spirit is for the care and benefit of God's children.

John 16:13-14 *"But when he, the Spirit of truth, comes, he will guide you into all truth, He will not speak on his own; he will speak only what he hears, and he will tell you what is yet to come. He will bring glory to me by taking from what is mine and making it known to you."*

STEP 8
"Made a list of all the persons we had harmed and became willing to make amends to them all."

Up to now we've looked at our relationship with God and ourselves. We made the wonderful DISCOVERY of God's treasure for us in Step 1, Step 2, and Step 3. Making the DECISION to ask God for His help in replacing our shortcomings with spiritual principles is the work in Step 4 through Step 7. Now we look at our relationship with others and work Step 8 through Step 12, to obtain the DESIRES of our hearts by becoming the authentic persons God created us to be!

Step 8 asks us to make a list of people who have been harmed by our compulsive and self-destructive behavior and then challenges us to become willing to make amends. As we prepare to apologize, we learn productive ways of dealing with guilt such as making amends and taking responsibility for our behavior. It's important to use the help and support of sponsors, counselors, and group members as we share our thoughts, feelings and challenges with Step 8. We can ask the Holy Spirit to reveal to us the names of those we've hurt. We can ask God for understanding of all the possible ways we have caused harm. He will reveal them to us and will help us understand everything necessary to continue.

READ ECCLESIASTES 4:9-12
As you prepare for Step 8, be willing to accept the love and support of others.
It will help you stay focused on "doing the next right thing."

The Spiritual Principles in Step 8 are self-discipline, self-control, honesty, and integrity.

"Thy rod and Thy staff, they comfort me."

The shepherd uses his rod to count and carefully examine each and every sheep. In the Old Testament this was referred to as passing "under the rod". The shepherd opens the fleece with his rod and examines his sheep for disease, wounds, or any sign of trouble. The shepherd knows his sheep and he calls them by name. Read Ezekiel 20:37. Our Heavenly Father keeps a good eye on His children. He knows **you** by name.

1. How did you handle your problems when you were a child?

2. Who knew you the best when you were a child?

3. Did this person tell you the truth about life, your strengths and limitations, and your family? Why or why not?

> Psalm 139:23-24 *"O Lord, you have searched me and you know me. You know when I sit and when I rise; you perceive my thoughts from afar. You discern my going out and my lying down; you are familiar with all my ways. Before a word is on my tongue you know it completely, O Lord."*

4. If you passed "under the rod" today, what would cause your Shepherd some concern?

5. When has God used His Word (His rod) to expose a problem in your life?

The shepherd's rod is his weapon of *power, authority, and defense.* He uses it as an instrument of protection for both himself and his sheep and is prepared for any situation. The shepherd throws the rod, or club, with amazing speed and accuracy. And it works! We can count on the Word of God in any situation. And it works!

6. Give an example of when God's Word protected or warned you about danger.

7. Have you used Scripture to help you fight off self-destructive temptations? Please explain.

8. How often do you read your Bible?

STEP 8 "Made a list of all the persons we had harmed and became willing to make amends to them all."

1. What feelings do you have about doing this Step?

___resentments	___relief	___forgiveness	
___guilt	___grudges	___fear	
___shame	___hope	___anxiety	___other

2. Use this space to write about one or two of your feelings concerning Step 8.

Remember, you have the comforter by your side.

3. Start by making your list.

- Don't worry right now about how and when you will make your amends.
- You don't need to worry about leaving someone off the list. Just write down who comes to mind....
- Your Step 4 inventory can help you with your list.

God created us with INSTINCTS
These instincts are **material security, emotional security, sexual desire,**
and the **desire for companionship/community**.

If these instincts become misdirected,
they can drive us, dominate us, and insist on ruling our lives.

The Twelve Steps and the Twelve Traditions (pages 70-72) says this about humility.
"For thousands of years we have been demanding more than our share of security, prestige, and romance. When we seemed to be succeeding, we drank to dream still greater dreams. When we were frustrated, even in part, we drank until oblivion. Never was there enough of what we thought we wanted.
In all these strivings, so many of them well-intentioned, our crippling handicap has been our lack of humility. We lacked the perspective to see that character-building and spiritual values had to come first, and that material satisfactions were not the purpose of living...."

Whom I have harmed:	How I harmed them:	How this harmed myself :

Studying David's Twenty-Third Psalm along with this Step 8 reminds us that the Holy Spirit is our comforter.

4. In working Step 8 and Step 9 we recognize the pain we've caused others and become willing to take responsibility to relieve the pain. How do you feel about taking responsibility at this time?

"Thy rod and Thy staff, they comfort me."
STEP 8 "Made a list of all the persons we had harmed and became willing to make amends to them all."

MATTHEW 6:14-15

____

____

MATTHEW 7:3-5

____

____

____

MARK 11:25

____

____

LUKE 6:27-28 (READ THROUGH VERSE 32)

____

____

____

LUKE 6:37 (READ THROUGH VERSE 38)

____

____

LUKE 10:27 (READ THROUGH VERSE 37)

____

____

____

LUKE 19:8

____

____

____

WEEK ONE WELLNESS CHECK-IN

Rate your physical, psychological, emotional, and spiritual health

- Examine your health in each area of your life. Give each behavior a number from 1-5 (#5 means very well).
- Be HONEST. It's helpful to know the *truth* about your recovery health in order to take care of yourself.
- Circle **one** BEHAVIOR in each area that you are willing to work on daily for the next week.

MY BIOLOGICAL HEALTH (PHYSICAL)

MY RECOVERY DATE:		NUMBER OF CONTINOUS DAYS	
Nutrition- when and what you eat		Physical /dental exams & appointments	
Water		Medications/ daily vitamins	
Identifying/reducing emotional eating		Stress management/keeping it simple	
Sleep/rest (too much, too little)		Eliminating/reducing caffeine	
Exercise (easy does it)		Eliminating/reducing sugar	
Pacing your activities (too much, too little)		Other:	

MY PSYCHOLOGICAL HEALTH (MY THOUGHTS & BEHAVIOR)

Managing denial/ defense mechanisms		Music/art/school work	
Positive vs. Negative thinking		Journaling thoughts & behaviors	
Reducing obsessive thoughts		Making phone calls (sponsor, hotline)	
Daily structure/ being on time		Self-help meetings	
Making amends (promptly admit)		Building self esteem	
Money management		Other:	

MY EMOTIONAL/RELATIONAL HEALTH

Letting go of enabling people		Connecting with family in healthy way	
Managing emotions		Self care	
Spending time with **safe** people		Relaxation exercises	
Setting boundaries		Healthy sexual relations	
Having fun		Journaling feelings/ talking about them	
To Thine Own Self Be True. My "yes" is "yes," and my "no" is "no."		Other:	

MY SPIRITUAL HEALTH

Telling the truth to myself and others		Loving myself/ self-forgiveness	
Service to others		Church / Bible study	
Prayer		Serenity Prayer	
Meditation and/or quiet time with God		Gratitude list, affirmations	
Utilizing the Steps /Spiritual Principles		Enjoying nature	
Balance in everyday life (avoiding extremes)		Seeking/finding my purpose, finding what matters	

- Recognize emotional triggers and <u>change behavior.</u>
- Recognize anxiety and <u>practice relaxation techniques.</u>
- Recognize sleeping / eating habits that are slipping and <u>practice self-care.</u>

WEEK ONE RELAPSE PREVENTION EXERCISE

Checklist of addiction/codependency symptoms which can lead to relapse.

On a 1 to 5 scale (0 meaning not present, 5 meaning it is problematic), how would you assess each of the following symptoms? Put an X on the line to indicate your answer. Enter your plan to make changes. Include behaviors you want to continue in order to remain healthy.

Exhaustion EXAMPLE- 0________________________X______3________________________________5
PLAN- Naps on the weekends are helping. I need to eat more fresh food to feel my best.

1. Exhaustion: Allowing yourself to become overly tired or in poor health.
   0____3____5

   PLAN____

2. Dishonesty: Rationalizing- making excuses for doing what you know you should not do.
   0____3____5

   PLAN____

3. Impatience: Things are not happening fast enough.
   0____3____5

   PLAN____

4. Argumentativeness: "If I could just make you understand."
   0____3____5

   PLAN____

5. Frustration: At people or because things in general don't seem to be going "right."
   0____3____5

   PLAN____

6. Self-Pity: "Why do these things happen to me?"
   0____3____5

   PLAN____

7. Cockiness: Got it made- I can handle it. "It will never again happen to me."
   0____3____5

   PLAN____

8. Expecting too much from others: "I've changed; why hasn't everyone else?"
   0____3____5

   PLAN____

9. Not being able to say "no": " I don't want the person to feel mad, sad, disappointed, etc."
   0____3____5

   PLAN____

10. People-pleasing: Wanting to be liked is the motive behind your behavior.
    0____3____5

    PLAN____

Note: Do I need to talk to my Psalm-Partner, therapist, sponsor, or friend about my relapse risk?

Expand on your plan to make changes. Include behaviors you want to continue in order to remain healthy.

____

____

____

____

____

____

____

____

____

____

____

____

____

____

____

____

____

____

____

"Thy rod and Thy staff, they comfort me."

The ROD: it becomes a rod of discipline for the wayward sheep headed towards a poisonous weed or about to venture too far off on its own. The shepherd is likely to use the rod for this purpose most often. We have tried to fill our inner hungers from the outside by venturing too far off into our addictions, compulsions and codependent patterns. His WORD fills us from the inside out.

1. Have you been disciplined recently? What happened?

2. Did you feel comfort at the time? Why or why not?

DISCIPLINE by Melody Beattie

Children need discipline to feel secure; so do adults.
Discipline means understanding there are logical consequences to our behavior.
Discipline means taking responsibility for our behavior and the consequences.
Discipline means learning to wait for what we want.
Discipline means being willing to work for and toward what we want.
Discipline means learning and practicing new behaviors.
Discipline means being where we need to be when we need to be there, despite our feelings.
Discipline is the day-to-day performing of tasks, whether these are recovery behaviors or washing the dishes.
Discipline involves trusting that our goals will be reached though we cannot see them.
Discipline can be grueling. We may feel afraid, confused, and uncertain. Later, we will see the purpose.
But this clarity of sight usually does not come during the time of discipline.
We may not even believe we're moving forward.
But we are.

3. Is it hard for you to stay on track?

4. What are you learning about yourself concerning discipline?

Isaiah 45:19…. "…I, the LORD, speak the truth; I declare what is right." Our

Shepherd keeps us near so He can look upon us.
5. Read Isaiah 64:8-9. Write your thoughts here.

STEP 8 "Made a list of all the persons we had harmed and became willing to make amends to them all."

Step 8 is based on the principle that we can only be restored to newness as we acknowledge and make amends for the emotional, sexual, relational, and physical damage of the past. Read Scripture on Step 8 and continue to add to your list of people you have harmed.

Ephesians 4:25 "Therefore each of you must put off falsehood and speak truthfully to his neighbor, for we are all members of one body."
1. What does this verse mean to you?

Ephesians 4:28 "He who has been stealing must steal no longer, but must work, doing something useful with his own hands, that he may have something to share with those in need."
2. What does this verse mean to you?

Luke 6:37 "Do not judge and you will not be judged. Do not condemn, and you will not be condemned. Forgive, and you will be forgiven."
3. What does this verse mean to you?

HARM: We need to strive to understand all the possible ways to cause harm.
It's been called "instincts in collision." On page 80 in the 12 x 12 ,The Twelve Steps and Twelve Traditions, it states: "To define the word "harm" in a practical way, we might call it the result of instincts in collision, which cause physical, mental, emotional, or spiritual damage to people".

When making your list it helps to think about deep emotional pain caused by neglect, exploitation, withdrawal, manipulation, and gossip.

4. Have you abandoned friendships?

5. Have you let someone else take the blame for a relationship coming to an end because you didn't wantto maintain it any longer?

6. Did you harm someone with your irritability, coldness, and irresponsibility?

7. Did you neglect anybody while you were focused on the addict in the family, which may have been you? Included in Step 8 are those we have harmed after we entered recovery.

"Thy rod and Thy staff, they comfort me."
STEP 8 "Made a list of all the persons we had harmed and became willing to make amends to them all."

PHILIPPIANS 2:3-4

____

____

____

PHILIPPIANS 4:5

____

____

1 THESSALONIANS 3:12

____

____

2 TIMOTHY 1:7

____

____

JAMES 4:11-12

____

____

____

JAMES 5:9

____

____

EPHESIANS 4:32

____

____

WEEK TWO WELLNESS CHECK-IN

Rate your physical, psychological, emotional, and spiritual health

- Examine your health in each area of your life. Give each behavior a number from 1-5 (#5 means very well).
- Be HONEST. It's helpful to know the *truth* about your recovery health in order to take care of yourself.
- Circle **one** BEHAVIOR in each area that you are willing to work on daily for the next week.

MY BIOLOGICAL HEALTH (PHYSICAL)

MY RECOVERY DATE:		NUMBER OF CONTINOUS DAYS	
Nutrition- when and what you eat		Physical /dental exams & appointments	
Water		Medications/ daily vitamins	
Identifying/reducing emotional eating		Stress management/keeping it simple	
Sleep/rest (too much, too little)		Eliminating/reducing caffeine	
Exercise (easy does it)		Eliminating/reducing sugar	
Pacing your activities (too much, too little)		Other:	

MY PSYCHOLOGICAL HEALTH (MY THOUGHTS & BEHAVIOR)

Managing denial/ defense mechanisms		Music/art/school work	
Positive vs. Negative thinking		Journaling thoughts & behaviors	
Reducing obsessive thoughts		Making phone calls (sponsor, hotline)	
Daily structure/ being on time		Self-help meetings	
Making amends (promptly admit)		Building self esteem	
Money management		Other:	

MY EMOTIONAL/RELATIONAL HEALTH

Letting go of enabling people		Connecting with family in healthy way	
Managing emotions		Self care	
Spending time with **safe** people		Relaxation exercises	
Setting boundaries		Healthy sexual relations	
Having fun		Journaling feelings/ talking about them	
To Thine Own Self Be True. My "yes" is "yes," and my "no" is "no."		Other:	

MY SPIRITUAL HEALTH

Telling the truth to myself and others		Loving myself/ self-forgiveness	
Service to others		Church / Bible study	
Prayer		Serenity Prayer	
Meditation and/or quiet time with God		Gratitude list, affirmations	
Utilizing the Steps /Spiritual Principles		Enjoying nature	
Balance in everyday life (avoiding extremes)		Seeking/finding my purpose, finding what matters	

- Recognize emotional triggers and <u>change behavior.</u>
- Recognize anxiety and <u>practice relaxation techniques.</u>
- Recognize sleeping / eating habits that are slipping and <u>practice self-care.</u>

169

WEEK TWO RELAPSE PREVENTION EXERCISE

Checklist of addiction/codependency symptoms which can lead to relapse.

On a 1 to 5 scale (0 meaning not present, 5 meaning it is problematic), how would you assess each of the following symptoms? Put an X on the line to indicate your answer. Enter your plan to make changes. Include behaviors you want to continue in order to remain healthy.

Exhaustion   EXAMPLE- 0________________________X______3________________________________5
PLAN- Naps on the weekends are helping. I need to eat more fresh food to feel my best.

1. Exhaustion: Allowing yourself to become overly tired or in poor health.
0______________________________________3____5

PLAN____

2. Dishonesty: Rationalizing- making excuses for doing what you know you should not do.
0______________________________________3____5

PLAN____

3. Impatience: Things are not happening fast enough.
0______________________________________3____5

PLAN____

4. Argumentativeness: "If I could just make you understand."
0______________________________________3____5

PLAN____

5. Frustration: At people or because things in general don't seem to be going "right."
0______________________________________3____5

PLAN____

6. Self-Pity: "Why do these things happen to me?"
0______________________________________3____5

PLAN____

7. Cockiness: Got it made- I can handle it. "It will never again happen to me."
0______________________________________3____5

PLAN____

8. Expecting too much from others: "I've changed; why hasn't everyone else?"
0______________________________________3____5

PLAN____

9. Not being able to say "no": " I don't want the person to feel mad, sad, disappointed, etc."
0______________________________________3____5

PLAN____

10. People-pleasing: Wanting to be liked is the motive behind your behavior.
0______________________________________3____5

PLAN____

Note: Do I need to talk to my Psalm-Partner, therapist, sponsor, or friend about my relapse risk?

Expand on your plan to make changes. Include behaviors you want to continue in order to remain healthy.

____

____

____

____

____

____

____

____

____

____

____

____

____

____

____

____

____

____

____

____

The shepherd's staff plays an important part in sheep management and it always brings comfort.

<u>**Comfort**</u> *= to soothe in distress or sorrow, to ease the misery or grief of, to bring consolation or hope to, to give a sense of ease, to help, to aid, to encourage, a state of ease and quiet enjoyment free from worry, pain, or trouble.*

The Comforter, the Holy Spirit, draws us together in healthy relationships and brings us the REAL feel-good we've always wanted.

1. Describe a time in your life when you were genuinely comforted by someone else. How did it feel?

2. Describe a time when you comforted someone else. Include how it made you feel.

3. Healthy comfort is radically different from the <u>automatic loss of self</u> that codependents feel when they:
a. compulsively try to **fix** another person,
b. help others with unspoken strings attached
c. help or comfort others to gain approval,
d.____

4. What's the difference between comforting and codependency?

5. Describe a time when you were on either side of codependent behavior. Did someone end up angry or hurt?

6. Do you need God's comfort today? Write about it here and share it with your PSALM-Partner or group.

STEP 8 "Made a list of all the persons we had harmed and became willing to make amends to them all."

Read James 3:5-10.
1. What does James say about the tongue?

James recognized that stinging words leave their mark. We have all been on both sides of the hurt that words can cause.
2. Whom have you hurt with your words? Give examples.

Read Proverbs 16:28-29.
3. Have you lead someone down a path that was not good?

Prayer for the Victims of Addiction
O blessed Lord; you ministered to all who came to you. Look with compassion upon all who through addiction have lost their health and freedom. Restore to them the assurance of your unfailing mercy; remove from them the fears that beset them; strengthen them in the work of their recovery, and to those who care for them, give patient understanding and persevering love. Amen.
The Book of Common Prayer

4. Write out your prayer to The Lord on this day.

Leave room for God in all you do. Do not look for God to show up in a particular way, but *do look for Him*.
5. Are you listening to God? Are you ignoring him? He lovingly continues to treat you as His child.

6. Who is supporting you in your recovery? Who can you thank today with your words?

"Thy rod and Thy staff, they comfort me."
STEP 8 "Made a list of all the persons we had harmed, and became willing to make amends to them all."

1 PETER 2:19 (READ THROUGH VERSE 22)

____

____

1 PETER 2:23

____

____

1 PETER 3:8-9 (READ THROUGH VERSE 12)

____

____

____

1 JOHN 2:9 (READ THROUGH VERSE 11)

____

____

1 JOHN 4:20 (READ VERSE 19 THROUGH 21)

____

____

PSALM 133:1 (READ WHOLE CHAPTER)

____

____

PROVERBS 15:4

____

____

____

WEEK THREE WELLNESS CHECK-IN

Rate your physical, psychological, emotional, and spiritual health

- Examine your health in each area of your life. Give each behavior a number from 1-5 (#5 means very well).
- Be HONEST. It's helpful to know the *truth* about your recovery health in order to take care of yourself.
- Circle **one** BEHAVIOR in each area that you are willing to work on daily for the next week.

MY BIOLOGICAL HEALTH (PHYSICAL)

MY RECOVERY DATE:		NUMBER OF CONTINOUS DAYS	
Nutrition- when and what you eat		Physical /dental exams & appointments	
Water		Medications/ daily vitamins	
Identifying/reducing emotional eating		Stress management/keeping it simple	
Sleep/rest (too much, too little)		Eliminating/reducing caffeine	
Exercise (easy does it)		Eliminating/reducing sugar	
Pacing your activities (too much, too little)		Other:	

MY PSYCHOLOGICAL HEALTH (MY THOUGHTS & BEHAVIOR)

Managing denial/ defense mechanisms		Music/art/school work	
Positive vs. Negative thinking		Journaling thoughts & behaviors	
Reducing obsessive thoughts		Making phone calls (sponsor, hotline)	
Daily structure/ being on time		Self-help meetings	
Making amends (promptly admit)		Building self esteem	
Money management		Other:	

MY EMOTIONAL/RELATIONAL HEALTH

Letting go of enabling people		Connecting with family in healthy way	
Managing emotions		Self care	
Spending time with **safe** people		Relaxation exercises	
Setting boundaries		Healthy sexual relations	
Having fun		Journaling feelings/ talking about them	
To Thine Own Self Be True. My "yes" is "yes," and my "no" is "no."		Other:	

MY SPIRITUAL HEALTH

Telling the truth to myself and others		Loving myself/ self-forgiveness	
Service to others		Church / Bible study	
Prayer		Serenity Prayer	
Meditation and/or quiet time with God		Gratitude list, affirmations	
Utilizing the Steps /Spiritual Principles		Enjoying nature	
Balance in everyday life (avoiding extremes)		Seeking/finding my purpose, finding what matters	

- Recognize emotional triggers and <u>change behavior.</u>
- Recognize anxiety and <u>practice relaxation techniques.</u>
- Recognize sleeping / eating habits that are slipping and <u>practice self-care.</u>

WEEK THREE RELAPSE PREVENTION EXERCISE
Checklist of addiction/codependency symptoms which can lead to relapse.

On a 1 to 5 scale (0 meaning not present, 5 meaning it is problematic), how would you assess each of the following symptoms? Put an X on the line to indicate your answer. Enter your plan to make changes. Include behaviors you want to continue in order to remain healthy.

<u>Exhaustion</u> EXAMPLE- 0________________________________X______3______________________________5
PLAN- Naps on the weekends are helping. I need to eat more fresh food to feel my best.

11. <u>Exhaustion:</u> Allowing yourself to become overly tired or in poor health.
0____3______________________________________5

PLAN____

12. <u>Dishonesty:</u> Rationalizing- making excuses for doing what you know you should not do.
0____3______________________________________5

PLAN____

13. <u>Impatience:</u> Things are not happening fast enough.
0____3______________________________________5

PLAN____

14. <u>Argumentativeness:</u> "If I could just make you understand."
0____3______________________________________5

PLAN____

15. <u>Frustration:</u> At people or because things in general don't seem to be going "right."
0____3______________________________________5

PLAN____

16. <u>Self-Pity:</u> "Why do these things happen to me?"
0____3______________________________________5

PLAN____

17. <u>Cockiness:</u> Got it made- I can handle it. "It will never again happen to me."
0____3______________________________________5

PLAN____

18. <u>Expecting too much from others:</u> "I've changed; why hasn't everyone else?"
0____3______________________________________5

PLAN____

19. <u>Not being able to say "no":</u> " I don't want the person to feel mad, sad, disappointed, etc."
0____3______________________________________5

PLAN____

20. <u>People-pleasing:</u> Wanting to be liked is the motive behind your behavior.
0____3______________________________________5

PLAN____

Note: Do I need to talk to my Psalm-Partner, therapist, sponsor, or friend about my relapse risk?

WEEK THREE RELAPSE PREVENTION EXERCISE

Expand on your plan to make changes. Include behaviors you want to continue in order to remain healthy.

____

____

____

____

____

____

____

____

____

____

____

____

____

____

____

____

____

____

____

____

"Thy rod and Thy staff, they comfort me."

The staff of the shepherd is uniquely for the comfort of his sheep. The shepherd uses his staff to gently lift a newborn lamb to reunite it with its mother. Where there is one, there is usually hundreds of ewes lambing at the same time. The staff in the skillful shepherd's hand dances from lamb to lamb to prevent the odor of his hands from interfering with drawing his sheep together into intimate relationships. The Holy Spirit wants to draw you close to Him and others. The Holy Spirit is all about relationships!

1. When was the last time you wanted to isolate from friends and family?

2. What makes you feel like running and hiding?

3. Why doesn't it work in the long run?

4. Can you think of a time when the Holy Spirit, the staff of God, helped get you out of a jam?
It will strengthen your faith to share the special ways your Shepherd has shown His love for you.

5. Name some present relationships where you find comfort? .

STEP 8 "Made a list of all the persons we had harmed and became willing to make amends to them all."

How can we forgive and make amends to those whom we feel have ***offended us*** in the past? Step 8 has two parts with two lists. One is labeled FORGIVENESS and the other is AMENDS. If you have been violated by others, the willingness to forgive can be attained when you pass through the stages of grief, shock, denial, anger, depression, sadness, and then forgiveness.

1. Do you need to share about a past hurt with your counselor, PSALM-Partner or sponsor?

Focus on only **your** part in making an amends or offering forgiveness.

WHO DO YOU NEED TO FORGIVE?	WHO DO YOU NEED TO MAKE AMENDS TO?
FORGIVENESS	AMENDS
	DO NOT MAKE AMENDS YET, WAIT UNTIL STEP 9 TO MAKE YOUR AMENDS.

2. Have you been blaming God? Write about it here.

3. Do you owe God an amends? Write about it here.

4. Have you been blaming yourself? Write about it here.

5. Do you owe yourself an amends? Write about it here.

6. What obstacles are interfering with completing your list?
    ___forgiveness?
    ___purposeful forgetting? "I did not hurt anybody but myself."
    ___fear of the outcome?
    ___pride? Search your motives and actions.
    ___other obstacles:

7. How many amends do you have on your list today?

"Thy rod and Thy staff, they comfort me."
STEP 8 "Made a list of all the persons we had harmed and willing to make amends to them all."

ROMANS 2:1

____

____

ROMANS 12:14

____

____

ROMANS 12:17

____

____

ROMANS 13:8 (READ THROUGH VERSE 10)

____

____

ROMANS 14:10 (READ FROM VERSE 7)

____

____

ROMANS 14:19

____

____

1 CORINTHIANS 13:6 (READ WHOLE CHAPTER)

____

____

____

"Thy rod and Thy staff, they comfort me."
STEP 8 "Made a list of all the persons we had harmed and willing to make amends to them all."

WEEK FOUR WELLNESS CHECK-IN

Rate your physical, psychological, emotional, and spiritual health

- Examine your health in each area of your life. Give each behavior a number from 1-5 (#5 means very well).
- Be HONEST. It's helpful to know the *truth* about your recovery health in order to take care of yourself.
- Circle **one** BEHAVIOR in each area that you are willing to work on daily for the next week.

MY BIOLOGICAL HEALTH (PHYSICAL)

MY RECOVERY DATE:		NUMBER OF CONTINOUS DAYS	
Nutrition- when and what you eat		Physical /dental exams & appointments	
Water		Medications/ daily vitamins	
Identifying/reducing emotional eating		Stress management/keeping it simple	
Sleep/rest (too much, too little)		Eliminating/reducing caffeine	
Exercise (easy does it)		Eliminating/reducing sugar	
Pacing your activities (too much, too little)		Other:	

MY PSYCHOLOGICAL HEALTH (MY THOUGHTS & BEHAVIOR)

Managing denial/ defense mechanisms		Music/art/school work	
Positive vs. Negative thinking		Journaling thoughts & behaviors	
Reducing obsessive thoughts		Making phone calls (sponsor, hotline)	
Daily structure/ being on time		Self-help meetings	
Making amends (promptly admit)		Building self esteem	
Money management		Other:	

MY EMOTIONAL/RELATIONAL HEALTH

Letting go of enabling people		Connecting with family in healthy way	
Managing emotions		Self care	
Spending time with **safe** people		Relaxation exercises	
Setting boundaries		Healthy sexual relations	
Having fun		Journaling feelings/ talking about them	
To Thine Own Self Be True. My "yes" is "yes," and my "no" is "no."		Other:	

MY SPIRITUAL HEALTH

Telling the truth to myself and others		Loving myself/ self-forgiveness	
Service to others		Church / Bible study	
Prayer		Serenity Prayer	
Meditation and/or quiet time with God		Gratitude list, affirmations	
Utilizing the Steps /Spiritual Principles		Enjoying nature	
Balance in everyday life (avoiding extremes)		Seeking/finding my purpose, finding what matters	

- Recognize emotional triggers and <u>change behavior.</u>
- Recognize anxiety and <u>practice relaxation techniques.</u>
- Recognize sleeping / eating habits that are slipping and <u>practice self-care.</u>

WEEK FOUR RELAPSE PREVENTION EXERCISE
Checklist of addiction/codependency symptoms which can lead to relapse.

On a 1 to 5 scale (0 meaning not present, 5 meaning it is problematic), how would you assess each of the following symptoms? Put an X on the line to indicate your answer. Enter your plan to make changes. Include behaviors you want to continue in order to remain healthy.

Exhaustion EXAMPLE- 0________________________________X______3_____________________________________5
PLAN- Naps on the weekends are helping. I need to eat more fresh food to feel my best.

1. Exhaustion: Allowing yourself to become overly tired or in poor health.
0____3____5

PLAN____

2. Dishonesty: Rationalizing- making excuses for doing what
0____3____5

PLAN____

3. Impatience: Things are not happening fast enough.
0____3____5

PLAN____

4. Argumentativeness: "If I could just make you understand."
0____3____5

PLAN____

5. Frustration: At people or because things in general don't seem to be going "right."
0____3____5

PLAN____

6. Self-Pity: "Why do these things happen to me?"
0____3____5

PLAN____

7. Cockiness: Got it made- I can handle it. "It will never again happen to me."
0____3____5

PLAN____

8. Expecting too much from others: "I've changed; why hasn't everyone else?"
0____3____5

PLAN____

9. Not being able to say "no": " I don't want the person to feel mad, sad, disappointed, etc."
0____3____5

PLAN____

10. People-pleasing: Wanting to be liked is the motive behind your behavior.
0____3____5

PLAN____

Note: Do I need to talk to my Psalm-Partner, therapist, sponsor, or friend about my relapse risk?

WEEK FOUR RELAPSE PREVENTION EXERCISE

Expand on your plan to make changes. Include behaviors you want to continue in order to remain healthy.

PSALM 23 "Thy rod and Thy staff, they comfort me."

STEP 8 "Made a list of all the persons we had harmed and became willing to make amends to them all."

COMPLETION

My favorite Scripture for Chapter 8: (write it here)

_______ I understand Chapter 8 and will continue to use it daily.
_______ I completed the Bible study in a ***Psalm 23*** group.
_______ I worked with a PSALM-Partner this month to study Chapter 8.

Psalm Partner NAME: ____

Psalm Partner Phone # ____

Today's date ____

My Signature _______________________________ **PSALM-Partner** _________________

BIBLE STUDY AT A GLANCE

MATTHEW 5:43-48	ROMANS 14:7-10	PROVERBS 14:1	
MATTHEW 6:14-15	I CORINTHIANS 4:5	PROVERBS 14:30	
MATTHEW 7:3-5	I CORINTHIANS 13		
MATTHEW 18:21-35	PHILIPPIANS 2:3-4		
MATTHEW 22:36-40	PHILIPPIANS 4:5		
MARK 11:25	I THESSALONIANS 3:12-13		
LUKE 6:37-38	2 TIMOTHY 1:7		
LUKE 10:25-37	JAMES 4:11-12		
LUKE 19:8	JAMES 5:9		
JOHN 13:34-35	I PETER 2:19-23		
ROMANS 2:1	I PETER3:8-12		
ROMANS 12:9	I JOHN 2:9-11		
ROMANS 12:14	I JOHN 4:19-21		
ROMANS 12:17	PSALM 133		
ROMANS 13:8-10	PROVERBS 10:12		

The Lord is My Shepherd:

A 12 Step Journey through PSALM 23

CHAPTER NINE

PSALM 23
"Thou dost prepare a table before me
in the presence of my enemies;"

STEP 9
"Made direct amends to such people wherever possible,
except when to do so would injure them or others."

"Thou dost prepare a table before me in the presence of my enemies;"

The good shepherd takes special care to prepare the "table" for the arrival of his flocks. The high mountain country of the summer ranges may have been remote and hard to reach but a good manager knows the trek provides the best provisions for his flock. Just before they arrive, he inspects the table to rid it of potential enemies. The enemies include poisonous weeds, animals of prey, and snakes. ***Jesus is doing the same thing for His fold.*** The believer's enemies can be categorized as the world, the flesh, and the devil.

The Lord is spreading for us the banquet of spiritual blessings; the provision of His Word, His blessings, His assurances, His Omnipotence, and His LOVE.

STEP 9
"Made direct amends to such people wherever possible,
except when to do so would injure them or others."

In Step 9 we make a sincere effort to offer apology for past actions and attempt to right our past wrongs. We hear over and over that the Twelve Steps are written in numerical order for a reason. We need <u>Step 4 and Step 5</u> <u>to learn about our personal responsibility</u> and we need <u>Step 6 and Step 7 to develop humility</u>. The making of amends in Step 9 needs to be approached cautiously by codependent people. The amends should never be installment payments for false shame or false guilt (situations over which we have no real control.) Step 9 happens over time as a process.

The second part of this step is important because we do not want to "injure them or others". Do not offer amends to those who would be more hurt by our action than helped.

There are five categories of persons to whom we may consider making amends:
1. Those we may turn to immediately.
2. Those whom a partial disclosure can be made.
3. Those to be deferred until later.
4. Those we should never contact such as old relationships where we should keep the doors closed.
5. Those we cannot contact directly due to death or other circumstances.

<table><tr><td>THE ESSENCE OF STEP 9 CAN BE DESCRIBED IN THE WORD
"FREEDOM".</td></tr></table>

The Spiritual Principles in Step 9 are humility, love, and forgiveness

Preparation of the table is a major part of the good shepherd's care and concern. With an eagle-eye, he carefully inspects the range for any signs of blue camas, one of the poisonous weeds. The deadly leaf will leave a lamb stiff, paralyzed, and then dead after merely a few nibbles. The shepherd decides whether to plan his grazing program to avoid the weeds or take steps to eradicate them. Read Isaiah 1:19.

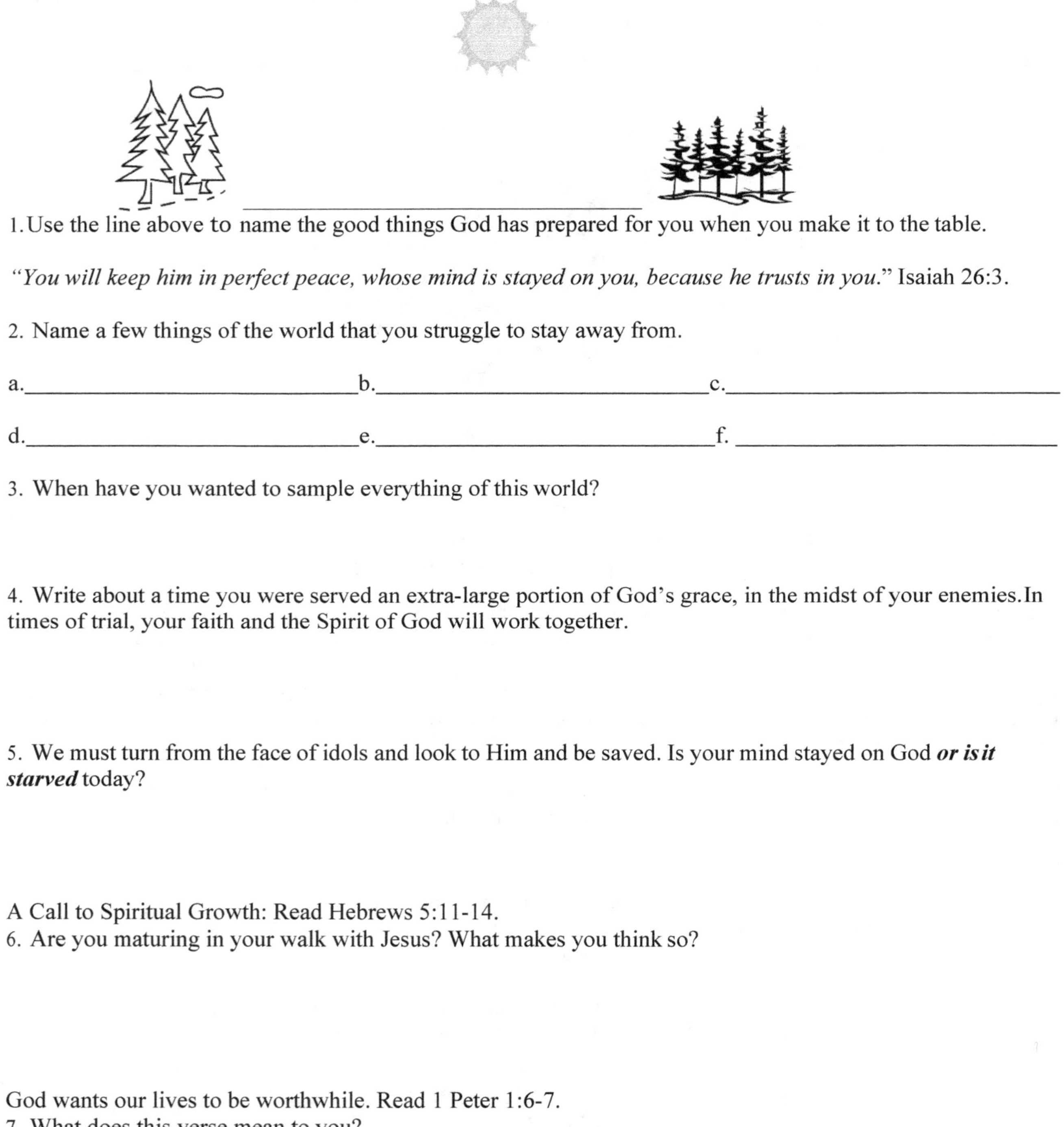

1. Use the line above to name the good things God has prepared for you when you make it to the table.

"You will keep him in perfect peace, whose mind is stayed on you, because he trusts in you." Isaiah 26:3.

2. Name a few things of the world that you struggle to stay away from.

a.________________________ b.________________________ c.________________________

d.________________________ e.________________________ f. ________________________

3. When have you wanted to sample everything of this world?

4. Write about a time you were served an extra-large portion of God's grace, in the midst of your enemies. In times of trial, your faith and the Spirit of God will work together.

5. We must turn from the face of idols and look to Him and be saved. Is your mind stayed on God ***or is it starved*** today?

A Call to Spiritual Growth: Read Hebrews 5:11-14.
6. Are you maturing in your walk with Jesus? What makes you think so?

God wants our lives to be worthwhile. Read 1 Peter 1:6-7.
7. What does this verse mean to you?

**STEP 9 "Made direct amends to such people wherever possible,
except when to do so would injure them or others."**

By nature, the process of Step 9 is one-sided. Preparation with another person in recovery is very important in understanding that the way things *feel* is not necessarily the way things *are*. Just because we feel afraid doesn't mean there's really something to fear.

1. What fears or expectations do you have about your amends?

2. As you are reconciled with your own conscience? What lingering remnants of guilt and remorse must you put to rest?

Review the five categories of persons to whom we may consider making amends.

   1. Those we may turn to immediately.
   Who is in category #1?

   2. Those whom a partial disclosure can be made.
   Who is in category #2?

   3. Those to be deferred until later.
   Who is in category #3?

   4. Those we should never contact such as old relationships where we should keep the doors closed.
   Who is in category #4?

   5. Those we cannot contact directly due to death or other circumstances.
   Who is in category #5?

Discuss your five categories with your sponsor, PSALM-Partner, your group, or someone you trust.
Date: _______________________

**Thou dost prepare a table before me in the presence of my enemies;"
STEP 9 "Made direct amends to such people wherever possible,
except when to do so would injure them or others."**

MATTHEW 5:7, 11 (READ VERSES 3-11)

____

____

____

MATTHEW 5:23-24

____

____

____

MATTHEW 7:12

____

____

MATTHEW 12:37 (READ FROM VERSE 35)

____

____

LUKE 6:27-28 (READ THROUGH VERSE 36)

____

____

____

ROMANS 12:18-19 (READ THROUGH VERSE 21)

____

____

____

____

Rate your physical, psychological, emotional, and spiritual health

- Examine your health in each area of your life. Give each behavior a number from 1-5 (#5 means very well).
- Be HONEST. It's helpful to know the *truth* about your recovery health in order to take care of yourself.
- Circle **one** BEHAVIOR in each area that you are willing to work on daily for the next week.

MY BIOLOGICAL HEALTH (PHYSICAL)

MY RECOVERY DATE:		NUMBER OF CONTINOUS DAYS	
Nutrition- when and what you eat		Physical /dental exams & appointments	
Water		Medications/ daily vitamins	
Identifying/reducing emotional eating		Stress management/keeping it simple	
Sleep/rest (too much, too little)		Eliminating/reducing caffeine	
Exercise (easy does it)		Eliminating/reducing sugar	
Pacing your activities (too much, too little)		Other:	

MY PSYCHOLOGICAL HEALTH (MY THOUGHTS & BEHAVIOR)

Managing denial/ defense mechanisms		Music/art/school work	
Positive vs. Negative thinking		Journaling thoughts & behaviors	
Reducing obsessive thoughts		Making phone calls (sponsor, hotline)	
Daily structure/ being on time		Self-help meetings	
Making amends (promptly admit)		Building self esteem	
Money management		Other:	

MY EMOTIONAL/RELATIONAL HEALTH

Letting go of enabling people		Connecting with family in healthy way	
Managing emotions		Self care	
Spending time with **safe** people		Relaxation exercises	
Setting boundaries		Healthy sexual relations	
Having fun		Journaling feelings/ talking about them	
To Thine Own Self Be True. My "yes" is "yes," and my "no" is "no."		Other:	

MY SPIRITUAL HEALTH

Telling the truth to myself and others		Loving myself/ self-forgiveness	
Service to others		Church / Bible study	
Prayer		Serenity Prayer	
Meditation and/or quiet time with God		Gratitude list, affirmations	
Utilizing the Steps /Spiritual Principles		Enjoying nature	
Balance in everyday life (avoiding extremes)		Seeking/finding my purpose, finding what matters	

- Recognize emotional triggers and <u>change behavior.</u>
- Recognize anxiety and <u>practice relaxation techniques.</u>
- Recognize sleeping / eating habits that are slipping and <u>practice self-care.</u>

Checklist of addiction/codependency symptoms which can lead to relapse.

On a 1 to 5 scale (0 meaning not present, 5 meaning it is problematic), how would you assess each of the following symptoms? Put an X on the line to indicate your answer. Enter your plan to make changes. Include behaviors you want to continue in order to remain healthy.

<u>Exhaustion</u>   EXAMPLE- 0________________________X______3________________________________5
PLAN- Naps on the weekends are helping. I need to eat more fresh food to feel my best.

1. <u>Exhaustion:</u> Allowing yourself to become overly tired or in poor health.
0____3____5

PLAN____

2. <u>Dishonesty:</u> Rationalizing- making excuses for doing what you know you should not do.
0____3____5

PLAN____

3. <u>Impatience:</u> Things are not happening fast enough.
0____3____5

PLAN____

4. <u>Argumentativeness:</u> "If I could just make you understand."
0____3____5

PLAN____

5. <u>Frustration:</u> At people or because things in general don't seem to be going "right."
0____3____5

PLAN____

6. <u>Self-Pity:</u> "Why do these things happen to me?"
0____3____5

PLAN____

7. <u>Cockiness:</u> Got it made- I can handle it. "It will never again happen to me."
0____3____5

PLAN____

8. <u>Expecting too much from others:</u> "I've changed; why hasn't everyone else?"
0____3____5

PLAN____

9. <u>Not being able to say "no":</u> " I don't want the person to feel mad, sad, disappointed, etc."
0____3____5

PLAN____

10. <u>People-pleasing:</u> Wanting to be liked is the motive behind your behavior.
0____3____5

PLAN____

Note: Do I need to talk to my Psalm-Partner, therapist, sponsor, or friend about my relapse risk?

WEEK ONE RELAPSE PREVENTION EXERCISE

Expand on your plan to make changes. Include behaviors you want to continue in order to remain healthy.

"Thou dost prepare a table before me in the presence of my enemies;"

Animals of prey are watching every movement of the sheep, ***waiting for a chance*** to make a quick attack. If the flock is frightened into a stampede, sheep are badly injured. Cougars seem to play with a vulnerable sheep much like a housecat would play with a mouse. These attacks often occur in silence because sheep become utterly numb with fear and they do not utter a peep. The attentive shepherd keeps his eye out for these predators and will trap or hunt them down so the flock can rest in peace. God has prepared a table for us but many of us get into difficulty over our heads.

1. When have you been unable to call or cry out for help?

2. Do you stay silent when you are fear-stricken? Give an example.

3. Who in your family also keeps silent when there is trouble?

4. What does God say about fear?

Relapse prevention is part of our recovery and it helps us to live "under the influence" of God.   5. Are you headed for a relapse? Are you engaged in an old, self-destructive behavior such as keeping a secret, staying in denial, doing someone else's inventory or magical thinking?

6. What are **you** doing to prevent relapse?

7. Journal Project:
Ask **other** people in recovery how God has helped them in the presence of their enemies. Without naming names, record what you are learning about relapse prevention.

**STEP 9 "Made direct amends to such people wherever possible,
except when to do so would injure them or others."**

Making amends includes going back and settling emotional accounts. When we have judged someone harshly, we need to re-examine our relationship with that person.
Read Acts 15:38-39 and 2 Timothy 4:11. Paul *changed his opinion* of John Mark.

1. Have you cut a relationship off because of a dispute?

2. In recovery it is ok to ***change your mind***. When we put our recovery first, we may have to *change our mind* about something when we notice it is interfering with our recovery. For example, "I planned to stay for the wedding reception, but now I see that it is not the best thing for me and my recovery. I am going to have to leave early." Are you open to this possibility?

3. Have you been labeled as irresponsible for changing your mind in the past, when you were NOT in recovery?

4. When we get caught off guard and get sucked into our self-destructive behaviors, we may trample the unseen needs of others. **Who** is most apt to get hurt if you relapse?

5. Are you afraid you will relapse?

Recovery tip: NEVER IGNORE A CRAVING. Notice it, give it a number from one to five, with five meaning the craving is strong, and then tell *someone safe* how you are feeling.

6. Every time we tell the truth, we are allowing trust to be re-established. Trust can be recovered over time by means of TRUTH AND GRACE. When has telling the truth strengthened your recovery?

7. Use your resentment list to see if you have harmed anyone because of your resentment.

WEEK TWO BIBLE STUDY

"Thou dost prepare a table before me in the presence of my enemies;"
STEP 9 "Made direct amends to such people wherever possible,
except when to do so would injure them or others."

COLOSSIANS 3:12-13

____

____

____

____

COLOSSIANS 3:18-21

____

____

____

____

COLOSSIANS 4:5-6

____

____

____

____

1 THESSALONIANS 5:15 (READ FROM VERSE 13)

____

____

____

PHILEMON 13-14 (READ VERSES 8-17)

____

____

____

HEBREWS 12:14-15

____

____

____

____

Rate your physical, psychological, emotional, and spiritual health

- Examine your health in each area of your life. Give each behavior a number from 1-5 (#5 means very well).
- Be HONEST. It's helpful to know the *truth* about your recovery health in order to take care of yourself.
- Circle **one** BEHAVIOR in each area that you are willing to work on daily for the next week.

MY BIOLOGICAL HEALTH (PHYSICAL)

MY RECOVERY DATE:		NUMBER OF CONTINOUS DAYS	
Nutrition- when and what you eat		Physical /dental exams & appointments	
Water		Medications/ daily vitamins	
Identifying/reducing emotional eating		Stress management/keeping it simple	
Sleep/rest (too much, too little)		Eliminating/reducing caffeine	
Exercise (easy does it)		Eliminating/reducing sugar	
Pacing your activities (too much, too little)		Other:	

MY PSYCHOLOGICAL HEALTH (MY THOUGHTS & BEHAVIOR)

Managing denial/ defense mechanisms		Music/art/school work	
Positive vs. Negative thinking		Journaling thoughts & behaviors	
Reducing obsessive thoughts		Making phone calls (sponsor, hotline)	
Daily structure/ being on time		Self-help meetings	
Making amends (promptly admit)		Building self esteem	
Money management		Other:	

MY EMOTIONAL/RELATIONAL HEALTH

Letting go of enabling people		Connecting with family in healthy way	
Managing emotions		Self care	
Spending time with **safe** people		Relaxation exercises	
Setting boundaries		Healthy sexual relations	
Having fun		Journaling feelings/ talking about them	
To Thine Own Self Be True. My "yes" is "yes," and my "no" is "no."		Other:	

MY SPIRITUAL HEALTH

Telling the truth to myself and others		Loving myself/ self-forgiveness	
Service to others		Church / Bible study	
Prayer		Serenity Prayer	
Meditation and/or quiet time with God		Gratitude list, affirmations	
Utilizing the Steps /Spiritual Principles		Enjoying nature	
Balance in everyday life (avoiding extremes)		Seeking/finding my purpose, finding what matters	

- Recognize emotional triggers and <u>change behavior.</u>
- Recognize anxiety and <u>practice relaxation techniques.</u>
- Recognize sleeping / eating habits that are slipping and <u>practice self-care.</u>

WEEK TWO RELAPSE PREVENTION EXERCISE
Checklist of addiction/codependency symptoms which can lead to relapse.

On a 1 to 5 scale (0 meaning not present, 5 meaning it is problematic), how would you assess each of the following symptoms? Put an X on the line to indicate your answer. Enter your plan to make changes. Include behaviors you want to continue in order to remain healthy.

<u>Exhaustion</u>   EXAMPLE- 0________________________________X_______3____5
PLAN- Naps on the weekends are helping. I need to eat more fresh food to feel my best.

1. <u>Exhaustion:</u> Allowing yourself to become overly tired or in poor health.
0____3____5

PLAN____

2. <u>Dishonesty:</u> Rationalizing- making excuses for doing what you know you should not do.
0____3____5

PLAN____

3. <u>Impatience:</u> Things are not happening fast enough.
0____3____5

PLAN____

4. <u>Argumentativeness:</u> "If I could just make you understand."
0____3____5

PLAN____

5. <u>Frustration:</u> At people or because things in general don't seem to be going "right."
0____3____5

PLAN____

6. <u>Self-Pity:</u> "Why do these things happen to me?"
0____3____5

PLAN____

7. <u>Cockiness:</u> Got it made- I can handle it. "It will never again happen to me."
0____3____5

PLAN____

8. <u>Expecting too much from others:</u> "I've changed; why hasn't everyone else?"
0____3____5

PLAN____

9. <u>Not being able to say "no":</u> " I don't want the person to feel mad, sad, disappointed, etc."
0____3____5

PLAN____

10. <u>People-pleasing:</u> Wanting to be liked is the motive behind your behavior.
0____3____5

PLAN____

Note: Do I need to talk to my Psalm-Partner, therapist, sponsor, or friend about my relapse risk?

WEEK TWO RELAPSE PREVENTION EXERCISE

Expand on your plan to make changes. Include behaviors you want to continue in order to remain healthy.

____

____

____

____

____

____

____

____

____

____

____

____

____

____

____

____

____

____

____

"Thou dost prepare a table before me in the presence of my enemies;"

The good shepherd makes sure to clear out debris of leaves and twigs from the water holes. He must plug up the snake holes present so that deadly snakes can't strike the sheep while they are grazing. It is all part of his work as he prepares the table for his sheep in the summer months.

1. Do you believe that God has prepared a way for you to get to the table? Please explain.

2. Are you taking advantage of the table which has been set for you by The Good Shepherd? Expand on your answer.

3. Now think of your physical health. Are you drinking water and eating right?

4. What are you doing in excess?

5. Can you rest in Him, with confidence of His care in your present situation? Are you in enemy territory?

6. Have you tasted a big serving of joy and security of Christ Himself? Give examples.

WEEK THREE STEP 9

**STEP 9 "Made direct amends to such people wherever possible,
except when to do so would injure them or others."**

The process of making and receiving amends invites new acceptance and respect in all of our relationships.
Having an open mind takes practice.

1. How do you respond to the amends **of others**?

2. Have you ever let someone off the hook, only to find him/her still dangling there in your mind a minute, day
or week later? What do you do?

It takes courage to say we are sorry. It hurts our pride.
3. Have you made a sincere effort to make amends to the people you have harmed in category #1?

4. Refer to the description of the categories. What progress have you made?

CATEGORY #1 Do it now.	PERSON Example: Sister	PLAN While at Starbucks, I will make amends for gossiping to our brother about her losing her job.	TIME FRAME Next Saturday
CATEGORY #2 Partial amends.	Example: Sue	I will tell her I am sorry for the way I cut off the relationship. It was not fair to her and it was because of my personal problems. I may do it by phone or letter.	By the end of the month
CATEGORY #3 Not now.	Example: Ex-boss	I will make amends for quitting my job w/o notice.	Defer to later
CATEGORY #4 No contact.	Example: old boyfriend	I never returned his belongings to him. I will donate $40 to the charity of my choice as my amends.	When I get my next check.
CATEGORY #5 Person is gone.	Example: Mom, who died in 2009	I will volunteer 4 hours at the senior center to make amends for my harsh words to her.	In the month of December.

When we make amends for the harm we have caused, we are helping others.
5. What things do you like to do to help others?

"Thou dost prepare a table before me in the presence of my enemies;"
STEP 9 "Made direct amends to such people wherever possible,
except when to do so would injure them or others."

PSALMS 90:17

____

____

PSALMS 126:5-6

____

____

____

PROVERBS 3:27

____

____

PROVERBS 12:18-20

____

____

____

PROVERBS 15:1-4

____

____

____

PROVERBS 16:7

____

____

____

Rate your physical, psychological, emotional, and spiritual health

- Examine your health in each area of your life. Give each behavior a number from 1-5 (#5 means very well).
- Be HONEST. It's helpful to know the *truth* about your recovery health in order to take care of yourself.
- Circle **one** BEHAVIOR in each area that you are willing to work on daily for the next week.

MY BIOLOGICAL HEALTH (PHYSICAL)

MY RECOVERY DATE:		NUMBER OF CONTINOUS DAYS	
Nutrition- when and what you eat		Physical /dental exams & appointments	
Water		Medications/ daily vitamins	
Identifying/reducing emotional eating		Stress management/keeping it simple	
Sleep/rest (too much, too little)		Eliminating/reducing caffeine	
Exercise (easy does it)		Eliminating/reducing sugar	
Pacing your activities (too much, too little)		Other:	

MY PSYCHOLOGICAL HEALTH (MY THOUGHTS & BEHAVIOR)

Managing denial/ defense mechanisms		Music/art/school work	
Positive vs. Negative thinking		Journaling thoughts & behaviors	
Reducing obsessive thoughts		Making phone calls (sponsor, hotline)	
Daily structure/ being on time		Self-help meetings	
Making amends (promptly admit)		Building self esteem	
Money management		Other:	

MY EMOTIONAL/RELATIONAL HEALTH

Letting go of enabling people		Connecting with family in healthy way	
Managing emotions		Self care	
Spending time with **safe** people		Relaxation exercises	
Setting boundaries		Healthy sexual relations	
Having fun		Journaling feelings/ talking about them	
To Thine Own Self Be True. My "yes" is "yes," and my "no" is "no."		Other:	

MY SPIRITUAL HEALTH

Telling the truth to myself and others		Loving myself/ self-forgiveness	
Service to others		Church / Bible study	
Prayer		Serenity Prayer	
Meditation and/or quiet time with God		Gratitude list, affirmations	
Utilizing the Steps /Spiritual Principles		Enjoying nature	
Balance in everyday life (avoiding extremes)		Seeking/finding my purpose, finding what matters	

- Recognize emotional triggers and <u>change behavior.</u>
- Recognize anxiety and <u>practice relaxation techniques.</u>
- Recognize sleeping / eating habits that are slipping and <u>practice self-care.</u>

WEEK THREE RELAPSE PREVENTION EXERCISE
Checklist of addiction/codependency symptoms which can lead to relapse.

On a 1 to 5 scale (0 meaning not present, 5 meaning it is problematic), how would you assess each of the following symptoms? Put an X on the line to indicate your answer. Enter your plan to make changes. Include behaviors you want to continue in order to remain healthy.

<u>Exhaustion</u> EXAMPLE- 0________________________________X______3____5
PLAN- Naps on the weekends are helping. I need to eat more fresh food to feel my best.

1. <u>Exhaustion:</u> Allowing yourself to become overly tired or in poor health.
0____3____5

PLAN____

2. <u>Dishonesty:</u> Rationalizing- making excuses for doing what you know you should not do.
0____3____5

PLAN____

3. <u>Impatience:</u> Things are not happening fast enough.
0____3____5

PLAN____

4. <u>Argumentativeness:</u> "If I could just make you understand."
0____3____5

PLAN____

5. <u>Frustration:</u> At people or because things in general don't seem to be going "right."
0____3____5

PLAN____

6. <u>Self-Pity:</u> "Why do these things happen to me?"
0____3____5

PLAN____

7. <u>Cockiness:</u> Got it made- I can handle it. "It will never again happen to me."
0____3____5

PLAN____

8. <u>Expecting too much from others:</u> "I've changed; why hasn't everyone else?"
0____3____5

PLAN____

9. <u>Not being able to say "no":</u> " I don't want the person to feel mad, sad, disappointed, etc."
0____3____5

PLAN____

10. <u>People-pleasing:</u> Wanting to be liked is the motive behind your behavior.
0____3____5

PLAN____

Note: Do I need to talk to my Psalm-Partner, therapist, sponsor, or friend about my relapse risk?

Expand on your plan to make changes. Include behaviors you want to continue in order to remain healthy.

"Thou dost prepare a table before me in the presence of my enemies;"

The highlight of the year for the shepherd is to see his beloved sheep thriving on the high, rich summer range. It comes with devotion and sacrifice. Jesus, our Shepherd, told us Himself, that He had come that we might have life and have it more abundantly. Jesus paid the price and sacrificed Himself for us so that we may be with Him forever. He is pleased when we flourish and walk in awareness of His presence. For this to be possible we need to sacrifice our **pride** and **selfishness**.

1. Enter a prayer to your Shepherd.

2. Are there people, places or things preventing you from accepting the serene contentment of His care? Are you able to sacrifice your pride? Are you able to sacrifice your selfishness? Give examples.

3. List some of the things that God has shown you through this line in the poem.

4. Come to the table. List the friends and recovery support people who also gather at the table? "And let us consider how we may spur one another on toward love and good deeds" (Hebrews 10:24)

5. The banquet table provides all we need. Are you experiencing freedom in your recovery? Review the Promises listed on page 6. Which of the Twelve Promises are you experiencing?

6. What are you doing to keep in tune with God? What meetings do you attend?

**STEP 9. "Made direct amends to such people wherever possible,
except when to do so would injure them or others."**

Preparing yourself spiritually to make amends requires turning to God for the willingness, power and love.

1. Do you owe amends to people who have also harmed you?

2. Have you forgiven them all? Which ones have you not forgiven yet?
   Spend time at the table so that Jesus can change the attitude of your heart.

3. Have you accepted God's forgiveness?

God wants to transform us.

> "Come now, let us reason together," says the Lord.
>   Though your sins are like scarlet, they shall be as white as snow;
>   though they are red as crimson, they shall be like wool.
>   If you are willing and obedient, you will eat the best from the land;
>   But if you resist and rebel, you will be devoured by the sword.
>   For the mouth of the Lord has spoken"   Isaiah 1:18-20

4. What are your immediate plans for making amends to yourself?

5. Do you have any long-range plans that might fit as an amends to yourself? A few examples include returning to school or starting a photo album or scrapbook to record your future walk with the Lord.

6. Have you experienced freedom by working Step 9?

"Thou dost prepare a table before me in the presence of my enemies;"
STEP 9 "Made direct amends to such people wherever possible,
except when to do so would injure them or others."

MATTHEW 5:7, 11 (READ VERSES 3-11)

____

____

____

MATTHEW 5:23-24

____

____

____

MATTHEW 7:12

____

____

____

MATTHEW 12:37 (READ FROM VERSE 35)

____

____

____

LUKE 6:27-28 (READ THROUGH VERSE 36)

____

____

____

ROMANS 12:18-19 (READ THROUGH VERSE 21)

____

____

ROMANS 14:19

____

____

____

Rate your physical, psychological, emotional, and spiritual health

- Examine your health in each area of your life. Give each behavior a number from 1-5 (#5 means very well).
- Be HONEST. It's helpful to know the *truth* about your recovery health in order to take care of yourself.
- Circle **one** BEHAVIOR in each area that you are willing to work on daily for the next week.

MY BIOLOGICAL HEALTH (PHYSICAL)

MY RECOVERY DATE:		NUMBER OF CONTINOUS DAYS	
Nutrition- when and what you eat		Physical /dental exams & appointments	
Water		Medications/ daily vitamins	
Identifying/reducing emotional eating		Stress management/keeping it simple	
Sleep/rest (too much, too little)		Eliminating/reducing caffeine	
Exercise (easy does it)		Eliminating/reducing sugar	
Pacing your activities (too much, too little)		Other:	

MY PSYCHOLOGICAL HEALTH (MY THOUGHTS & BEHAVIOR)

Managing denial/ defense mechanisms		Music/art/school work	
Positive vs. Negative thinking		Journaling thoughts & behaviors	
Reducing obsessive thoughts		Making phone calls (sponsor, hotline)	
Daily structure/ being on time		Self-help meetings	
Making amends (promptly admit)		Building self esteem	
Money management		Other:	

MY EMOTIONAL/RELATIONAL HEALTH

Letting go of enabling people		Connecting with family in healthy way	
Managing emotions		Self care	
Spending time with **safe** people		Relaxation exercises	
Setting boundaries		Healthy sexual relations	
Having fun		Journaling feelings/ talking about them	
To Thine Own Self Be True. My "yes" is "yes," and my "no" is "no."		Other:	

MY SPIRITUAL HEALTH

Telling the truth to myself and others		Loving myself/ self-forgiveness	
Service to others		Church / Bible study	
Prayer		Serenity Prayer	
Meditation and/or quiet time with God		Gratitude list, affirmations	
Utilizing the Steps /Spiritual Principles		Enjoying nature	
Balance in everyday life (avoiding extremes)		Seeking/finding my purpose, finding what matters	

- Recognize emotional triggers and <u>change behavior.</u>
- Recognize anxiety and <u>practice relaxation techniques.</u>
- Recognize sleeping / eating habits that are slipping and <u>practice self-care.</u>

WEEK FOUR RELAPSE PREVENTION EXERCISE

Checklist of addiction/codependency symptoms which can lead to relapse.

On a 1 to 5 scale (0 meaning not present, 5 meaning it is problematic), how would you assess each of the following symptoms? Put an X on the line to indicate your answer. Enter your plan to make changes. Include behaviors you want to continue in order to remain healthy.

Exhaustion EXAMPLE- 0________________________X______3_______________________5
PLAN- Naps on the weekends are helping. I need to eat more fresh food to feel my best.

1. Exhaustion: Allowing yourself to become overly tired or in poor health.
0____3__________________________________5

PLAN____

2. Dishonesty: Rationalizing- making excuses for doing what you know you should not do.
0____3__________________________________5

PLAN____

3. Impatience: Things are not happening fast enough.
0____3__________________________________5

PLAN____

4. Argumentativeness: "If I could just make you understand."
0____3__________________________________5

PLAN____

5. Frustration: At people or because things in general don't seem to be going "right."
0____3__________________________________5

PLAN____

6. Self-Pity: "Why do these things happen to me?"
0____3__________________________________5

PLAN____

7. Cockiness: Got it made- I can handle it. "It will never again happen to me."
0____3__________________________________5

PLAN____

8. Expecting too much from others: "I've changed; why hasn't everyone else?"
0____3__________________________________5

PLAN____

9. Not being able to say "no": " I don't want the person to feel mad, sad, disappointed, etc."
0____3__________________________________5

PLAN____

10. People-pleasing: Wanting to be liked is the motive behind your behavior.
0____3__________________________________5

PLAN____

Note: Do I need to talk to my Psalm-Partner, therapist, sponsor, or friend about my relapse risk?

WEEK FOUR RELAPSE PREVENTION EXERCISE

Expand on your plan to make changes. Include behaviors you want to continue in order to remain healthy.

PSALM 23
"Thou dost prepare a table before me in the presence of my enemies;"

**STEP 9 "Made direct amends to such people whenever possible,
except when to do so would injure them or others."**

COMPLETION

My favorite Scripture for Chapter 9: Write it here

________I understand Chapter 9 and will continue to use it daily.
________I studied and completed the Bible study in a ***PSALM 23*** group.
________I worked with a PSALM-Partner this month to study Chapter 9.

NAME: ____

Phone # ____

Today's date ____

My Signature ______________________ PSALM-Partner ______________________

BIBLE STUDY AT A GLANCE

MATTHEW 5:9	COLOSSIANS 3:18-21	PROVERBS 16:6-7	
MATTHEW 5:23-24	COLOSSIANS 4:5-6	PROVERBS 16:20-24	
MATTHEW 7:12	I THESSALONIANS 5:15	PROVERBS 25:11	
MATTHEW 12:35-37	PHILEMON 8-17		
LUKE 6:27-36	HEBREWS 12:14-15		
ROMANS 12:18-21	JAMES 3:17-18		
ROMANS 14:19	I PETER 1:22		
ROMANS 15:2	I JOHN 3:17-19		
ROMANS 15:5-7	PSALM 51:14-17		
I CORINTHIANS 8:1-3	PSALM 90:17		
GALATIANS 6:7-10	PSALM 126:5-6		
PHILIPPIANS 1:9-11	PROVERBS 3:27		
PHILIPPIANS 4:2	PROVERBS 12:18-20		
COLOSSIANS 3:12-13	PROVERBS 15:1-4		

The Lord is My Shepherd:

A 12 Step Journey through PSALM 23

CHAPTER TEN

†

PSALM 23
"Thou has anointed my head with oil; My cup overflows."

STEP 10
"Continued to take personal inventory, and when we were
wrong, promptly admitted it."

"Thou hast anointed my head with oil; My cup overflows."

The high meadows of the tablelands are lush and green for the sheep of a good shepherd. While away from the home ranch in the summer, the sheep have intimate close contact with their shepherd, and he tends to their every need. Hordes of insects emerge during the warm weather causing serious problems for the flock. Their shepherd comes prepared with oil to smear over the nose and head of his sheep to protect them from the parasites. Once the oil has been applied, the relief is immediate and the sheep relax, feed, and lie down.

We need the continuous anointing of God's gracious Spirit. The Holy Spirit can give us the attitudes of Christ and makes it possible for us to act and react with calmness to the things that bug us. We do not need the mind of the media, our friends, or even our parents. We need to believe and accept the anointing of Christ's gracious Spirit upon our minds. Read Philippians 4:8 where we are instructed in this matter.

STEP 10. "Continued to take personal inventory and when we were wrong promptly admitted it."

Step 10 is the first of the three maintenance Steps. We continue the work of Step 4 through Step 9 which helps us with honesty, forgiveness, and responsibility. But even such profound changes are not guaranteed to be permanent. We use Step 10 to create and maintain continuous awareness of what we are feeling, thinking and doing. Your personal, Weekly Wellness Check-in is a tool to help you prevent relapse.

Step 10 also addresses RIGHT AND WRONG. Unlike the process contained in Step 4 through Step 9 of cleaning up the wreckage of the **past,** Step 10 keeps us ***current***. We must be ever vigilant in self-examination and accurate self-appraisal as we continue to be honest. This helps us pay attention to our actions and our motives. When the effects are harmful or hurtful to others, we promptly take responsibility for the harm caused and make amends.

Step 10 is a maintenance Step that encourages us to continue to monitor our attitudes and behaviors in order to strike a balance from living in the extremes and/or engaging in unproductive ways that may contribute to relapse.

The Spiritual Principles in Step 10 are self-discipline, self-control, honesty, and integrity.

"Thou hast anointed my head with oil; My cup overflows."

Summertime is fly time and the winged parasites can readily turn the summer months into a time of torture for sheep. The nose-fly buzzes about the sheep's head, attempting to deposit eggs in the mucous membranes of the sheep's nose. The eggs hatch and the worm-like larvae travel up the nasal passages into the sheep's head. They burrow into the flesh and cause severe inflammation and intense irritation. The good shepherd brings oil for his sheep. Without it, sheep are known to beat their heads against trees or rocks and in extreme cases kill themselves for relief. The entire flock is disturbed and *panicky*. At the first sign of flies, the protective shepherd smears an antidote of handmade oil over the head and nose of his beloved sheep. It brings peace of mind to the sheep, the flock, and the shepherd.

It is the daily anointing of God's gracious Spirit upon our minds
that delivers us from our tempers, frustrations, and irritableness.

1. What has been bugging you lately?

2. When have you been *panicky* because of someone else's temper or frustration?

3. Do you have ANTs, ***A****utomatic **N**egative **T**houghts,* marching through your mind?

4. Name a few ANTs that march through your mind. For example, "I <u>should</u> be able to do this", "This <u>always</u> happens to me", "I will <u>never</u> get this right!"

Where there is one ANT there are surely more to come.
5. Have you noticed how the thoughts keep coming? Give an example of your thoughts.

Your body and emotional responses do not depend on whether your thoughts are true or not true.

6. How do the negative thoughts make you feel? How does your body respond? Are the thoughts really true?

STEP 10 "Continued to take personal inventory and when we were wrong promptly admitted it."

A few questions to ask in a personal inventory: Answer the questions today. Date: _______________

1. Have I sought out guidance from the Lord today?

2. Have I been resentful, selfish, dishonest or afraid?

3. Have I set myself up for disappointment?

4. Have I kept something to myself that I should have discussed with my sponsor, a trusted friend or my group?

5. What did I do today that I want to be sure to repeat?

6. Do I believe that God is strong when I am weak? Explain.

7. Have I been worrying about yesterday or tomorrow?

8. Have I been taking somebody else's inventory? This question could be on the codependency symptom checklist.... It's easier to look at the behavior of someone else than it is to take an honest look at ourselves. Keep your eyes focused on yourself and your behavior. How hard is that for you to do?

"Thou hast anointed my head with oil; My cup overflows."
STEP 10 "Continued to take personal inventory, and when we were wrong promptly admitted it."

MATTHEW 5:8

____

____

MARK 14:38

____

____

LUKE 6:41-42

____

____

____

ROMANS 12:3

____

____

____

ROMANS 16:19(READ THROUGH VERSE 20)

____

____

1 CORINTHIANS 3:10(READ THROUGH VERSE 16)

____

____

GALATIANS 4:9

____

____

____

Rate your physical, psychological, emotional, and spiritual health

- Examine your health in each area of your life. Give each behavior a number from 1-5 (#5 means very well).
- Be HONEST. It's helpful to know the *truth* about your recovery health in order to take care of yourself.
- Circle **one** BEHAVIOR in each area that you are willing to work on daily for the next week.

MY BIOLOGICAL HEALTH (PHYSICAL)

MY RECOVERY DATE:		NUMBER OF CONTINOUS DAYS	
Nutrition- when and what you eat		Physical /dental exams & appointments	
Water		Medications/ daily vitamins	
Identifying/reducing emotional eating		Stress management/keeping it simple	
Sleep/rest (too much, too little)		Eliminating/reducing caffeine	
Exercise (easy does it)		Eliminating/reducing sugar	
Pacing your activities (too much, too little)		Other:	

MY PSYCHOLOGICAL HEALTH (MY THOUGHTS & BEHAVIOR)

Managing denial/ defense mechanisms		Music/art/school work	
Positive vs. Negative thinking		Journaling thoughts & behaviors	
Reducing obsessive thoughts		Making phone calls (sponsor, hotline)	
Daily structure/ being on time		Self-help meetings	
Making amends (promptly admit)		Building self esteem	
Money management		Other:	

MY EMOTIONAL/RELATIONAL HEALTH

Letting go of enabling people		Connecting with family in healthy way	
Managing emotions		Self care	
Spending time with **safe** people		Relaxation exercises	
Setting boundaries		Healthy sexual relations	
Having fun		Journaling feelings/ talking about them	
To Thine Own Self Be True. My "yes" is "yes," and my "no" is "no."		Other:	

MY SPIRITUAL HEALTH

Telling the truth to myself and others		Loving myself/ self-forgiveness	
Service to others		Church / Bible study	
Prayer		Serenity Prayer	
Meditation and/or quiet time with God		Gratitude list, affirmations	
Utilizing the Steps /Spiritual Principles		Enjoying nature	
Balance in everyday life (avoiding extremes)		Seeking/finding my purpose, finding what matters	

- Recognize emotional triggers and <u>change behavior.</u>
- Recognize anxiety and <u>practice relaxation techniques.</u>
- Recognize sleeping / eating habits that are slipping and <u>practice self-care.</u>

WEEK ONE RELAPSE PREVENTION EXERCISE
Checklist of addiction/codependency symptoms which can lead to relapse.

On a 1 to 5 scale (0 meaning not present, 5 meaning it is problematic), how would you assess each of the following symptoms? Put an X on the line to indicate your answer. Enter your plan to make changes. Include behaviors you want to continue in order to remain healthy.

<u>Exhaustion</u>   EXAMPLE- 0________________________X______3____5
        PLAN- Naps on the weekends are helping. I need to eat more fresh food to feel my best.

1. <u>Exhaustion:</u> Allowing yourself to become overly tired or in poor health.
   0____3____5

   PLAN____

2. <u>Dishonesty:</u> Rationalizing- making excuses for doing what you know you should not do.
   0____3____5

   PLAN____

3. <u>Impatience:</u> Things are not happening fast enough.
   0____3____5

   PLAN____

4. <u>Argumentativeness:</u> "If I could just make you understand."
   0____3____5

   PLAN____

5. <u>Frustration:</u> At people or because things in general don't seem to be going "right."
   0____3____5

   PLAN____

6. <u>Self-Pity:</u> "Why do these things happen to me?"
   0____3____5

   PLAN____

7. <u>Cockiness:</u> Got it made- I can handle it. "It will never again happen to me."
   0____3____5

   PLAN____

8. <u>Expecting too much from others:</u> "I've changed; why hasn't everyone else?"
   0____3____5

   PLAN____

9. <u>Not being able to say "no":</u> " I don't want the person to feel mad, sad, disappointed, etc."
   0____3____5

   PLAN____

10. <u>People-pleasing:</u> Wanting to be liked is the motive behind your behavior.
    0____3____5

    PLAN____

Note: Do I need to talk to my Psalm-Partner, therapist, sponsor, or friend about my relapse risk?

WEEK ONE RELAPSE PREVENTION EXERCISE

Expand on your plan to make changes. Include behaviors you want to continue in order to remain healthy.

1. Read and write Philippians 4:8.

2. When has your behavior in the past week reflected the fact that *your* Shepherd has anointed your head with oil? Maybe you experienced God doing for you what you could not do for yourself.

3. How does it feel?

4. What is your plan for reflection every day?

5. Assessment of yesterday - day_________________   date _________________

Start with your Negatives	End with your Positives
_________________________	_________________________
_________________________	_________________________
_________________________	_________________________
_________________________	_________________________
_________________________	_________________________

6. God is renewing our minds with TRUTH. God's Word is the measuring stick for our inventory. Read Mark 13:28-31. *"Sky and earth will wear out; my words won't wear out."* from The Message. Write your thoughts.

7. Read Mark 13:32-37. He who stands firm will be saved. Step 10 reminds us that persistence is essential. Have you been sleeping on the job?

8. What have you done this week that you are especially proud of?

STEP 10. "Continued to take personal inventory and when we were wrong promptly admitted it."

Matthew 12:43-45 The Message
"When a defiling evil spirit is expelled from someone, it drifts along through the desert looking for an oasis, some unsuspecting soul it can be-devil. When it doesn't find anyone, it says, 'I'll go back to my old haunt.' On return it finds the person spotlessly clean, but vacant. It then runs out and rounds up seven other spirits more evil than itself and they all move in, whooping it up. That person ends up far worse off than if he'd never gotten cleaned up in the first place."

1. How do these verses apply to recovery?

Use Step 10 to keep your house clean and occupied.

> Watch your thoughts because they become your actions.
> Watch your actions because they become your habits.
> Watch your habits because they become your character.
> Watch your character because it is your destiny.
>   From Reflections by the Old-Timers, Our AA Legacy to the Faith Community

2. Any **character defect** named in Step 4 such as doubt, anxiety, worry, jealousy, etc., may try to cause you trouble. Is there anything you need to take care of today to protect your recovery? It is easier to take care of such things now instead of letting them fester.

3. What relationships are still causing you some trouble?

4. What will you do to make sure your house is occupied?

5. What is your Spiritual condition today? Use the **Weekly Wellness Check-in** to make sure you are keeping your life in balance.

"Thou hast anointed my head with oil; My cup overflows."
STEP 10. "Continued to take personal inventory, and when we were wrong promptly admitted it."

GALATIANS 5:1

____

____

____

EPHESIANS 5:15-16

____

____

____

PHILIPPIANS 2:14-15

____

____

____

COLOSSIANS 3:2-3 (READ FROM VERSE 1)

____

____

____

1 THESSALONIANS 5:17-22

____

____

____

2 THESSALONIANS 3:3-5

____

____

____

____

Rate your physical, psychological, emotional, and spiritual health

- Examine your health in each area of your life. Give each behavior a number from 1-5 (#5 means very well).
- Be HONEST. It's helpful to know the *truth* about your recovery health in order to take care of yourself.
- Circle **one** BEHAVIOR in each area that you are willing to work on daily for the next week.

MY BIOLOGICAL HEALTH (PHYSICAL)

MY RECOVERY DATE:		NUMBER OF CONTINOUS DAYS	
Nutrition- when and what you eat		Physical /dental exams & appointments	
Water		Medications/ daily vitamins	
Identifying/reducing emotional eating		Stress management/keeping it simple	
Sleep/rest (too much, too little)		Eliminating/reducing caffeine	
Exercise (easy does it)		Eliminating/reducing sugar	
Pacing your activities (too much, too little)		Other:	

MY PSYCHOLOGICAL HEALTH (MY THOUGHTS & BEHAVIOR)

Managing denial/ defense mechanisms		Music/art/school work	
Positive vs. Negative thinking		Journaling thoughts & behaviors	
Reducing obsessive thoughts		Making phone calls (sponsor, hotline)	
Daily structure/ being on time		Self-help meetings	
Making amends (promptly admit)		Building self esteem	
Money management		Other:	

MY EMOTIONAL/RELATIONAL HEALTH

Letting go of enabling people		Connecting with family in healthy way	
Managing emotions		Self care	
Spending time with **safe** people		Relaxation exercises	
Setting boundaries		Healthy sexual relations	
Having fun		Journaling feelings/ talking about them	
To Thine Own Self Be True. My "yes" is "yes," and my "no" is "no."		Other:	

MY SPIRITUAL HEALTH

Telling the truth to myself and others		Loving myself/ self-forgiveness	
Service to others		Church / Bible study	
Prayer		Serenity Prayer	
Meditation and/or quiet time with God		Gratitude list, affirmations	
Utilizing the Steps /Spiritual Principles		Enjoying nature	
Balance in everyday life (avoiding extremes)		Seeking/finding my purpose, finding what matters	

- Recognize emotional triggers and <u>change behavior.</u>
- Recognize anxiety and <u>practice relaxation techniques.</u>
- Recognize sleeping / eating habits that are slipping and <u>practice self-care.</u>

WEEK TWO RELAPSE PREVENTION EXERCISE

Checklist of addiction/codependency symptoms which can lead to relapse.

On a 1 to 5 scale (0 meaning not present, 5 meaning it is problematic), how would you assess each of the following symptoms? Put an X on the line to indicate your answer. Enter your plan to make changes. Include behaviors you want to continue in order to remain healthy.

Exhaustion   EXAMPLE- 0_______________________X_______3_________________________________5
   PLAN- Naps on the weekends are helping. I need to eat more fresh food to feel my best.

1. Exhaustion: Allowing yourself to become overly tired or in poor health.
   0____3__________________________________5

   PLAN____

2. Dishonesty: Rationalizing- making excuses for doing what you know you should not do.
   0____3__________________________________5

   PLAN____

3. Impatience: Things are not happening fast enough.
   0____3__________________________________5

   PLAN____

4. Argumentativeness: "If I could just make you understand."
   0____3__________________________________5

   PLAN____

5. Frustration: At people or because things in general don't seem to be going "right."
   0____3__________________________________5

   PLAN____

6. Self-Pity: "Why do these things happen to me?"
   0____3__________________________________5

   PLAN____

7. Cockiness: Got it made- I can handle it. "It will never again happen to me."
   0____3__________________________________5

   PLAN____

8. Expecting too much from others: "I've changed; why hasn't everyone else?"
   0____3__________________________________5

   PLAN____

9. Not being able to say "no": " I don't want the person to feel mad, sad, disappointed, etc."
   0____3__________________________________5

   PLAN____

10. People-pleasing: Wanting to be liked is the motive behind your behavior.
   0____3__________________________________5

   PLAN____

Note: Do I need to talk to my Psalm-Partner, therapist, sponsor, or friend about my relapse risk?

Expand on your plan to make changes. Include behaviors you want to continue in order to remain healthy.

Surely one of the most meaningful aspects about Jesus is that HE does for us what no one else can do. No one else can satisfy our hearts, no one else can solve the problems of the mind like Jesus does.

1. Have you ever tried to satisfy your heart by seeking the approval of another person?

2. Why doesn't it work in the long run?

We are His guests at the banquet table. The overflowing cup symbolizes the superabundance the host has in store for his guests. Jesus likened the kingdom of heaven to a wedding banquet in Matthew 22:1-2. Those who follow God's way of life can enjoy unlimited blessings as guests in the kingdom of God.

3. Use this opportunity to make a gratitude list. What are you grateful for?

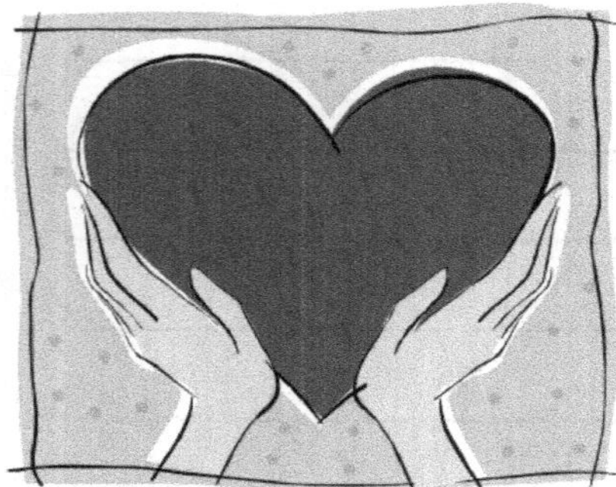

4. Make a list of your gifts and strengths.

5. When did you discovery your strengths?

6. Which strengths are particularly helpful in your recovery?

7. Is there anything or anybody that keeps you from using, acknowledging, or enjoying your gifts?

STEP 10. "Continued to take personal inventory and when we were wrong promptly admitted it."

The Oxford Group's Five "C's" were used to describe the group's life changing principles and practices:
Confidence, Confession, Conviction, Conversion, and Continuance.

1. What do these words mean to your recovery? Use scripture and personal experience.
Confidence:

Confession:

Conviction:

Conversion:

Continuance:

ALAnon, the 12 Step program for family members affected by someone else's drinking, speaks of three C's; "You didn't **CAUSE** it," "You can't **CONTROL** it.," and "You can't **CURE** it."

2. How do the three C's help families?

3. How do they help you?

4. What unhealthy thoughts and behaviors does your RECOVERY protect you from, in the present and the future?

Present	Future
_______________________	_______________________
_______________________	_______________________
_______________________	_______________________
_______________________	_______________________
_______________________	_______________________
_______________________	_______________________
_______________________	_______________________
_______________________	_______________________

"Thou hast anointed my head with oil; My cup overflows."
STEP 10. "Continued to take personal inventory, and when we were wrong promptly admitted it."

2 TIMOTHY 2:23-24 (READ VERSES 20-26)

____

____

____

____

HEBREWS 2:1 (READ THROUGH VERSE 3)

____

____

____

HEBREWS 3:12-13 (READ FROM VERSE 7)

____

____

____

HEBREWS 4:13

____

____

____

HEBREWS 10:35 (READ THROUGH VERSE 38)

____

____

____

HEBREWS 12:28

____

____

____

JAMES 1:13-14

____

____

____

Rate your physical, psychological, emotional, and spiritual health

- Examine your health in each area of your life. Give each behavior a number from 1-5 (#5 means very well).
- Be HONEST. It's helpful to know the *truth* about your recovery health in order to take care of yourself.
- Circle **one** BEHAVIOR in each area that you are willing to work on daily for the next week.

MY BIOLOGICAL HEALTH (PHYSICAL)

MY RECOVERY DATE:		NUMBER OF CONTINOUS DAYS	
Nutrition- when and what you eat		Physical /dental exams & appointments	
Water		Medications/ daily vitamins	
Identifying/reducing emotional eating		Stress management/keeping it simple	
Sleep/rest (too much, too little)		Eliminating/reducing caffeine	
Exercise (easy does it)		Eliminating/reducing sugar	
Pacing your activities (too much, too little)		Other:	

MY PSYCHOLOGICAL HEALTH (MY THOUGHTS & BEHAVIOR)

Managing denial/ defense mechanisms		Music/art/school work	
Positive vs. Negative thinking		Journaling thoughts & behaviors	
Reducing obsessive thoughts		Making phone calls (sponsor, hotline)	
Daily structure/ being on time		Self-help meetings	
Making amends (promptly admit)		Building self esteem	
Money management		Other:	

MY EMOTIONAL/RELATIONAL HEALTH

Letting go of enabling people		Connecting with family in healthy way	
Managing emotions		Self care	
Spending time with **safe** people		Relaxation exercises	
Setting boundaries		Healthy sexual relations	
Having fun		Journaling feelings/ talking about them	
To Thine Own Self Be True. My "yes" is "yes," and my "no" is "no."		Other:	

MY SPIRITUAL HEALTH

Telling the truth to myself and others		Loving myself/ self-forgiveness	
Service to others		Church / Bible study	
Prayer		Serenity Prayer	
Meditation and/or quiet time with God		Gratitude list, affirmations	
Utilizing the Steps /Spiritual Principles		Enjoying nature	
Balance in everyday life (avoiding extremes)		Seeking/finding my purpose, finding what matters	

- Recognize emotional triggers and <u>change behavior.</u>
- Recognize anxiety and <u>practice relaxation techniques.</u>
- Recognize sleeping / eating habits that are slipping and <u>practice self-care.</u>

WEEK THREE RELAPSE PREVENTION EXERCISE

Checklist of addiction/codependency symptoms which can lead to relapse.

On a 1 to 5 scale (0 meaning not present, 5 meaning it is problematic), how would you assess each of the following symptoms? Put an X on the line to indicate your answer. Enter your plan to make changes. Include behaviors you want to continue in order to remain healthy.

Exhaustion EXAMPLE- 0______________________X______3___________________________5
PLAN- Naps on the weekends are helping. I need to eat more fresh food to feel my best.

1. Exhaustion: Allowing yourself to become overly tired or in poor health.
 0___________________________________3____5

 PLAN____

2. Dishonesty: Rationalizing- making excuses for doing what you know you should not do.
 0___________________________________3____5

 PLAN____

3. Impatience: Things are not happening fast enough.
 0___________________________________3____5

 PLAN____

4. Argumentativeness: "If I could just make you understand."
 0___________________________________3____5

 PLAN____

5. Frustration: At people or because things in general don't seem to be going "right."
 0___________________________________3____5

 PLAN____

6. Self-Pity: "Why do these things happen to me?"
 0___________________________________3____5

 PLAN____

7. Cockiness: Got it made- I can handle it. "It will never again happen to me."
 0___________________________________3____5

 PLAN____

8. Expecting too much from others: "I've changed; why hasn't everyone else?"
 0___________________________________3____5

 PLAN____

9. Not being able to say "no": " I don't want the person to feel mad, sad, disappointed, etc."
 0___________________________________3____5

 PLAN____

10. People-pleasing: Wanting to be liked is the motive behind your behavior.
 0___________________________________3____5

 PLAN____

Note: Do I need to talk to my Psalm-Partner, therapist, sponsor, or friend about my relapse risk?

Expand on your plan to make changes. Include behaviors you want to continue in order to remain healthy.

____

____

____

____

____

____

____

____

____

____

____

____

____

____

____

____

____

____

____

"Thou hast anointed my head with oil; My cup overflows."

"The Sovereign LORD comes with power, and His arm rules for Him .... He tends His flock like a shepherd: He gathers the lambs in His arms and carries them close to His heart; He gently leads those that have young." Isa. 40:10-11. Think about how your Shepherd has cared for you. Never stop talking about HIS faithfulness.

1. Are you one who sees the cup half full, or half empty? Are you similar to one or both of your parents in this regard?

2. Developing patience. Read and write Romans 5:3-4

     The shepherd tenderly cared for the delicate, ill and weak sheep, Isaiah 40:11; Ezekiel 34:3-4, 16; Zechariah 11:9. Our Shepherd, the Lord Jesus, also cares for us, and meets our needs. *"I will feed my flock, and I will cause them to lie down, saith the Lord GOD. I will seek that which was lost, and bring again that which was driven away, and will bind up that which was broken, and will strengthen that which was sick."* Ezekiel 34:15-16 KJV

3. When was the last time your Shepherd cared for you as written in Ezekiel?

Romans 5:3-4 from The Message; *"There's more to come: We continue to shout our praise even when we're hemmed in with troubles, because we know how troubles can develop passionate patience in us, and how that patience in turn forges the tempered steel of virtue, keeping us alert for whatever God will do next. In alert expectancy such as this, we're never left feeling shortchanged. Quite the contrary- we can't round up enough containers to hold everything God generously pours into our lives though the Holy Spirit."*
4. What is overflowing out of your life that you can share with others?

5. Are you involved in service at this time?

6. Do you have a PSALM-Partner? Do you speak to someone about your recovery on a regular basis?

Service and accountability are important in your recovery.

---

7. Write your short-term and long-term plans for service.

STEP 10. "Continued to take personal inventory and when we were wrong promptly admitted it."

It's impossible to choose relapse behavior AND recovery behavior at the same time.

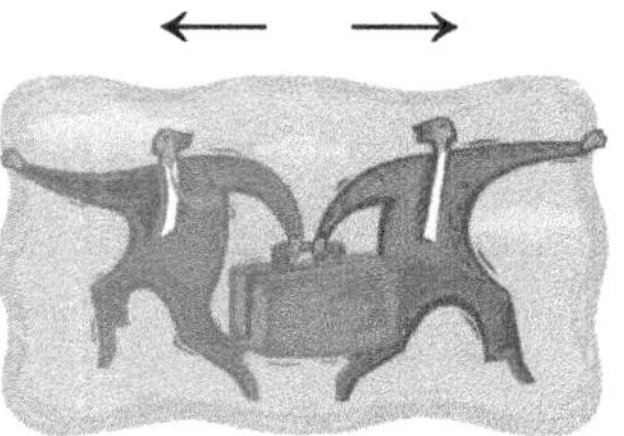

ADDICTION & RELAPSE   **VS**   **RECOVERY & REPAIR**

1. Write as many behaviors as you can think of in each column.

Your list of behaviors will serve as a relapse prevention tool. Refer to this list often. Use your journal. **Keep watch for self-centeredness and self-will.**

Have you heard about Addiction Interaction Disorder? In studies by Dr. Patrick Carnes, many facts have been discovered:

- Less than 13% of addicts have only one addiction,
- Substantial recovery is more successful when all addictions present are addressed,
- Addictions do not merely coexist, but actually interact with each other.

2. Do you need to take these facts into account for your own recovery? Remember, process addictions such as gambling, shopping, spending/debting, hoarding, eating disorders, work, and many more can lead us in wrong directions.

Optimal health and a balanced lifestyle using Scripture and the Spiritual Principles of the 12 Steps can keep us free from other obsessions, addictions, and compulsive behaviors.

"Thou hast anointed my head with oil; My cup overflows."
STEP 10. "Continued to take personal inventory, and when we were wrong promptly admitted it."

ROMANS 14:19

____

____

ROMANS 15:2

____

____

ROMANS 15:7

____

____

1CORINTHIANS 8:12-13 (READ FROM VERSE 9)

____

____

____

GALATIONS 6:8 (READ VERSES 7-10)

____

____

PHILIPPIANS 1:9-10 (READ THROUGH VERSE 11)

____

____

PHILIPPIANS 4:2

____

____

____

WEEK FOUR WELLNESS CHECK-IN

Rate your physical, psychological, emotional, and spiritual health

- Examine your health in each area of your life. Give each behavior a number from 1-5 (#5 means very well).
- Be HONEST. It's helpful to know the *truth* about your recovery health in order to take care of yourself.
- Circle **one** BEHAVIOR in each area that you are willing to work on daily for the next week.

MY BIOLOGICAL HEALTH (PHYSICAL)

MY RECOVERY DATE:		NUMBER OF CONTINOUS DAYS	
Nutrition- when and what you eat		Physical /dental exams & appointments	
Water		Medications/ daily vitamins	
Identifying/reducing emotional eating		Stress management/keeping it simple	
Sleep/rest (too much, too little)		Eliminating/reducing caffeine	
Exercise (easy does it)		Eliminating/reducing sugar	
Pacing your activities (too much, too little)		Other:	

MY PSYCHOLOGICAL HEALTH (MY THOUGHTS & BEHAVIOR)

Managing denial/ defense mechanisms		Music/art/school work	
Positive vs. Negative thinking		Journaling thoughts & behaviors	
Reducing obsessive thoughts		Making phone calls (sponsor, hotline)	
Daily structure/ being on time		Self-help meetings	
Making amends (promptly admit)		Building self esteem	
Money management		Other:	

MY EMOTIONAL/RELATIONAL HEALTH

Letting go of enabling people		Connecting with family in healthy way	
Managing emotions		Self care	
Spending time with **safe** people		Relaxation exercises	
Setting boundaries		Healthy sexual relations	
Having fun		Journaling feelings/ talking about them	
To Thine Own Self Be True. My "yes" is "yes," and my "no" is "no."		Other:	

MY SPIRITUAL HEALTH

Telling the truth to myself and others		Loving myself/ self-forgiveness	
Service to others		Church / Bible study	
Prayer		Serenity Prayer	
Meditation and/or quiet time with God		Gratitude list, affirmations	
Utilizing the Steps /Spiritual Principles		Enjoying nature	
Balance in everyday life (avoiding extremes)		Seeking/finding my purpose, finding what matters	

- Recognize emotional triggers and <u>change behavior.</u>
- Recognize anxiety and <u>practice relaxation techniques.</u>
- Recognize sleeping / eating habits that are slipping and <u>practice self-care.</u>

WEEK FOUR RELAPSE PREVENTION EXERCISE

Checklist of addiction/codependency symptoms which can lead to relapse.

On a 1 to 5 scale (0 meaning not present, 5 meaning it is problematic), how would you assess each of the following symptoms? Put an X on the line to indicate your answer. Enter your plan to make changes. Include behaviors you want to continue in order to remain healthy.

<u>Exhaustion</u>   EXAMPLE- 0________________________X_______3________________________________5
             PLAN- Naps on the weekends are helping. I need to eat more fresh food to feel my best.

1. <u>Exhaustion:</u> Allowing yourself to become overly tired or in poor health.
    0____3____5

    PLAN____

2. <u>Dishonesty:</u> Rationalizing- making excuses for doing what you know you should not do.
    0____3____5

    PLAN____

3. <u>Impatience:</u> Things are not happening fast enough.
    0____3____5

    PLAN____

4. <u>Argumentativeness:</u> "If I could just make you understand."
    0____3____5

    PLAN____

5. <u>Frustration:</u> At people or because things in general don't seem to be going "right."
    0____3____5

    PLAN____

6. <u>Self-Pity:</u> "Why do these things happen to me?"
    0____3____5

    PLAN____

7. <u>Cockiness:</u> Got it made- I can handle it. "It will never again happen to me."
    0____3____5

    PLAN____

8. <u>Expecting too much from others:</u> "I've changed; why hasn't everyone else?"
    0____3____5

    PLAN____

9. <u>Not being able to say "no":</u> " I don't want the person to feel mad, sad, disappointed, etc."
    0____3____5

    PLAN____

10. <u>People-pleasing:</u> Wanting to be liked is the motive behind your behavior.
    0____3____5

    PLAN____

Note: Do I need to talk to my Psalm-Partner, therapist, sponsor, or friend about my relapse risk?

WEEK FOUR RELAPSE PREVENTION EXERCISE

Expand on your plan to make changes. Include behaviors you want to continue in order to remain healthy.

PSALM 23 "Thou hast anointed my head with oil; my cup overflows."

STEP 10. "Continued to take personal inventory, and when we were wrong promptly admitted it."

COMPLETION

My favorite Scripture for Chapter 10: Write it here.

________I understand Chapter 10 and will continue to use it daily.
________I studied and completed the Bible study in a *Psalm 23* group.
________I worked with a PSALM-Partner this month to study Chapter 10.

NAME: ____

Phone # ____

Today's date____

My Signature ____PSALM-Partner ____________________________

BIBLE STUDY AT A GLANCE

MATTHEW 5:8	GALATIANS 5:1	HEBREWS 4:12-13	PSALMS 24:3-5
MATTHEW 26:71-75	GALATIANS 5:13-15	HEBREWS 10:35-38	PSALMS 68:5,6
MARK 14:38	EPHESIANS 4:26-32	HEBREWS 12:25	PSALMS 85:8-9
LUKE 6:41-42	EPHESIANS 5:15-16	HEBREWS 12:28	PSALMS 101:2-4
JOHN 17: 15-17	PHILIPPIANS 2:14-15	JAMES 1:13-14	PSALMS 103:8-18
ROMANS 12:3	PHILIPPIANS 4:8-9	JAMES 1:19	PROVERBS 12:1
ROMANS 12:16	COLOSSIANS 3:1-3	JAMES 1:21-25	
ROMANS 16: 19-20	I THESSALONIANS 5:17-22	I PETER 2:11	
I CORINTHIANS 3:10-16	2 THESSALONIANS 3:3-5	2 PETER 3:17-18	
I CORINTHIANS 6:12	I TIMOTHY 4:7-8	I JOHN 2:3	
I CORINTHIANS 10:6-13	2 TIMOTHY 2:3-7	I JOHN 2:15-17	
I CORINTHIANS 10: 23-24	2 TIMOTHY2:20-26	2 JOHN 8	
2 CORINTHIANS 10: 17-18	HEBREWS 2:1-3	GENESIS 31:45-55	
GALATIANS 4: 9	HEBREWS 3:7-13		

The Lord is My Shepherd:

A 12 Step Journey through PSALM 23

CHAPTER ELEVEN

†

PSALM 23
"Surely goodness and loving-kindness will follow me
all the days of my life."

STEP 11
"Sought through prayer and meditation to improve our
conscious contact with God, praying only for knowledge of
His will for us and the power to carry it out."

PSALM 23
"Surely goodness and loving-kindness shall follow me all the days of my life."

Summer is moving into autumn. Soon the good shepherd will drive his flock from the tablelands and back to the home ranch for the winter. The autumn days can quickly fluctuate from warm Indian-summer weather to blizzards of sleet and hail leaving the shepherd and his flock chilled, wet, and cold. The shepherd is always prepared and *on time*. A spoonful of *handmade mixture* for the lamb or ewe that has succumbed to the weather puts the chilled creature back on its feet. The shepherd is skilled, and the sheep are under his management.

The flock is in a state of strength and wellness at this time of the year. With autumn comes the season of mating known as the season of the rut. There will be great battles between the rams for possession of the ewes. Their necks swell and grow strong and the crashing of heads can be heard both day and night. Combat can be deadly, so the shepherd is prepared to intervene.

We have a privileged position. He is the one thing that we need. God makes the first move. He takes the initiative by calling us and leading us to a place of rest and safety.

It's not because we're seeking God; He is seeking us.

STEP 11. "Sought through prayer and meditation to improve our conscious contact with God, praying only for knowledge of His will for us and the power to carry that out."

In Step 11 we work to develop spirituality and we invest in our serenity and peace of mind in recovery. Step 2 is where we began to develop our conscious awareness of Jesus as our Higher Power. Now we are reaching out to the Lord to strengthen and improve our intimate and personal relationship with Him as our precious Shepherd. Group members, when sharing about Step 11, refer to prayer, meditation on God's Word, conscious contact, and God's will. As recovering persons, we use the Holy Bible, our support groups, retreats, recovery literature and our church. Bill Wilson, from A.A., found great peace and encouragement through the Bible and the book, *My Utmost for His Highest*, by Oswald Chambers.

God's quiet voice sometimes is so faint that we forget that He is near.

But not to worry: He cannot forget us.

The Spiritual Principles for Step 11 are commitment, humility, courage, and faith.

"Surely goodness and loving-kindness shall follow me all the days of my life."

What a statement! Can it really be true? Can a twisted life really be made right? Read Ezekiel 37:1-6.

1. Do you find yourself doing things <u>for</u> God in an effort to make your own life right?

2. Some of us have had the strange, stubborn notion that we can live certain parts of our lives without God. Why is it hard to give up control?

3. Do you really believe that God will do in you what you cannot do? Have you ever suddenly realized that God is doing for you what you can not do for yourself? Review The Promises.

God knows how to make things right

Ezekiel 34:4-6: From The Message:
God, the Master, told the dry bones, "Watch this; I'm bringing the breath of life to you and you'll come to life. I'll attach sinews to you, put meat on your bones, cover you with skin, and breathe life into you. You'll come alive and you'll realize that I am God."

4. Our victory in our recovery program is entirely at the initiative of God. He bought you and brought you into his flock. When did you join the flock? Write about it here.

5. Write about a time when change or pain in your life turned out to have benefits after Jesus took you through to the other end. These stories are important, keep remembering and sharing them.

6. When Jesus recovers us in the here and now, we can't help but share the gospel and His ultimate sacrifice for us. Thank Him now.

"Surely goodness and loving-kindness shall follow me all the days of my life."

STEP 11. "Sought through prayer and meditation to improve our conscious contact with God, praying only for knowledge of His will for us and the power to carry that out."

Prayer is the highest expression of our dependence and faith on God. We can use the acronym ACTS: Acclamation, Confession, Thanksgiving, and Supplication when we pray to our Lord as taught in the Lord's Prayer. Often, it's after we have exhausted all our energy trying to solve a problem that we approach God to seek His wisdom and strength. Even if it isn't our first line of defense in every instance, prayer will change YOU. It'll change your vision. We can ask for anything--even the most difficult things. *"Do not be anxious about anything, but in everything, by prayer and petition, with thanksgiving, present your requests to God"* Phil. 4:6. Even "Jesus, help!" will prompt the Holy Spirit to intercede for us.

1. Read Romans 8:26-27. Write it here.

2. Does knowing that the Holy Spirit intercedes for you make praying easier? Why or why not?

3. What has your prayer life been like in the last month?

4. Journaling your prayers is an awesome way of seeing how God responds when you enter into a relationship and conscious contact with Him. Use this chart to journal your prayers. Enter the Date, Prayer, God's answer, and the date of answered prayer. You can make your own chart in the future.

Entry date	My prayer	God's answer	Date answered

5. What is this experience like for you?

**"Surely goodness and loving-kindness shall follow me all the days of my life."
STEP 11. "Sought through prayer and meditation to improve our conscious contact with God,
praying only for knowledge of His will for us and the power to carry that out."**

MATTHEW 21:22 (READ FROM VERSE 21)

____

____

MARK 9:37

____

____

LUKE 6:20-22 (READ THROUGH VERSE 26)

____

____

____

JOHN 15:26

____

____

ACTS 6:7

____

____

ROMANS 8:17 (READ FROM VERSE 14)

____

____

2 CORINTHIANS 8:5 (READ FROM VERSE 1)

____

____

____

Rate your physical, psychological, emotional, and spiritual health

- Examine your health in each area of your life. Give each behavior a number from 1-5 (#5 means very well).
- Be HONEST. It's helpful to know the *truth* about your recovery health in order to take care of yourself.
- Circle **one** BEHAVIOR in each area that you are willing to work on daily for the next week.

MY BIOLOGICAL HEALTH (PHYSICAL)

MY RECOVERY DATE:		NUMBER OF CONTINOUS DAYS	
Nutrition- when and what you eat		Physical /dental exams & appointments	
Water		Medications/ daily vitamins	
Identifying/reducing emotional eating		Stress management/keeping it simple	
Sleep/rest (too much, too little)		Eliminating/reducing caffeine	
Exercise (easy does it)		Eliminating/reducing sugar	
Pacing your activities (too much, too little)		Other:	

MY PSYCHOLOGICAL HEALTH (MY THOUGHTS & BEHAVIOR)

Managing denial/ defense mechanisms		Music/art/school work	
Positive vs. Negative thinking		Journaling thoughts & behaviors	
Reducing obsessive thoughts		Making phone calls (sponsor, hotline)	
Daily structure/ being on time		Self-help meetings	
Making amends (promptly admit)		Building self esteem	
Money management		Other:	

MY EMOTIONAL/RELATIONAL HEALTH

Letting go of enabling people		Connecting with family in healthy way	
Managing emotions		Self care	
Spending time with **safe** people		Relaxation exercises	
Setting boundaries		Healthy sexual relations	
Having fun		Journaling feelings/ talking about them	
To Thine Own Self Be True. My "yes" is "yes," and my "no" is "no."		Other:	

MY SPIRITUAL HEALTH

Telling the truth to myself and others		Loving myself/ self-forgiveness	
Service to others		Church / Bible study	
Prayer		Serenity Prayer	
Meditation and/or quiet time with God		Gratitude list, affirmations	
Utilizing the Steps /Spiritual Principles		Enjoying nature	
Balance in everyday life (avoiding extremes)		Seeking/finding my purpose, finding what matters	

- Recognize emotional triggers and <u>change behavior.</u>
- Recognize anxiety and <u>practice relaxation techniques.</u>
- Recognize sleeping / eating habits that are slipping and <u>practice self-care.</u>

WEEK ONE RELAPSE PREVENTION EXERCISE
Checklist of addiction/codependency symptoms which can lead to relapse.

On a 1 to 5 scale (0 meaning not present, 5 meaning it is problematic), how would you assess each of the following symptoms? Put an X on the line to indicate your answer. Enter your plan to make changes. Include behaviors you want to continue in order to remain healthy.

<u>Exhaustion</u>   EXAMPLE- 0________________________X______3_________________________________5
PLAN- Naps on the weekends are helping. I need to eat more fresh food to feel my best.

1. <u>Exhaustion:</u> Allowing yourself to become overly tired or in poor health.
0____3____5

PLAN____

2. <u>Dishonesty:</u> Rationalizing- making excuses for doing what you know you should not do.
0____3____5

PLAN____

3. <u>Impatience:</u> Things are not happening fast enough.
0____3____5

PLAN____

4. <u>Argumentativeness:</u> "If I could just make you understand."
0____3____5

PLAN____

5. <u>Frustration:</u> At people or because things in general don't seem to be going "right."
0____3____5

PLAN____

6. <u>Self-Pity:</u> "Why do these things happen to me?"
0____3____5

PLAN____

7. <u>Cockiness:</u> Got it made- I can handle it. "It will never again happen to me."
0____3____5

PLAN____

8. <u>Expecting too much from others:</u> "I've changed; why hasn't everyone else?"
0____3____5

PLAN____

9. <u>Not being able to say "no":</u> " I don't want the person to feel mad, sad, disappointed, etc."
0____3____5

PLAN____

10. <u>People-pleasing:</u> Wanting to be liked is the motive behind your behavior.
0____3____5

PLAN____

Note: Do I need to talk to my Psalm-Partner, therapist, sponsor, or friend about my relapse risk?

WEEK ONE RELAPSE PREVENTION EXERCISE

Expand on your plan to make changes. Include behaviors you want to continue in order to remain healthy.

____

____

____

____

____

____

____

____

____

____

____

____

____

____

____

____

____

____

____

____

____

"Surely goodness and loving-kindness shall follow me all the days of my life."

The season of the rut brings changes in the flock. The rams strut proudly across the pastures and are ready to fight head to head for the favor of the ewes. The shepherd is ready, and he has a remedy. In this case it is not oil or a liquid mixture as used to cure the chill; it is simply grease. The shepherd chases down the rams and smears their heads with generous quantities of grease. The lubricant causes the rams to slide off each other with little or no damage. They may even feel dumb founded at the end of the ritual, but the tension dissipates, and the shepherd is happy. Think of a time when you went head to head with someone.

1. Who was badly bruised?

Jesus told the twelve disciples about the coming of the Comforter- the Spirit of Truth.
2. What do you know about the Holy Spirit?

3. Can you think of a time when you ran on self-will and the Lord followed you in goodness and mercy?

God in His GOODNESS supplies all of our needs and in His MERCY, He supplies forgiveness for all of our sins. And how long does this coverage last? David confidently wrote "all the days of my life".

4. Write a thank you note to your Shepherd. What do you love about HIM?

STEP 11. "Sought through prayer and meditation to improve our conscious contact with God, praying only for knowledge of His will for us and the power to carry that out."

For the next week, practice three to five minutes of meditation a day. Do whatever helps you to achieve these three goals: **Sitting still, feeling comfort, and having a straight spine.**

- It is usually a good idea to take a few slow, deep breaths before you begin.
- Some people like to close their eyes; others prefer to focus on an object: perhaps the flame of a candle, the setting of the sun, the ocean, or your garden.
- Let the busy thoughts drain out of your mind as you become still.
- Focus your attention on one of the lines of David's poem. There might be one that you prefer at this time.
- Focus on what your Shepherd is whispering to you about His care and love for YOU.

1. Enter your notes here:

2. Is this something you will use as part of your **Relapse Prevention/ Recovery Plan**? Cherish the growth you've made in recovery… and protect it.

"Surely goodness and loving-kindness shall follow me all the days of my life."
STEP 11. "Sought through prayer and meditation to improve our conscious contact with God,
praying only for knowledge of His will for us and the power to carry that out."

ACTS 6:7

____

____

____

ROMANS 8:17 (READ FROM VERSE 14)

____

____

____

2 CORINTHIANS 8:5 (READ FROM VERSE 1)

____

____

____

COLOSSIANS 1:13-14

____

____

____

COLOSSIANS 3:1-2

____

____

____

1 TIMOTHY 4:12-13 (READ VERSES 11-16)

____

____

____

HEBREWS 4:15-16

____

____

____

Rate your physical, psychological, emotional, and spiritual health

- Examine your health in each area of your life. Give each behavior a number from 1-5 (#5 means very well).
- Be HONEST. It's helpful to know the *truth* about your recovery health in order to take care of yourself.
- Circle **one** BEHAVIOR in each area that you are willing to work on daily for the next week.

MY BIOLOGICAL HEALTH (PHYSICAL)

MY RECOVERY DATE:		NUMBER OF CONTINOUS DAYS	
Nutrition- when and what you eat		Physical /dental exams & appointments	
Water		Medications/ daily vitamins	
Identifying/reducing emotional eating		Stress management/keeping it simple	
Sleep/rest (too much, too little)		Eliminating/reducing caffeine	
Exercise (easy does it)		Eliminating/reducing sugar	
Pacing your activities (too much, too little)		Other:	

MY PSYCHOLOGICAL HEALTH (MY THOUGHTS & BEHAVIOR)

Managing denial/ defense mechanisms		Music/art/school work	
Positive vs. Negative thinking		Journaling thoughts & behaviors	
Reducing obsessive thoughts		Making phone calls (sponsor, hotline)	
Daily structure/ being on time		Self-help meetings	
Making amends (promptly admit)		Building self esteem	
Money management		Other:	

MY EMOTIONAL/RELATIONAL HEALTH

Letting go of enabling people		Connecting with family in healthy way	
Managing emotions		Self care	
Spending time with **safe** people		Relaxation exercises	
Setting boundaries		Healthy sexual relations	
Having fun		Journaling feelings/ talking about them	
To Thine Own Self Be True. My "yes" is "yes," and my "no" is "no."		Other:	

MY SPIRITUAL HEALTH

Telling the truth to myself and others		Loving myself/ self-forgiveness	
Service to others		Church / Bible study	
Prayer		Serenity Prayer	
Meditation and/or quiet time with God		Gratitude list, affirmations	
Utilizing the Steps /Spiritual Principles		Enjoying nature	
Balance in everyday life (avoiding extremes)		Seeking/finding my purpose, finding what matters	

- Recognize emotional triggers and <u>change behavior.</u>
- Recognize anxiety and <u>practice relaxation techniques.</u>
- Recognize sleeping / eating habits that are slipping and <u>practice self-care.</u>

WEEK TWO RELAPSE PREVENTION EXERCISE
Checklist of addiction/codependency symptoms which can lead to relapse.

On a 1 to 5 scale (0 meaning not present, 5 meaning it is problematic), how would you assess each of the following symptoms? Put an X on the line to indicate your answer. Enter your plan to make changes. Include behaviors you want to continue in order to remain healthy.

<u>Exhaustion</u>   EXAMPLE- 0________________________________X______3____5
PLAN- Naps on the weekends are helping. I need to eat more fresh food to feel my best.

1. <u>Exhaustion:</u> Allowing yourself to become overly tired or in poor health.
0____3____5

PLAN____

2. <u>Dishonesty:</u> Rationalizing- making excuses for doing what you know you should not do.
0____3____5

PLAN____

3. <u>Impatience:</u> Things are not happening fast enough.
0____3____5

PLAN____

4. <u>Argumentativeness:</u> "If I could just make you understand."
0____3____5

PLAN____

5. <u>Frustration:</u> At people or because things in general don't seem to be going "right."
0____3____5

PLAN____

6. <u>Self-Pity:</u> "Why do these things happen to me?"
0____3____5

PLAN____

7. <u>Cockiness:</u> Got it made- I can handle it. "It will never again happen to me."
0____3____5

PLAN____

8. <u>Expecting too much from others:</u> "I've changed; why hasn't everyone else?"
0____3____5

PLAN____

9. <u>Not being able to say "no":</u> " I don't want the person to feel mad, sad, disappointed, etc."
0____3____5

PLAN____

10. <u>People-pleasing:</u> Wanting to be liked is the motive behind your behavior.
0____3____5

PLAN____

Note: Do I need to talk to my Psalm-Partner, therapist, sponsor, or friend about my relapse risk?

Expand on your plan to make changes. Include behaviors you want to continue in order to remain healthy.

____

____

____

____

____

____

____

____

____

____

____

____

____

____

____

____

____

____

____

____

"Surely goodness and loving-kindness shall follow me all the days of my life."

David declares, "**Surely**…" He denotes a *fact*. He didn't write, "**Sometimes**…, or "**If we measure up**". He declared, "**Surely** goodness and loving-kindness shall follow me all the days of my life."

1. Does your Bible translation use other words in this line of David's Psalm??

2. Have you allowed this *fact* to comfort you? What parts of your life are getting healthier?

3. Which relationships are getting better?

This is the 11th line in the poem. We need to study the beginning, middle and end of the poem again and again to really get this *fact* into our bones.

"Surely goodness and loving-kindness shall follow me all the days of my life."

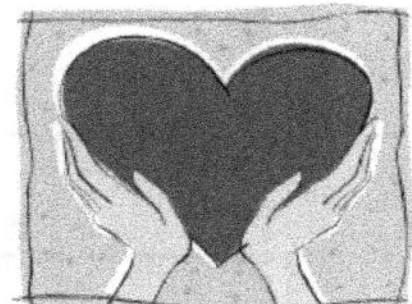

THIS PROMISE FILLS THE ***DESIRES*** OF OUR HEARTS!!!

God is **good**! As Jesus said with such utter finality, "*No one* is good-except God." Luke 18:19
4. Do you have any doubt that God's goodness shall follow you?

For the one who is truly in Christ's care, no difficulty can arise without eventual good coming out of the chaos.
5. Write Romans 8:28.

God is love. He is as loving as we need Him to be. The PSALMS are filled with affirmations of God's love for us. David writes, *"I... rejoice in your **love**"* PSALMS 31:7. *"You are forgiving and good, O Lord, aboundingin **love** to all who call to you"* PSALMS 86:5.

Nothing can separate us from God's goodness and love.
6. In what area of your life do you need God's special care today?

STEP 11. "Sought through prayer and meditation to improve our conscious contact with God, praying only for knowledge of His will for us and the power to carry that out."

Self-soothing is very important in recovery. We have a variety of ways to comfort ourselves without addictive or self-destructive behavior. This is a form of stress management and relapse prevention.

	THINGS I CAN DO WHEN I AM ALONE	THINGS I CAN DO WHEN I AM WITH OTHERS
Example: DURING THE DAY	**Example**: 1. during the day I like to work on my scrapbooks 2. walk my dogs 3. practice positive thoughts, affirmations	**Example:** 1. go to exercise class 2. have tea with a friend 3. talk on the phone
DURING THE DAY	1.______________ 2.______________ 3.______________ 4.______________ 5.______________	1.______________ 2.______________ 3.______________ 4.______________ 5.______________
DURING THE NIGHT	1.______________ 2.______________ 3.______________ 4.______________ 5.______________	1.______________ 2.______________ 3.______________ 4.______________ 5______________

2. Positive Thoughts:______ What Bible verses support these truthful thoughts?______

1. Jesus loves me. ______________________________________

2. I am lovable. ______________________________________

3. I deserve to be loved. ______________________________________

4. I can learn. ______________________________________

5. I can succeed. ______________________________________

6. I deserve to be content and happy. ______________________________________

7. Mistakes are okay; I can learn from my mistakes. ______________________________________

"Surely goodness and loving-kindness shall follow me all the days of my life."
STEP 11. "Sought through prayer and meditation to improve our conscious contact with God,
praying only for knowledge of His will for us and the power to carry that out."

PSALMS 1:1-3

____

____

PSALMS 16:7-8

____

____

PSALMS 25:4-5

____

____

PSALMS 119:105-106

____

____

____

PROVERBS 3:5-6

____

____

____

PROVERBS 16:20

____

____

MATTHEW 5:19-20

____

____

____

Rate your physical, psychological, emotional, and spiritual health

- Examine your health in each area of your life. Give each behavior a number from 1-5 (#5 means very well).
- Be HONEST. It's helpful to know the *truth* about your recovery health in order to take care of yourself.
- Circle **one** BEHAVIOR in each area that you are willing to work on daily for the next week.

MY BIOLOGICAL HEALTH (PHYSICAL)

MY RECOVERY DATE:		NUMBER OF CONTINOUS DAYS	
Nutrition- when and what you eat		Physical /dental exams & appointments	
Water		Medications/ daily vitamins	
Identifying/reducing emotional eating		Stress management/keeping it simple	
Sleep/rest (too much, too little)		Eliminating/reducing caffeine	
Exercise (easy does it)		Eliminating/reducing sugar	
Pacing your activities (too much, too little)		Other:	

MY PSYCHOLOGICAL HEALTH (MY THOUGHTS & BEHAVIOR)

Managing denial/ defense mechanisms		Music/art/school work	
Positive vs. Negative thinking		Journaling thoughts & behaviors	
Reducing obsessive thoughts		Making phone calls (sponsor, hotline)	
Daily structure/ being on time		Self-help meetings	
Making amends (promptly admit)		Building self esteem	
Money management		Other:	

MY EMOTIONAL/RELATIONAL HEALTH

Letting go of enabling people		Connecting with family in healthy way	
Managing emotions		Self care	
Spending time with **safe** people		Relaxation exercises	
Setting boundaries		Healthy sexual relations	
Having fun		Journaling feelings/ talking about them	
To Thine Own Self Be True. My "yes" is "yes," and my "no" is "no."		Other:	

MY SPIRITUAL HEALTH

Telling the truth to myself and others		Loving myself/ self-forgiveness	
Service to others		Church / Bible study	
Prayer		Serenity Prayer	
Meditation and/or quiet time with God		Gratitude list, affirmations	
Utilizing the Steps /Spiritual Principles		Enjoying nature	
Balance in everyday life (avoiding extremes)		Seeking/finding my purpose, finding what matters	

- Recognize emotional triggers and <u>change behavior.</u>
- Recognize anxiety and <u>practice relaxation techniques.</u>
- Recognize sleeping / eating habits that are slipping and <u>practice self-care.</u>

WEEK THREE RELAPSE PREVENTION EXERCISE

Checklist of addiction/codependency symptoms which can lead to relapse.

On a 1 to 5 scale (0 meaning not present, 5 meaning it is problematic), how would you assess each of the following symptoms? Put an X on the line to indicate your answer. Enter your plan to make changes. Include behaviors you want to continue in order to remain healthy.

<u>Exhaustion</u>   EXAMPLE- 0________________________X______3________________________________5
PLAN- Naps on the weekends are helping. I need to eat more fresh food to feel my best.

1. <u>Exhaustion:</u> Allowing yourself to become overly tired or in poor health.
0____3____5

PLAN____

2. <u>Dishonesty:</u> Rationalizing- making excuses for doing what you know you should not do.
0____3____5

PLAN____

3. <u>Impatience:</u> Things are not happening fast enough.
0____3____5

PLAN____

4. <u>Argumentativeness:</u> "If I could just make you understand."
0____3____5

PLAN____

5. <u>Frustration:</u> At people or because things in general don't seem to be going "right."
0____3____5

PLAN____

6. <u>Self-Pity:</u> "Why do these things happen to me?"
0____3____5

PLAN____

7. <u>Cockiness:</u> Got it made- I can handle it. "It will never again happen to me."
0____3____5

PLAN____

8. <u>Expecting too much from others:</u> "I've changed; why hasn't everyone else?"
0____3____5

PLAN____

9. <u>Not being able to say "no":</u> " I don't want the person to feel mad, sad, disappointed, etc."
0____3____5

PLAN____

10. <u>People-pleasing:</u> Wanting to be liked is the motive behind your behavior.
0____3____5

PLAN____

Note: Do I need to talk to my Psalm-Partner, therapist, sponsor, or friend about my relapse risk?

WEEK THREE RELAPSE PREVENTION EXERCISE

Expand on your plan to make changes. Include behaviors you want to continue in order to remain healthy.

"Surely goodness and loving-kindness shall follow me all the days of my life."

Under mismanagement sheep can be the most destructive livestock there is. The sheep can ruin and ravage land beyond remedy and they live with a gnawing hunger most of the year. Satan, like the heartless rancher, holds ownership over so many. The devil hates God and he is constantly messing with God's flock. Everything Satan does is designed to draw you and me away from God's love. According to John Milton, the devil is the prowling Wolf.

"Whom hunger drives to seek new haunt for prey,
watching where Shepherds pen their flocks at eve,
so climbs this grand thief into God's fold."

This enemy is the source of all our doubts about God's goodness. Satan is the one behind the subtle seduction to doubt our Shepherd's wise provision. The devil fills us with guilt over the past, while denying God's unfailing forgiveness.

Doubts come and go; we do not need to be dismayed by them. We should counter them by reminding ourselves **of their source** and remembering that what the devil says is **not true**- Satan is a liar. Then we can renew our minds and strengthen our hearts with the truth of God's Word.

1. What kind of situation causes you to have doubts?

2. Write Philippians 4:8, 9.

In a few years a flock under the care of The Good Shepherd will clean up and restore land as no other creature can. In other words, goodness and mercy follow The Good Shepherd's flocks. Soak yourself in this truth, know it from **firsthand experience**. Receive and experience the amazing grace of the Master, Jesus Christ, deep, deep within yourself. Then you will be warm and affectionate with goodness and mercy to others.

3. Do you leave a blessing behind you?

4. Is your life a pleasure to people or a pain?

5. Do you leave behind forgiveness – or bitterness?

6. Read Philippians 4:4-7.

STEP 11. "Sought through prayer and meditation to improve our conscious contact with God, praying only for knowledge of his will for us and the power to carry that out."

RUNNING TO WIN

Read Hebrews11:1-2. Faith in what we don't see.

The Message: *The fundamental fact of existence is that this trust in God, this faith, is the firm foundation under everything that makes life worth living. It's our handle on what we can't see. The act of faith is what distinguished our ancestors, set them above the crowd.*

1. How strong is your faith? Do you need to improve your conscious contact with God?

2. Now read Hebrews 12:1-3. What do you need to let go of to run the race with perseverance?

We are at our best when there is balance in our lives.

3. Think of having four tires on your car that need to be checked and filled with air every day for a smooth ride. Now think of that car as you and your life. Which area of your life, (or tire on your car) is low *right now*?

Physical health?

Psychological health?

Emotional health?

Spiritual health?

4. What area is the hardest for you to keep tuned up?

5. How has it affected the other tires?

6. What will you do today to persevere?

PUTT, PUTT, PUTT...

"Surely goodness and loving-kindness shall follow me all the days of my life."
STEP 11. "Sought through prayer and meditation to improve our conscious contact with God, as we understood Him, praying only for knowledge of His will for us and the power to carry that out."

COLOSSIANS 1:13-14

____

____

____

COLOSSIANS 3:1-2

____

____

____

COLOSSIANS 3:16 (READ VERSES 15-17)

____

____

____

____

1 TIMOTHY 4:12-13 (READ VERSES 11-16)

____

____

____

HEBREWS 4:15-16

____

____

____

____

WEEK FOUR WELLNESS CHECK-IN

Rate your physical, psychological, emotional, and spiritual health

- Examine your health in each area of your life. Give each behavior a number from 1-5 (#5 means very well).
- Be HONEST. It's helpful to know the *truth* about your recovery health in order to take care of yourself.
- Circle **one** BEHAVIOR in each area that you are willing to work on daily for the next week.

MY BIOLOGICAL HEALTH (PHYSICAL)

MY RECOVERY DATE:		NUMBER OF CONTINOUS DAYS	
Nutrition- when and what you eat		Physical /dental exams & appointments	
Water		Medications/ daily vitamins	
Identifying/reducing emotional eating		Stress management/keeping it simple	
Sleep/rest (too much, too little)		Eliminating/reducing caffeine	
Exercise (easy does it)		Eliminating/reducing sugar	
Pacing your activities (too much, too little)		Other:	

MY PSYCHOLOGICAL HEALTH (MY THOUGHTS & BEHAVIOR)

Managing denial/ defense mechanisms		Music/art/school work	
Positive vs. Negative thinking		Journaling thoughts & behaviors	
Reducing obsessive thoughts		Making phone calls (sponsor, hotline)	
Daily structure/ being on time		Self-help meetings	
Making amends (promptly admit)		Building self esteem	
Money management		Other:	

MY EMOTIONAL/RELATIONAL HEALTH

Letting go of enabling people		Connecting with family in healthy way	
Managing emotions		Self care	
Spending time with **safe** people		Relaxation exercises	
Setting boundaries		Healthy sexual relations	
Having fun		Journaling feelings/ talking about them	
To Thine Own Self Be True. My "yes" is "yes," and my "no" is "no."		Other:	

MY SPIRITUAL HEALTH

Telling the truth to myself and others		Loving myself/ self-forgiveness	
Service to others		Church / Bible study	
Prayer		Serenity Prayer	
Meditation and/or quiet time with God		Gratitude list, affirmations	
Utilizing the Steps /Spiritual Principles		Enjoying nature	
Balance in everyday life (avoiding extremes)		Seeking/finding my purpose, finding what matters	

- Recognize emotional triggers and <u>change behavior.</u>
- Recognize anxiety and <u>practice relaxation techniques.</u>
- Recognize sleeping / eating habits that are slipping and <u>practice self-care.</u>

WEEK FOUR RELAPSE PREVENTION EXERCISE
Checklist of addiction/codependency symptoms which can lead to relapse.

On a 1 to 5 scale (0 meaning not present, 5 meaning it is problematic), how would you assess each of the following symptoms? Put an X on the line to indicate your answer. Enter your plan to make changes. Include behaviors you want to continue in order to remain healthy.

Exhaustion   EXAMPLE- 0________________________X_______3____________________________________5
PLAN- Naps on the weekends are helping. I need to eat more fresh food to feel my best.

1. Exhaustion: Allowing yourself to become overly tired or in poor health.
0____3_____________________________________5

PLAN____

2. Dishonesty: Rationalizing- making excuses for doing what you know you should not do.
0____3_____________________________________5

PLAN____

3. Impatience: Things are not happening fast enough.
0____3_____________________________________5

PLAN____

4. Argumentativeness: "If I could just make you understand."
0____3_____________________________________5

PLAN____

5. Frustration: At people or because things in general don't seem to be going "right."
0____3_____________________________________5

PLAN____

6. Self-Pity: "Why do these things happen to me?"
0____3_____________________________________5

PLAN____

7. Cockiness: Got it made- I can handle it. "It will never again happen to me."
0____3_____________________________________5

PLAN____

8. Expecting too much from others: "I've changed; why hasn't everyone else?"
0____3_____________________________________5

PLAN____

9. Not being able to say "no": " I don't want the person to feel mad, sad, disappointed, etc."
0____3_____________________________________5

PLAN____

10. People-pleasing: Wanting to be liked is the motive behind your behavior.
0____3_____________________________________5

PLAN____

Note: Do I need to talk to my Psalm-Partner, therapist, sponsor, or friend about my relapse risk?

WEEK FOUR RELAPSE PREVENTION EXERCISE

Expand on your plan to make changes. Include behaviors you want to continue in order to remain healthy.

PSALM 23 "Surely goodness and loving-kindness shall follow me all the days of my life."

**STEP 11. "Sought through prayer and meditation to improve our conscious contact
with God, praying only for knowledge of his will for us
and the power to carry that out."**

COMPLETION

My favorite Scripture for Chapter 11: Write it here.

_______I understand Chapter 11and will continue to use it daily.
_______I studied and completed the Bible study in a *Psalm 23* group.
_______I worked with a PSALM-Partner this month to study Chapter 11.

NAME: ____

Phone # ____

Today's date____

My Signature ____PSALM-Partner _____________________

AT A GLANCE

MATTHEW 5:13-16	ACTS 6:7	PSALMS 1:1-3	
MATTHEW 5:19-20	ROMANS 8:14-17	PSALMS 16:7-8	
MATTHEW 6:2	ROMANS 8:26-27	PSALMS 25:4-5	
MATTHEW 6:5-8	ROMANS 8:28	PSALMS 37:7-9	
MATTHEW 7:7-8	2 CORINTHIANS 8:1-5	PSALMS 88:9	
MATTHEW 21:21-22	2 CORINTHIANS 9:6	PSALMS 119:105-106	
MARK 9:36-37	PHILIPPIANS 4:4-7	PROVERBS 3:5-6	
MARK 11:24	COLOSSIANS 1:13-14	PROVERBS 16:20	
LUKE 6:20-26	COLOSSIANS 3:1-4		
LUKE 6:46-49	COLOSSIANS 3:15-17		
LUKE 11:9-10	1TIMOTHY 4:11-16		
LUKE 12:27-34	HEBREWS 4:14-16		
JOHN 15: 26-29	HEBREWS 5:7		
JOHN 16:1	1 JOHN 4:10-16		

He Restores My Soul:

A 12 Step Journey through PSALM 23

CHAPTER TWELVE

†

PSALM 23
"And I will dwell in the house of the Lord forever."

STEP 12
"Having had a spiritual awakening as a result of these steps, we try to carry this message to others and to practice these principles in all our affairs."

PSALM 23
"And I will dwell in the house of the Lord forever".

The sheep owner is always moving his flock *forward* and is supplying green pastures for his sheep to find peace and plenty. During the winter, while back at the home ranch, the sheep continue to receive goodness and mercy from the master's expert, loving hands. These sheep are content and would rather be in *no other* place than in their master's flock. A sheep is as safe as its shepherd is adequate. Our Shepherd is perfectly adequate, and He assures us of spiritual safety not only for today, or even tomorrow, but on to Eternity.

We ache for His care and concern. The Good Shepherd declared, *"I am the door: by me if any man enter in, he shall be saved, and shall go in and out, and find pasture"* John 10:9.

STEP 12. "Having had a spiritual awakening as a result of these steps we try
to carry this message to others and to practice these principles in all our affairs."

Congratulations! Step 12 is the last Step but not the end of our journey. A.A. co-founder Bill Wilson called the solution: a "spiritual experience," later to be called a "spiritual awakening." It is this **spiritual awakening** and the verbs in this Step, **carry** and **practice** that outline the direction we will take as we study Step 12. The hard work of the first eleven steps results in a gift beyond measure. We have come to a new and intimate understanding of God that is an ongoing and unfolding experience. We **carry** the message by practicing the principle –attraction, not promotion. There are different ways to **carry** the message such as being a sponsor, speaking at meetings, telling your story, inviting an addict/codependent to a meeting, volunteering in a hospital or jail, service at the meetings, and focusing on the newcomers. Sharing our stories about our transformation helps the newcomer and it helps us appreciate our new sense of meaning and purpose. What we hear at meetings is really true: We keep our recovery by giving it away. As we **practice** applying spiritual principles in all our affairs, we can ask The Lord to help us. Knowing which spiritual principle to practice in any given situation is difficult. It takes effort and practice.

..... we need each other.

The Spiritual Principles for Step 12 are unconditional love, selflessness, and steadfastness.

"And I will dwell in the house of the Lord forever."

1. When, in the past year, did you feel most content **being led** by Jesus, your Shepherd?

Christ the Good Shepherd says, *"If anyone would come after me, he must deny himself and take up his cross and follow me."* Mark 8:34. The honest, difficult truth is that most of us simply do not want to do this, especially when we experience pain. We do not want to deny ourselves; we do not want to be led. We actually prefer to flee from pain and do our own thing, even when we know that it may take us straight into chaos, trouble and problems. *"We all, like sheep, have gone astray, each of us has turned to his own way; and the LORD has laid on him the iniquity of us all."* Isaiah 53:6.

2. Is there a worn-out trail from an old habit that takes you off God's path? Write the sequence of events and the thought process that takes place at the fork in the road.

Complete this sentence, "It usually starts with….. "

3. Why do you think you stay or return there?

4. What will you miss by returning to your old "stomping grounds?"

5. Who has your permission to tell you the truth when there is concern about your recovery? Giving a person this permission is part of a good relapse prevention program.

6. If you relapse, what would be the most helpful thing a friend or family member **could say** to help you get back into recovery?

7. What would you want them to **do?**

The Amplified version of the Old Testament reads,
"I will dwell in the 'presence' of the Lord forever."

**STEP 12. "Having had a spiritual awakening as a result of these steps we try
to carry this message to others and to practice these principles in all our affairs."**

Our *spiritual awakening* can be dramatic or gradual, but it is always continuous. It is different for everyone.

From the Author: In a sense, addressing the addictions, the pain, and/or the self-destructive relationships, *is only the beginning of our renewal.* In the film "The Wizard of Oz" there is a scene where the original black and white film got a color make-over. Dorothy's farmhouse from Kansas is twirled and hurled through the air as a result of a huge tornado. The house spins out of control with an abrupt landing for Dorothy in The Land of OZ; it was the end of the trip. My house spun out of control and my trip landed me in a twelve-step meeting, much to my surprise. Early recovery for me meant working with God on my house; my physical, emotional, psychological, and spiritual health. Then one day, an ordinary twenty-four-hour day during my third year of recovery, I walked outside my door, and just as Dorothy did after the film's make-over, saw everything IN LIVING COLOR! I wasn't in OZ or any other make-believe place, the Lord awakened my soul right there in Pleasanton, California with spiritual blessings rich with vibrant colors of joy, soft yellows of peace, and abundant colorful splashes of grace and mercy and security in Himself! I had an increased tendency to seek God's will rather than force things to happen my way, with the amazing ability to appreciate the world and people around me, rather than fearfully judge others based on past experiences. The Lord's promises were coming true!!!! And I, like Dorothy who rejoiced in returning home to Kansas, found MY dwelling place in the presence of the Lord FOREVER. I also found the unmistakable ability to be thankful to God for all of the above.

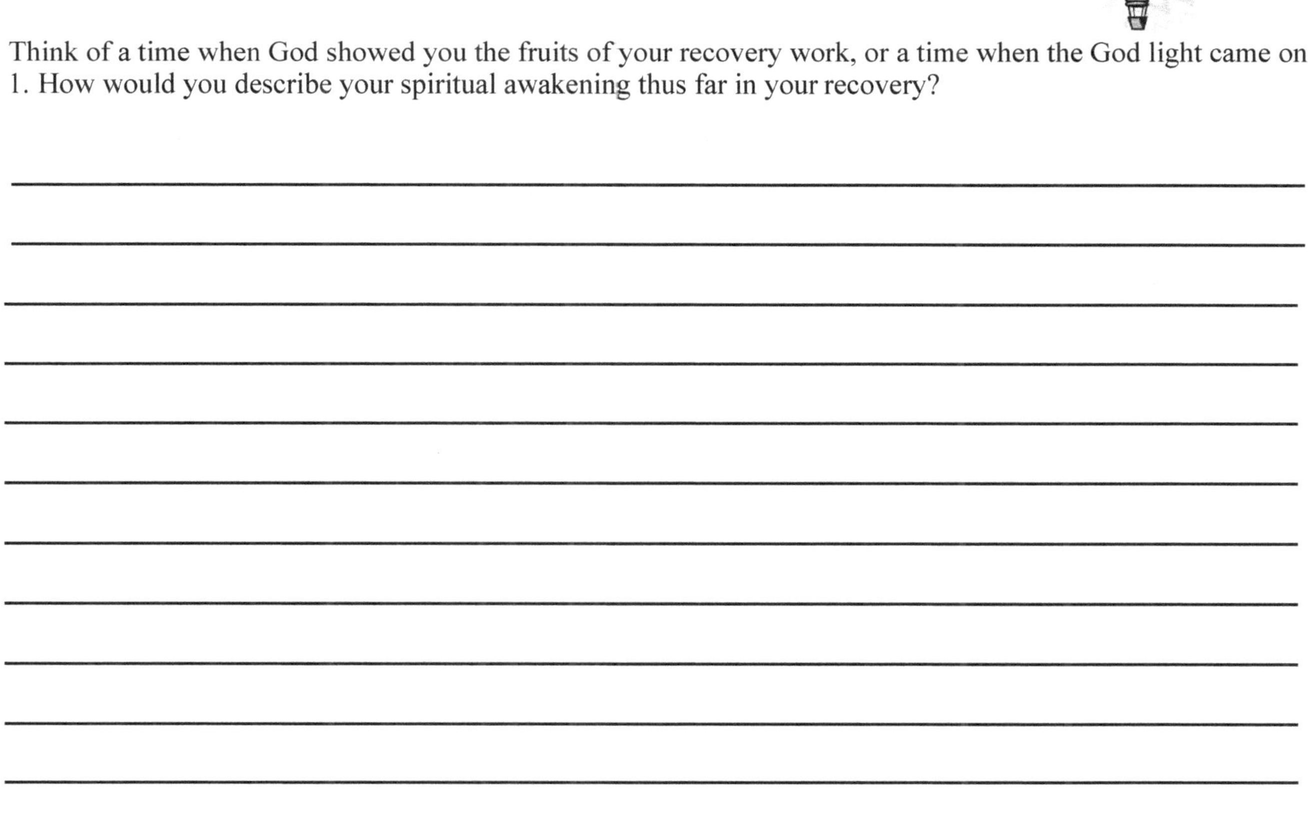

Think of a time when God showed you the fruits of your recovery work, or a time when the God light came on.
1. How would you describe your spiritual awakening thus far in your recovery?

"And I will dwell in the house of the Lord forever."
STEP 12. "Having had a spiritual awakening as a result of these steps we try
to carry this message to others and to practice these principles in all our affairs."

MATTHEW 24:14

MATTHEW 25:40

MATTHEW 28:19-20

MARK 5:19

LUKE 8:16

LUKE 14:13

JOHN 20:21

WEEK ONE WELLNESS CHECK-IN

Rate your physical, psychological, emotional, and spiritual health

- Examine your health in each area of your life. Give each behavior a number from 1-5 (#5 means very well).
- Be HONEST. It's helpful to know the *truth* about your recovery health in order to take care of yourself.
- Circle **one** BEHAVIOR in each area that you are willing to work on daily for the next week.

MY BIOLOGICAL HEALTH (PHYSICAL)

MY RECOVERY DATE:		NUMBER OF CONTINOUS DAYS	
Nutrition- when and what you eat		Physical /dental exams & appointments	
Water		Medications/ daily vitamins	
Identifying/reducing emotional eating		Stress management/keeping it simple	
Sleep/rest (too much, too little)		Eliminating/reducing caffeine	
Exercise (easy does it)		Eliminating/reducing sugar	
Pacing your activities (too much, too little)		Other:	

MY PSYCHOLOGICAL HEALTH (MY THOUGHTS & BEHAVIOR)

Managing denial/ defense mechanisms		Music/art/school work	
Positive vs. Negative thinking		Journaling thoughts & behaviors	
Reducing obsessive thoughts		Making phone calls (sponsor, hotline)	
Daily structure/ being on time		Self-help meetings	
Making amends (promptly admit)		Building self esteem	
Money management		Other:	

MY EMOTIONAL/RELATIONAL HEALTH

Letting go of enabling people		Connecting with family in healthy way	
Managing emotions		Self care	
Spending time with **safe** people		Relaxation exercises	
Setting boundaries		Healthy sexual relations	
Having fun		Journaling feelings/ talking about them	
To Thine Own Self Be True. My "yes" is "yes," and my "no" is "no."		Other:	

MY SPIRITUAL HEALTH

Telling the truth to myself and others		Loving myself/ self-forgiveness	
Service to others		Church / Bible study	
Prayer		Serenity Prayer	
Meditation and/or quiet time with God		Gratitude list, affirmations	
Utilizing the Steps /Spiritual Principles		Enjoying nature	
Balance in everyday life (avoiding extremes)		Seeking/finding my purpose, finding what matters	

- Recognize emotional triggers and <u>change behavior.</u>
- Recognize anxiety and <u>practice relaxation techniques.</u>
- Recognize sleeping / eating habits that are slipping and <u>practice self-care.</u>

WEEK ONE RELAPSE PREVENTION EXERCISE
Checklist of addiction/codependency symptoms which can lead to relapse.

On a 1 to 5 scale (0 meaning not present, 5 meaning it is problematic), how would you assess each of the following symptoms? Put an X on the line to indicate your answer. Enter your plan to make changes. Include behaviors you want to continue in order to remain healthy.

Exhaustion   EXAMPLE- 0________________________________X______3____5
PLAN- Naps on the weekends are helping. I need to eat more fresh food to feel my best.

1. Exhaustion: Allowing yourself to become overly tired or in poor health.
0____3____5

PLAN____

2. Dishonesty: Rationalizing- making excuses for doing what you know you should not do.
0____3____5

PLAN____

3. Impatience: Things are not happening fast enough.
0____3____5

PLAN____

4. Argumentativeness: "If I could just make you understand."
0____3____5

PLAN____

5. Frustration: At people or because things in general don't seem to be going "right."
0____3____5

PLAN____

6. Self-Pity: "Why do these things happen to me?"
0____3____5

PLAN____

7. Cockiness: Got it made- I can handle it. "It will never again happen to me."
0____3____5

PLAN____

8. Expecting too much from others: "I've changed; why hasn't everyone else?"
0____3____5

PLAN____

9. Not being able to say "no": " I don't want the person to feel mad, sad, disappointed, etc."
0____3____5

PLAN____

10. People-pleasing: Wanting to be liked is the motive behind your behavior.
0____3____5

PLAN____

Note: Do I need to talk to my Psalm-Partner, therapist, sponsor, or friend about my relapse risk?

WEEK ONE RELAPSE PREVENTION EXERCISE

Expand on your plan to make changes. Include behaviors you want to continue in order to remain healthy.

"And I will dwell in the house of the Lord forever".

Let's look at the Serenity Prayer in its entirety and reflect on the beautiful words of Reinhold Niebuhr:

God grant me the Serenity to accept the things I cannot change:

Courage to change the things I can; and Wisdom to know the difference....

Living one day at a time; Enjoying one moment at a time;

Accepting hardship as the pathway to peace;

Taking, as He did, this sinful world as it is, not as I would have it;

Trusting that He will make all things right, if I surrender to His Will;

That I may be reasonably happy in this life, and supremely

happy with Him forever in the next. Amen.

1. Which line can you relate to today?

2. Why?

3. Write and reflect on the birth of Jesus. When did you first understand that Christmas is about baby Jesus?

4. How do you celebrate Christmas?

**STEP 12. "Having had a spiritual awakening as a result of these steps we try
to carry this message to others and to practice these principles in all our affairs."**

Have you noticed how much of our recovery we learn from others; our sponsors, speakers, counselors, and recovering people sitting with us in various meetings? Even someone we think we have little in common with can, and often does, speak the very words we need to hear at that very moment. They carried the message without even knowing it!

1. When has that happened to you?

2. Who **carried** the message to you and was partly responsible for helping you get started in recovery?

3. What originally brought you to recovery? An addiction? Codependency? Your abusive childhood?

4. What was the precipitating event?

5. How long have you been in recovery?______________   Do you speak in meetings? ______________

---

1 Peter 2:9-10- THE MESSAGE- *"You are the ones chosen by God, chosen for the high calling of priestly work, chosen to be holy people, God's instruments to do his work and speak out for him, to tell others of the night-and-day difference he made for you- from nothing to something, from rejected to accepted."*

Keep sharing about how your life has been transformed because it may be the key that opens the door of God's grace, acceptance and love for a struggling person. God will use your message to bring glory to His name.

6. Write down your thoughts and experiences here.

7. Is there a topic or subject that you want to learn more about?

8. You may have a concern that you need to talk about. Who can you talk to?

"And I will dwell in the house of the Lord forever."
STEP 12. "Having had a spiritual awakening as a result of these steps we try
to carry this message to others and to practice these principles in all our affairs."

GALATIANS 6:1-2

____

____

____

GALATIANS 6:9-10

____

____

____

EPHESIANS 5:1-2

____

____

EPHESIANS 5:19-20

____

____

EPHESIANS 5:29

____

____

PHILIPPIANS 4:9

____

____

COLOSSIANS 4:5-6

____

____

Rate your physical, psychological, emotional, and spiritual health

- Examine your health in each area of your life. Give each behavior a number from 1-5 (#5 means very well).
- Be HONEST. It's helpful to know the *truth* about your recovery health in order to take care of yourself.
- Circle **one** BEHAVIOR in each area that you are willing to work on daily for the next week.

MY BIOLOGICAL HEALTH (PHYSICAL)

MY RECOVERY DATE:		NUMBER OF CONTINOUS DAYS	
Nutrition- when and what you eat		Physical /dental exams & appointments	
Water		Medications/ daily vitamins	
Identifying/reducing emotional eating		Stress management/keeping it simple	
Sleep/rest (too much, too little)		Eliminating/reducing caffeine	
Exercise (easy does it)		Eliminating/reducing sugar	
Pacing your activities (too much, too little)		Other:	

MY PSYCHOLOGICAL HEALTH (MY THOUGHTS & BEHAVIOR)

Managing denial/ defense mechanisms		Music/art/school work	
Positive vs. Negative thinking		Journaling thoughts & behaviors	
Reducing obsessive thoughts		Making phone calls (sponsor, hotline)	
Daily structure/ being on time		Self-help meetings	
Making amends (promptly admit)		Building self esteem	
Money management		Other:	

MY EMOTIONAL/RELATIONAL HEALTH

Letting go of enabling people		Connecting with family in healthy way	
Managing emotions		Self care	
Spending time with **safe** people		Relaxation exercises	
Setting boundaries		Healthy sexual relations	
Having fun		Journaling feelings/ talking about them	
To Thine Own Self Be True. My "yes" is "yes," and my "no" is "no."		Other:	

MY SPIRITUAL HEALTH

Telling the truth to myself and others		Loving myself/ self-forgiveness	
Service to others		Church / Bible study	
Prayer		Serenity Prayer	
Meditation and/or quiet time with God		Gratitude list, affirmations	
Utilizing the Steps /Spiritual Principles		Enjoying nature	
Balance in everyday life (avoiding extremes)		Seeking/finding my purpose, finding what matters	

- Recognize emotional triggers and <u>change behavior.</u>
- Recognize anxiety and <u>practice relaxation techniques.</u>
- Recognize sleeping / eating habits that are slipping and <u>practice self-care.</u>

WEEK TWO RELAPSE PREVENTION EXERCISE
Checklist of addiction/codependency symptoms which can lead to relapse.

On a 1 to 5 scale (0 meaning not present, 5 meaning it is problematic), how would you assess each of the following symptoms? Put an X on the line to indicate your answer. Enter your plan to make changes. Include behaviors you want to continue in order to remain healthy.

<u>Exhaustion</u> EXAMPLE- 0_________________________________X______3____5

PLAN- Naps on the weekends are helping. I need to eat more fresh food to feel my best.

1. <u>Exhaustion:</u> Allowing yourself to become overly tired or in poor health.
0____3____5

PLAN____

2. <u>Dishonesty:</u> Rationalizing- making excuses for doing what you know you should not do.
0____3____5

PLAN____

3. <u>Impatience:</u> Things are not happening fast enough.
0____3____5

PLAN____

4. <u>Argumentativeness:</u> "If I could just make you understand."
0____3____5

PLAN____

5. <u>Frustration:</u> At people or because things in general don't seem to be going "right."
0____3____5

PLAN____

6. <u>Self-Pity:</u> "Why do these things happen to me?"
0____3____5

PLAN____

7. <u>Cockiness:</u> Got it made- I can handle it. "It will never again happen to me."
0____3____5

PLAN____

8. <u>Expecting too much from others:</u> "I've changed; why hasn't everyone else?"
0____3____5

PLAN____

9. <u>Not being able to say "no":</u> " I don't want the person to feel mad, sad, disappointed, etc."
0____3____5

PLAN____

10. <u>People-pleasing:</u> Wanting to be liked is the motive behind your behavior.
0____3____5

PLAN____

Note: Do I need to talk to my Psalm-Partner, therapist, sponsor, or friend about my relapse risk?

WEEK TWO RELAPSE PREVENTION EXERCISE

Expand on your plan to make changes. Include behaviors you want to continue in order to remain healthy.

"And I will dwell in the house of the Lord forever."

The Twenty-Third Psalm covers every condition or circumstances in life: the joys, the sorrows, the testing, the victories, matters that are day-to-day and matters that are eternal.

1. What line of the Psalm ministers to you today?

God's grace is sufficient for you and your recovery. We can be sure that we will make it in our recovery because God began a work within us which is continuing each day we live. When God starts a project, He finishes it!!

2. Read Colossians.1:10-14 NKIV-*" ...that you may have a walk worthy of the Lord, fully pleasing Him, being fruitful in every good work and increasing in knowledge of God; strengthened with all might according to His glorious power, for all patience and longsuffering with joy; giving thanks to the Father who has qualified us to be partakers of the inheritance of the saints in the light. He has delivered us from the power of darkness and translated us into the kingdom of the Son of His love, in whom we have redemption through His blood, the forgiveness of sins."*

NOTES:

3. What thoughts, feelings or urges do you get that cause you to doubt the truth of Colossians 1:10-14?

4. What do you need to do to stay on track?

Because of the birth, death and resurrection of Jesus, you will end up with the Lord in Heaven forever. The joy of the Lord doesn't mean that we enjoy the difficult circumstances we face.

5. Is there a certain season of the year that is especially painful or difficult for you? Write about it here.

STEP 12. "Having had a spiritual awakening as a result of these steps we try to carry this message to others and to practice these principles in all our affairs."

We are His sheep. 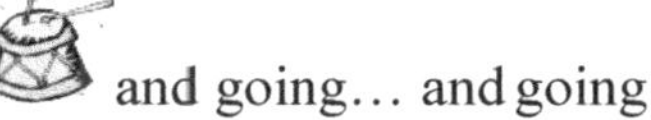 Baaa Baaaaa.

As we keep making the commitment, every day, every hour, every minute, to turn our lives over to the care of Jesus our Good Shepherd, we can know restoration, protection, and abundance while being led on the paths of righteousness for His names sake.

Step 12 has its own spiritual principles: **unconditional love, selflessness,** and **steadfastness. Unconditional love** is a gift we give and receive in recovery. We don't ask for anything in return, we merely extend ourselves. Sometimes the best way of loving and helping someone is to stop enabling them.

1. How are you practicing **unconditional love**?

We carry the message to help others find freedom from their pain and grow as individuals.
2. What does "principles over personalities" mean to you?

3. How do you practice the principle of **selflessness**?

Steadfastness: God's song keeps on going and going… and going.

The study of Step 4 in the **The Lord id My Shepherd: A 12 Step Journey through PSALM 23** workbook, refers to being in tune with God. God is steadfast. HE is the same yesterday, today and tomorrow. He's the same from generation to generation. Jesus came to show us how to live. Maybe each choice we make determines how in tune with God we are at any given time.

4. Are you in tune with God today?

5. When was the last time you were out of tune with God's rhythm?

David knew what it felt like to be loved by the Good Shepherd. Jesus came to give His life for us. JESUS LOVES YOU. Are you falling in love with the Shepherd?

"And I will dwell in the house of the Lord forever".
STEP 12. "Having had a spiritual awakening as a result of these steps we try
to carry this message to others and practice these principles in all our affairs."

MATTHEW 7:7-8

____

____

2 TIMOTHY 4:2

____

____

1 THESSALONIANS 5:11

____

____

1 THESSALONIANS 5:14

____

____

HEBREWS 3:13

____

____

HEBREWS 6:10-11

____

____

____

HEBREWS 10:24-25

____

____

____

____

WEEK THREE WELLNESS CHECK-IN

Rate your physical, psychological, emotional, and spiritual health

Examine your health in each area of your life. Give each behavior a number from 1-5 (#5 means very well). Be HONEST. It's helpful to know the *truth* about your recovery health in order to take care of yourself. Circle **one** BEHAVIOR in each area that you are willing to work on daily for the next week.

MY BIOLOGICAL HEALTH (PHYSICAL)

MY RECOVERY DATE:		NUMBER OF CONTINOUS DAYS	
Nutrition- when and what you eat		Physical /dental exams & appointments	
Water		Medications/ daily vitamins	
Identifying/reducing emotional eating		Stress management/keeping it simple	
Sleep/rest (too much, too little)		Eliminating/reducing caffeine	
Exercise (easy does it)		Eliminating/reducing sugar	
Pacing your activities (too much, too little)		Other:	

MY PSYCHOLOGICAL HEALTH (MY THOUGHTS & BEHAVIOR)

Managing denial/ defense mechanisms		Music/art/school work	
Positive vs. Negative thinking		Journaling thoughts & behaviors	
Reducing obsessive thoughts		Making phone calls (sponsor, hotline)	
Daily structure/ being on time		Self-help meetings	
Making amends (promptly admit)		Building self esteem	
Money management		Other:	

MY EMOTIONAL/RELATIONAL HEALTH

Letting go of enabling people		Connecting with family in healthy way	
Managing emotions		Self care	
Spending time with **safe** people		Relaxation exercises	
Setting boundaries		Healthy sexual relations	
Having fun		Journaling feelings/ talking about them	
To Thine Own Self Be True. My "yes" is "yes," and my "no" is "no."		Other:	

MY SPIRITUAL HEALTH

Telling the truth to myself and others		Loving myself/ self-forgiveness	
Service to others		Church / Bible study	
Prayer		Serenity Prayer	
Meditation and/or quiet time with God		Gratitude list, affirmations	
Utilizing the Steps /Spiritual Principles		Enjoying nature	
Balance in everyday life (avoiding extremes)		Seeking/finding my purpose, finding what matters	

- Recognize emotional triggers and <u>change behavior.</u>
- Recognize anxiety and <u>practice relaxation techniques.</u>
- Recognize sleeping / eating habits that are slipping and <u>practice self-care.</u>

WEEK THREE RELAPSE PREVENTION EXERCISE
Checklist of addiction/codependency symptoms which can lead to relapse.

On a 1 to 5 scale (0 meaning not present, 5 meaning it is problematic), how would you assess each of the following symptoms? Put an X on the line to indicate your answer. Enter your plan to make changes. Include behaviors you want to continue in order to remain healthy.

<u>Exhaustion</u> EXAMPLE- 0______________________________X________3________________________________5

        PLAN- Naps on the weekends are helping. I need to eat more fresh food to feel my best.

1. <u>Exhaustion:</u> Allowing yourself to become overly tired or in poor health.
   0____3____5

   PLAN____

2. <u>Dishonesty:</u> Rationalizing- making excuses for doing what you know you should not do.
   0____3____5

   PLAN____

3. <u>Impatience:</u> Things are not happening fast enough.
   0____3____5

   PLAN____

4. <u>Argumentativeness:</u> "If I could just make you understand."
   0____3____5

   PLAN____

5. <u>Frustration:</u> At people or because things in general don't seem to be going "right."
   0____3____5

   PLAN____

6. <u>Self-Pity:</u> "Why do these things happen to me?"
   0____3____5

   PLAN____

7. <u>Cockiness:</u> Got it made- I can handle it. "It will never again happen to me."
   0____3____5

   PLAN____

8. <u>Expecting too much from others:</u> "I've changed; why hasn't everyone else?"
   0____3____5

   PLAN____

9. <u>Not being able to say "no":</u> " I don't want the person to feel mad, sad, disappointed, etc."
   0____3____5

   PLAN____

10. <u>People-pleasing:</u> Wanting to be liked is the motive behind your behavior.
   0____3____5

   PLAN____

Note: Do I need to talk to my Psalm-Partner, therapist, sponsor, or friend about my relapse risk?

WEEK THREE RELAPSE PREVENTION EXERCISE

Expand on your plan to make changes. Include behaviors you want to continue in order to remain healthy.

"And I will dwell in the house of the Lord forever."

Use these Four Absolutes as your gauge for successful living.
1. What behaviors will you continue or eliminate in each absolute in order to prevent future barriers to God.

    a. Absolute Honesty:
Example: I will continue to truthfully count my days of sobriety. I will not lie or keep secrets.

    b. Absolute Purity:

    c. Absolute Unselfishness:

    d. Absolute Love:

2. Read and write 2 Corinthians 12:9

3. Read and write Philippians 4:6, 9

Plant your feet on 2 Corinthians 5:17

"THEREFORE IF ANY MAN IS IN CHRIST, HE IS A NEW CREATURE; THE OLD THINGS PASSED AWAY; BEHOLD, NEW THINGS HAVE COME,"

IT IS THE KEY TO RECOVERY.

WHEN THE DEVIL REMINDS YOU OF YOUR PAST, REMIND HIM OF HIS FUTURE!!!!

4. What will you do next time you feel bad or guilty about your past?

**STEP 12. "Having had a spiritual awakening as a result of these steps we try
to carry this message to others and to practice these principles in all our affairs."**

1. Write down as many things you can think of under each section. Who can you share this information with?

Accomplishments in your recovery	Short term goals for your recovery

2. WRITE A PRAYER TO GOD:

"And I will dwell in the house of the Lord forever".
STEP 12. "Having had a spiritual awakening as a result of these steps we try
to carry this message to others and practice these principles in all our affairs."

ACTS 4:33

____

____

____

ROMANS 12:11-12

____

____

____

ROMANS 15:5

____

____

____

2 CORINTHIANS 5:20

____

____

____

2 CORINTHIANS 9:13

____

____

____

MATTHEW 5:13-16

____

____

____

MATTHEW 6:2

____

____

____

WEEK FOUR WELLNESS CHECK-IN

Rate your physical, psychological, emotional, and spiritual health

- Examine your health in each area of your life. Give each behavior a number from 1-5 (#5 means very well).
- Be HONEST. It's helpful to know the _truth_ about your recovery health in order to take care of yourself.
- Circle **one** BEHAVIOR in each area that you are willing to work on daily for the next week.

MY BIOLOGICAL HEALTH (PHYSICAL)

MY RECOVERY DATE:		NUMBER OF CONTINOUS DAYS	
Nutrition- when and what you eat		Physical /dental exams & appointments	
Water		Medications/ daily vitamins	
Identifying/reducing emotional eating		Stress management/keeping it simple	
Sleep/rest (too much, too little)		Eliminating/reducing caffeine	
Exercise (easy does it)		Eliminating/reducing sugar	
Pacing your activities (too much, too little)		Other:	

MY PSYCHOLOGICAL HEALTH (MY THOUGHTS & BEHAVIOR)

Managing denial/ defense mechanisms		Music/art/school work	
Positive vs. Negative thinking		Journaling thoughts & behaviors	
Reducing obsessive thoughts		Making phone calls (sponsor, hotline)	
Daily structure/ being on time		Self-help meetings	
Making amends (promptly admit)		Building self esteem	
Money management		Other:	

MY EMOTIONAL/RELATIONAL HEALTH

Letting go of enabling people		Connecting with family in healthy way	
Managing emotions		Self care	
Spending time with **safe** people		Relaxation exercises	
Setting boundaries		Healthy sexual relations	
Having fun		Journaling feelings/ talking about them	
To Thine Own Self Be True. My "yes" is "yes," and my "no" is "no."		Other:	

MY SPIRITUAL HEALTH

Telling the truth to myself and others		Loving myself/ self-forgiveness	
Service to others		Church / Bible study	
Prayer		Serenity Prayer	
Meditation and/or quiet time with God		Gratitude list, affirmations	
Utilizing the Steps /Spiritual Principles		Enjoying nature	
Balance in everyday life (avoiding extremes)		Seeking/finding my purpose, finding what matters	

- Recognize emotional triggers and <u>change behavior.</u>
- Recognize anxiety and <u>practice relaxation techniques.</u>
- Recognize sleeping / eating habits that are slipping and <u>practice self-care.</u>

WEEK FOUR RELAPSE PREVENTION EXERCISE
Checklist of addiction/codependency symptoms which can lead to relapse.

On a 1 to 5 scale (0 meaning not present, 5 meaning it is problematic), how would you assess each of the following symptoms? Put an X on the line to indicate your answer. Enter your plan to make changes. Include behaviors you want to continue in order to remain healthy.

Exhaustion   EXAMPLE- 0________________________________X________3____5
PLAN- Naps on the weekends are helping. I need to eat more fresh food to feel my best.

1.   Exhaustion: Allowing yourself to become overly tired or in poor health.
0____3____5

PLAN____

2.   Dishonesty: Rationalizing- making excuses for doing what you know you should not do.
0____3____5

PLAN____

3.   Impatience: Things are not happening fast enough.
0____3____5

PLAN____

4.   Argumentativeness: "If I could just make you understand."
0____3____5

PLAN____

5.   Frustration: At people or because things in general don't seem to be going "right."
0____3____5

PLAN____

6.   Self-Pity: "Why do these things happen to me?"
0____3____5

PLAN____

7.   Cockiness: Got it made- I can handle it. "It will never again happen to me."
0____3____5

PLAN____

8.   Expecting too much from others: "I've changed; why hasn't everyone else?"
0____3____5

PLAN____

9.   Not being able to say "no": " I don't want the person to feel mad, sad, disappointed, etc."
0____3____5

PLAN____

10. People-pleasing: Wanting to be liked is the motive behind your behavior.
0____3____5

PLAN____

Note: Do I need to talk to my Psalm-Partner, therapist, sponsor, or friend about my relapse risk?

WEEK FOUR RELAPSE PREVENTION EXERCISE

Expand on your plan to make changes. Include behaviors you want to continue in order to remain healthy.

Psalm 23 "And I will dwell in the house of the Lord forever".

STEP 12. "Having had a spiritual awakening as a result of these steps we try
to carry this message to others and practice these principles in all our affairs."

COMPLETION

My favorite Scripture for Chapter 12: Write it here.

______I understand Chapter 12 and will continue to use it daily.
______I studied and completed the Bible study in a *Psalm 23* group.
______I worked with a PSALM-Partner this month to study Chapter 12.

NAME: _____________________________________

Phone # ___________________________________

Today's date_________________________________

My Signature _________________________________PSALM-Partner

AT A GLANCE

MATTHEW 24:14	GALATIANS 6:1-2	JAMES 2:16-17	
MATTHEW 25:40	GALATIANS 6:9-10	JAMES 3:13	
MATTHEW 28:19-20	EPHESIANS 5:1-2	1 PETER 4:8-11	
MARK 5:19-20	EPHESIANS 5:19-20	1 JOHN 3:17-18	
MARK 6:12	EPHESIANS 5:29	PSALM 71:15-18	
LUKE 8:16-18	PHILIPPIANS 4:9		
LUKE 14:12-14	COLOSSIANS 4:5-6		
JOHN 13:14	2 TIMOTHY 4:2		
JOHN 20:21	1 THESSALONIANS 5:11		
ACTS 4:33	1 THESSALONIANS 5:14		
ROMANS 12:1-8	HEBREWS 3:13		
ROMANS 12:11-13	HEBREWS 6:10-11		
ROMANS 15:5-6	HEBREWS 10:24-25		
2 CORINTHIANS 5:20	HEBREWS 12:1-3		
2 CORINTHIANS 9:13	HEBREWS 13:16		

STEP 4 WORKSHEET – MUSIC SHEET

PSALM 23 "He leads me beside the quiet waters."
STEP 4 "Made a searching and fearless moral inventory of ourselves."

APPENDIX A

STEP 4 WORKSHEET – MUSIC SHEET

PSALM 23 "He leads me beside the quiet waters."
STEP 4 "Made a searching and fearless moral inventory of ourselves."

APPENDIX A

STEP 4 WORKSHEET – MUSIC SHEET

PSALM 23 "He leads me beside the quiet waters."
STEP 4 "Made a searching and fearless moral inventory of ourselves."

APPENDIX A

STEP 4 WORKSHEET – MUSIC SHEET

PSALM 23 "He leads me beside the quiet waters."
STEP 4 "Made a searching and fearless moral inventory of ourselves."

APPENDIX A

STEP 4 WORKSHEET – MUSIC SHEET

PSALM 23 "He leads me beside the quiet waters."
STEP 4 "Made a searching and fearless moral inventory of ourselves."

APPENDIX A

STEP 4 WORKSHEET – MUSIC SHEET

PSALM 23 "He leads me beside the quiet waters."
STEP 4 "Made a searching and fearless moral inventory of ourselves."

APPENDIX A

STEP 4 WORKSHEET – MUSIC SHEET

PSALM 23 "He leads me beside the quiet waters."
STEP 4 "Made a searching and fearless moral inventory of ourselves."

APPENDIX A

STEP 4 WORKSHEET – MUSIC SHEET

PSALM 23 "He leads me beside the quiet waters."
STEP 4 "Made a searching and fearless moral inventory of ourselves."

APPENDIX A

STEP 4 WORKSHEET – MUSIC SHEET

PSALM 23 "He leads me beside the quiet waters."
STEP 4 "Made a searching and fearless moral inventory of ourselves."

APPENDIX A

STEP 4 WORKSHEET – MUSIC SHEET

PSALM 23 "He leads me beside the quiet waters."
STEP 4 "Made a searching and fearless moral inventory of ourselves."

APPENDIX B

Step 4 RESENTMENT INVENTORY CHART

Rationale for us:

Elements that may herald the need for implementation of effective Relapse Prevention Strategies are:

Unresolved resentments, Overwhelming fears and Character defects seen as justifiable qualities.

I'm Resentful at:	The Cause	How it affects me? "The wound"	What was (or is) my part in it? Character defects: What traits did I use for protection? (This is part of Step 5, wait until then to complete this column)
1. Example #1 MY UNCLE	Unemotional High expectations Never attended my games Always at work Physically abusive	Self Esteem Sense of comfort Security	Emotionally distant Perfectionism Entitlement Pleasing others
2. Example #2 BOB	His attention towards my wife Did not pay money he owed Took my job	Sex relations Financial security Inability to trust	Vengefulness/ revenge Lust Jealousy
3.			
4.			
5.			
6.			
7.			
8.			

APPENDIX B

Step 4 RESENTMENT INVENTORY CHART

Rationale for us:

Elements that may herald the need for implementation of effective Relapse Prevention Strategies are:

Unresolved resentments, Overwhelming fears and Character defects seen as justifiable qualities.

I'm Resentful at:	The Cause	How it affects me? "The wound"	What was (or is) my part in it? Character defects: What traits did I use for protection?
1.			
2.			
3.			
4.			
5.			
6.			
7.			
8.			

APPENDIX B

Step 4 RESENTMENT INVENTORY CHART

Rationale for us:

Elements that may herald the need for implementation of effective Relapse Prevention Strategies are:

Unresolved resentments, Overwhelming fears and Character defects seen as justifiable qualities.

I'm Resentful at:	The Cause	How it affects me? "The wound"	What was (or is) my part in it? Character defects: What traits did I use for protection?
1.			
2.			
3.			
4.			
5.			
6.			
7.			
8.			

APPENDIX B

Step 4 RESENTMENT INVENTORY CHART

Rationale for us:

Elements that may herald the need for implementation of effective Relapse Prevention Strategies are:

Unresolved resentments, Overwhelming fears and Character defects seen as justifiable qualities.

I'm Resentful at:	The Cause	How it affects me? "The wound"	What was (or is) my part in it? Character defects: What traits did I use for protection?
1.			
2.			
3.			
4.			
5.			
6.			
7.			
8.			

APPENDIX B

Step 4 RESENTMENT INVENTORY CHART

Rationale for us:

Elements that may herald the need for implementation of effective Relapse Prevention Strategies are:

Unresolved resentments, Overwhelming fears and Character defects seen as justifiable qualities.

I'm Resentful at:	The Cause	How it affects me? "The wound"	What was (or is) my part in it? Character defects: What traits did I use for protection?
1.			
2.			
3.			
4.			
5.			
6.			
7.			
8.			

APPENDIX C

STEP 4 WORKSHEET

PSALM 23 "He leads me beside the quiet waters."
STEP 4 "Made a searching and fearless moral inventory of ourselves."

MY RESENTMENTS / MY RELATIONSHIPS / MY FEARS:

APPENDIX C

STEP 4 WORKSHEET

PSALM 23 "He leads me beside the quiet waters."
STEP 4 "Made a searching and fearless moral inventory of ourselves."

MY RESENTMENTS / MY RELATIONSHIPS / MY FEARS:

APPENDIX C

STEP 4 WORKSHEET

PSALM 23 "He leads me beside the quiet waters."
STEP 4 "Made a searching and fearless moral inventory of ourselves."

MY RESENTMENTS / MY RELATIONSHIPS / MY FEARS:

APPENDIX C

STEP 4 WORKSHEET

PSALM 23 "He leads me beside the quiet waters."
STEP 4 "Made a searching and fearless moral inventory of ourselves."

MY RESENTMENTS / MY RELATIONSHIPS / MY FEARS:

APPENDIX C

STEP 4 WORKSHEET

PSALM 23 "He leads me beside the quiet waters."
STEP 4 "Made a searching and fearless moral inventory of ourselves."

MY RESENTMENTS / MY RELATIONSHIPS / MY FEARS:

APPENDIX C

STEP 4 WORKSHEET

PSALM 23 "He leads me beside the quiet waters."
STEP 4 "Made a searching and fearless moral inventory of ourselves."

MY RESENTMENTS / MY RELATIONSHIPS / MY FEARS:

APPENDIX C

STEP 4 WORKSHEET

PSALM 23 "He leads me beside the quiet waters."
STEP 4 "Made a searching and fearless moral inventory of ourselves."

MY RESENTMENTS / MY RELATIONSHIPS / MY FEARS:

APPENDIX C

STEP 4 WORKSHEET

PSALM 23 "He leads me beside the quiet waters."
STEP 4 "Made a searching and fearless moral inventory of ourselves."

MY RESENTMENTS / MY RELATIONSHIPS / MY FEARS:

APPENDIX C

STEP 4 WORKSHEET

PSALM 23 "He leads me beside the quiet waters."
STEP 4 "Made a searching and fearless moral inventory of ourselves."

MY RESENTMENTS / MY RELATIONSHIPS / MY FEARS:

APPENDIX C

STEP 4 WORKSHEET

PSALM 23 "He leads me beside the quiet waters."
STEP 4 "Made a searching and fearless moral inventory of ourselves."

MY RESENTMENTS / MY RELATIONSHIPS / MY FEARS:

Journal Notes

"Seek ye first the kingdom of God and His righteousness, and all these things shall be added unto you." Matthew 6:33 (ASV)
How do I feel today? How strong is my recovery? What spiritual principle will help me today? Do I need to ask for help?

Journal Notes

"Seek ye first the kingdom of God and His righteousness, and all these things shall be added unto you." Matthew 6:33 (ASV)
How do I feel today? How strong is my recovery? What spiritual principle will help me today? Do I need to ask for help?

Journal Notes

"Seek ye first the kingdom of God and His righteousness, and all these things shall be added unto you." Matthew 6:33 (ASV)
How do I feel today? How strong is my recovery? What spiritual principle will help me today? Do I need to ask for help?

Journal Notes

Journal Notes

"Seek ye first the kingdom of God and His righteousness, and all these things shall be added unto you." Matthew 6:33 (ASV)
How do I feel today? How strong is my recovery? What spiritual principle will help me today? Do I need to ask for help?

Journal Notes

Journal Notes

"Seek ye first the kingdom of God and His righteousness, and all these things shall be added unto you." Matthew 6:33 (ASV)
How do I feel today? How strong is my recovery? What spiritual principle will help me today? Do I need to ask for help?

Journal Notes

"Seek ye first the kingdom of God and His righteousness, and all these things shall be added unto you." Matthew 6:33 (ASV)
How do I feel today? How strong is my recovery? What spiritual principle will help me today? Do I need to ask for help?

Journal Notes

"Seek ye first the kingdom of God and His righteousness, and all these things shall be added unto you." Matthew 6:33 (ASV)
How do I feel today? How strong is my recovery? What spiritual principle will help me today? Do I need to ask for help?

Journal Notes

"Seek ye first the kingdom of God and His righteousness, and all these things shall be added unto you." Matthew 6:33 (ASV)
How do I feel today? How strong is my recovery? What spiritual principle will help me today? Do I need to ask for help?

Journal Notes

"Seek ye first the kingdom of God and His righteousness, and all these things shall be added unto you." Matthew 6:33 (ASV)
How do I feel today? How strong is my recovery? What spiritual principle will help me today? Do I need to ask for help?

Journal Notes

"Seek ye first the kingdom of God and His righteousness, and all these things shall be added unto you." Matthew 6:33 (ASV)
How do I feel today? How strong is my recovery? What spiritual principle will help me today? Do I need to ask for help?

Journal Notes

"Seek ye first the kingdom of God and His righteousness, and all these things shall be added unto you." Matthew 6:33 (ASV)
How do I feel today? How strong is my recovery? What spiritual principle will help me today? Do I need to ask for help?

Journal Notes

"Seek ye first the kingdom of God and His righteousness, and all these things shall be added unto you." Matthew 6:33 (ASV)
How do I feel today? How strong is my recovery? What spiritual principle will help me today? Do I need to ask for help?

Journal Notes

"Seek ye first the kingdom of God and His righteousness, and all these things shall be added unto you." Matthew 6:33 (ASV)
How do I feel today? How strong is my recovery? What spiritual principle will help me today? Do I need to ask for help?

Journal Notes

"Seek ye first the kingdom of God and His righteousness, and all these things shall be added unto you." Matthew 6:33 (ASV)
How do I feel today? How strong is my recovery? What spiritual principle will help me today? Do I need to ask for help?

Journal Notes

"Seek ye first the kingdom of God and His righteousness, and all these things shall be added unto you." Matthew 6:33 (ASV)
How do I feel today? How strong is my recovery? What spiritual principle will help me today? Do I need to ask for help?

Journal Notes

Journal Notes

"Seek ye first the kingdom of God and His righteousness, and all these things shall be added unto you." Matthew 6:33 (ASV)
How do I feel today? How strong is my recovery? What spiritual principle will help me today? Do I need to ask for help?

Journal Notes

"Seek ye first the kingdom of God and His righteousness, and all these things shall be added unto you." Matthew 6:33 (ASV)
How do I feel today? How strong is my recovery? What spiritual principle will help me today? Do I need to ask for help?

Journal Notes

"Seek ye first the kingdom of God and His righteousness, and all these things shall be added unto you." Matthew 6:33 (ASV)
How do I feel today? How strong is my recovery? What spiritual principle will help me today? Do I need to ask for help?

PHONE NUMBERS
HOTLINES, DOCTORS, IMPORTANT NUMBERS

<u>REFERENCES</u>

Alcoholics Anonymous, 4th ed., New York: Alcoholics Anonymous World Services, Inc., 2001. ISBN 978-1-893007-17-8.

Anderson, Neil T. and Quarles, Mike & Julia. *Freedom From Addiction.* Ventura, California, 1996. ISBN 0-8307-1856-6.

Beattie, Melody. *Codependent No More*, Center City, MN: Hazelden, 1987. ISBN 0-89486-402-5.

Carnes, Patrick. *Out of the Shadows: Understanding Sexual Addiction,* Minneapolis, MN: CompCare, 1983.

Dr. Bob and the Good Oldtimers, New York: Alcoholics Anonymous World Services, Inc., 1980. ISBN 0-916856-07-0.

Keller, Phillip. *A Shepherd Looks At Psalm 23:* Zondervan, Grand Rapids, Michigan. ISBN 0-310-21435-1

Lucado, Max. *Safe in the Shepherd's Arms,* Nashville, Tennessee, 2002. ISBN 1-4041-00253.

Miller, Keith J. *A Hunger for Healing,* New York, NY, 1991. ISBN 0-06-065716-2

Recovery Devotional Bible, *New International Version* 1993. Grand Rapids, Michigan.
Notice of copyright must appear on the title or copyright page as follows:
    Scripture taken from the HOLY BIBLE, INTERNATIONAL VERSION ®. Copyright © 1972, 1978, 1984, by International Bible Society. Used by permission of Zondervan. All rights reserved.

The Narcotics Anonymous Step Working Guides, 1998. Van Nuys, California Narcotics Anonymous World Services, Inc. ISBN 1-55776-370-4

Twelve Steps and Twelve Traditions, 1981. New York: Alcoholics Anonymous World Services, Inc. ISBN 0-916856-29-1.

Wilson, Jan R. and Wilson, Judith A. 1992. *ADDICTIONARY,* Center City MN. Hazelden. ISBN 1-56838-116-6

Our A.A. Legacy to the Faith Community, Compiled and Edited by Dick B., 2005, Winter Park, FL, ISBN 0-0767292-0-2